Praise for *HR and the New Hispanic Workforce*

"Hits on the true issues we face—solid real-world information. Goes way beyond HR to important, high-level organization and culture issues that we must consider. A valuable guide to navigating new and potentially turbulent organizational waters." —**Dr. Michael Fleming, Director, Organizational Development and Learning, Banner Good Samaritan Medical Center**

"An indispensable book, a tour de force, that empowers HR professionals to understand how Hispanics are transforming the dynamics of the American workplace. Provides an invaluable tool heretofore missing from the literature, and it could not have arrived at a more opportune moment!" —**Robert Coleman, Director, Total Rewards & Accountability, SVB Financial Group; faculty member, San Francisco State University, College of Extended Learning**

"Not only addresses the unique needs and concerns of the Hispanic worker but also provides the HR practitioner with strategies to address the crucial hiring, performance management, and recognition processes. A timely and invaluable resource to help us successfully manage the skills, knowledge, and talents of an emerging workforce." —**Debbie Benami-Rahm, M.S., M.H.C., President, DBR Career Services, Inc.**

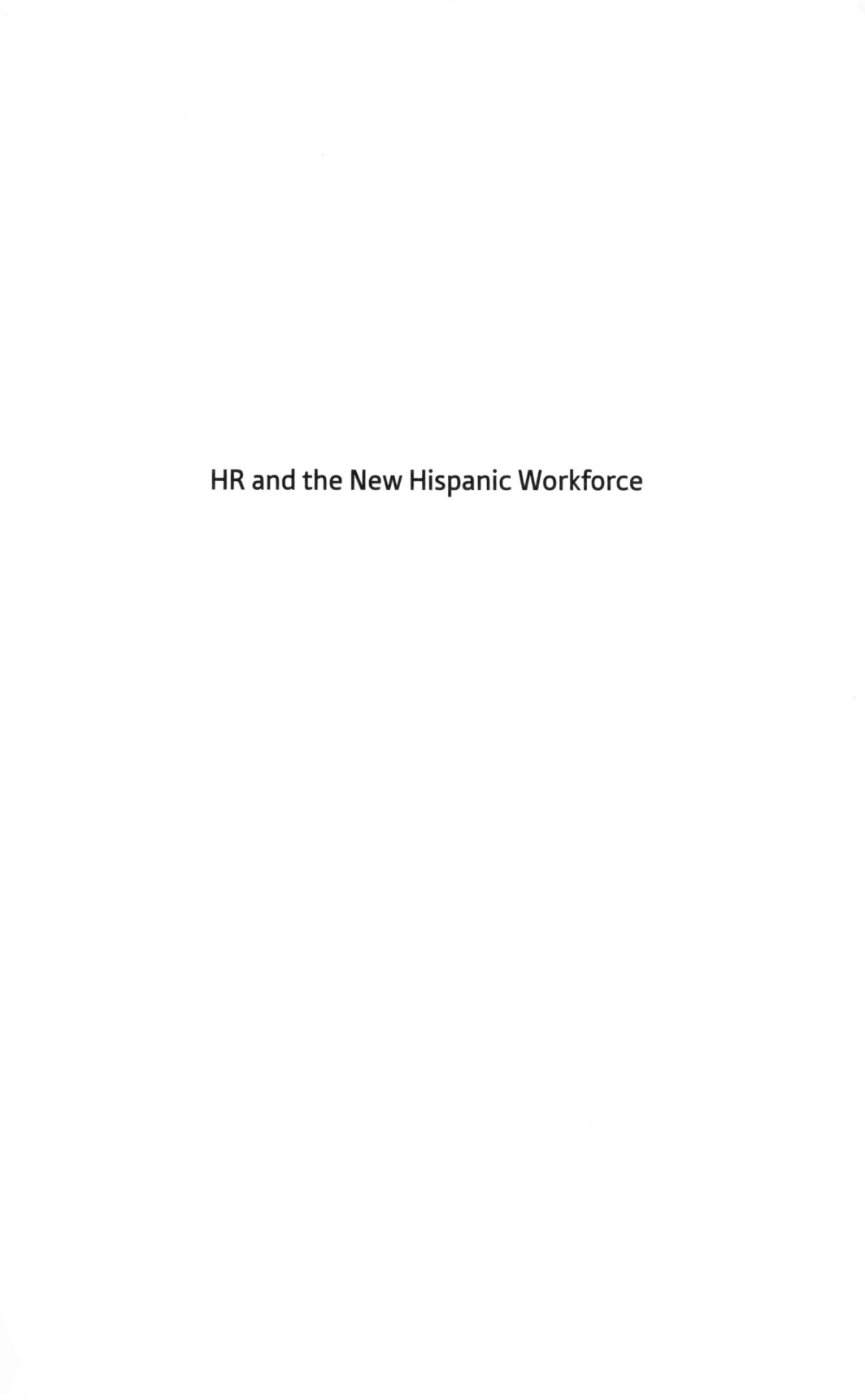

HR and the New Hispanic Workforce

HR AND THE *New* Hispanic *Workforce*

A COMPREHENSIVE GUIDE TO CULTIVATING
AND LEVERAGING EMPLOYEE SUCCESS

Louis E. V. Nevaer

Vaso Perimenis Ekstein, SPHR

Davies-Black Publishing
Mountain View, California

Published by Davies-Black Publishing, a division of CPP, Inc., 1055 Joaquin Road, 2nd Floor, Mountain View, CA 94043; 800-624-1765.

Special discounts on bulk quantities of Davies-Black books are available to corporations, professional associations, and other organizations. For details, contact the Director of Marketing and Sales at Davies-Black Publishing: 650-691-9123; fax 650-623-9271.

Copyright © 2007 by Davies-Black Publishing, a division of CPP, Inc. All rights reserved. No part of this book may be reproduced, stored in a retrieval system, or transmitted in any form by any means, electronic, mechanical, photocopying, recording, or otherwise, without written permission of the publisher, except in the case of brief quotations embodied in critical articles or reviews.

Davies-Black and its colophon are registered trademarks of CPP, Inc.

Visit the Davies-Black Publishing Web site at www.daviesblack.com.

Material from "Making Threats Credible" by Deepak Malhotra, *Negotiation* 8(3), March 2005, reprinted with permission of Harvard Business School Publishing. Material from The Media Audit reprinted with permission of International Demographics, Inc., TheMediaAudit.com. Material from *Strategic Human Resources: Frameworks for General Managers* by James N. Baron and David M. Kreps, © 1999 John Wiley & Sons, reprinted with permission of John Wiley & Sons. Material from "Speak to What Drives Them" by Anne Field, *Working Knowledge*, October 2003, reprinted with permission of Harvard Business School Publishing. Material from "Tips for Starting a Diversity Program," published by The Workplace Diversity Network, reprinted with permission of the Cornell University School of Industrial Labor Relations, Buffalo, New York.

11 10 09 08 07   10 9 8 7 6 5 4 3 2 1

Printed in the United States of America

Library of Congress Cataloging-in-Publication Data
Nevaer, Louis E. V.
HR and the new Hispanic workforce : a comprehensive guide to cultivating and leveraging employee success / Louis E. V. Nevaer and Vaso Perimenis Ekstein
      p. cm.
Includes bibliographical references and index.
ISBN 978-0-89106-189-2 (alk. paper)
1. Hispanic Americans—Employment. 2. Personnel management. I. Ekstein, Vaso Perimenis. II. Title.
HD8081.H7N48 2007
658.30089′68073—dc22
                                                                                            2006038285

FIRST EDITION
First printing 2007

*For Diego and Annalies Stork-Sanchez, who,
I expect, will enter the workforce in about 2025.*
Louis E. V. Nevaer

*For Jason and Sofia, my husband and daughter,
who are the loves of my life.*
Vaso Perimenis Ekstein

Contents

A Note on Terminology — xi
Acknowledgments — xiii
About the Authors — xv

Introduction — 1

1 Employee Selection — 13
How to Find, Attract, and Select the Best Hispanic Candidates

2 HR Policies — 67
Why Employee Policies and Manuals Are Necessary

3 Performance Management — 103
How to Evaluate the Performance of Hispanic Employees

4 Training and Development — 139
How Successful Companies Nurture Their Hispanic Workforce

5 Employee Relations and Retention — 181
How to Keep Hispanic Employees Challenged and Satisfied

Appendix 1: *Hispanic* Versus *Latino* in the Workplace — 237
Appendix 2: Important Hispanic Dates and Events — 239
Appendix 3: Organizations for Hispanic Employees — 249

Notes — 261
Index — 275

A Note on Terminology

In dealing with the Hispanic workforce, it is helpful for HR professionals to understand distinctions between the terms *Hispanic* and *Latino*. Most people consider *Hispanic* to be the more inclusive term; "Latinos" make up only 22 percent of all U.S. Hispanics, according to surveys conducted by Hispanic Economics.[1] (An analogy: While all New Yorkers are American, not all Americans are New Yorkers.)

The Pew Hispanic Center reported similar findings in a 2000 poll. In a choice between *Latino* and *Hispanic,* 53 percent of respondents had no preference, but 34 percent preferred *Hispanic*. The response, however, varied by particular areas within the United States. Respondents in California and the Northeast were more likely to prefer *Latino;* those in Texas and the South, *Hispanic*.[2]

Aside from the choice between the two terms, many simply prefer identification with their country of origin, as in Mexican, Cuban, or Guatamalan.

Note that *Hispanic* is a cultural-linguistic identity that has evolved over eleven centuries; *Latino* is a more recent term, emerging in the United States as part of the American civil rights movement in the 1970s. In the United States, *Hispanic* was first used during the Nixon administration in 1970 to denote people in the United States who spoke Spanish. The Census Bureau used *Hispanic* on a small number of its long census forms that year. A decade later, the bureau added it to all forms; in 2000 it added *Latino*.[3]

We feel that the designation *Hispanic,* as a historic identification for related cultural and linguistic traditions, is best suited to describing the phenomenon we witness in the United States today: the emergence of a bilingual consumer market and the continental integration of English and Spanish Americas through economic trade pacts and demographic changes. In addition, the more inclusive, apolitical term to use in a corporate setting is *Hispanic*. Primarily for that reason, we have chosen to use *Hispanic* over *Latino* to cover the HR considerations for this growing population group within the United States

See Appendix 1 for further discussion on *Hispanic* versus *Latino* terminology.

Acknowledgments

I am indebted to the steadfast support and valuable insights offered by Milton Alexander White, who patiently reviewed portions of the manuscript for this book. Although offering a dissenting opinion on some observations made in the text, his enthusiasm for this project was heartening.

—Louis E. V. Nevaer

I am truly blessed to have such a supportive husband who has encouraged me along the way, thus allowing me to change course in my career. This book would not have been written without his support, forbearance, cheer, and love.

I also owe my gratitude to the many colleagues with whom I have worked throughout the years who have helped me hone my skills and develop a deep appreciation for my craft.

—Vaso Perimenis Ekstein

The Society for Human Resource Management (SHRM) is the world's largest association devoted to human resource management. Representing more than 210,000 individual members, the Society's mission is both to serve human resource management professionals and to advance the profession. Founded in 1948, SHRM currently has more than 550 affiliated chapters within the United States and members in more than 100 countries. Visit SHRM Online at www.shrm.org.

About the Authors

Louis E. V. Nevaer is one of the nation's leading authorities on Hispanics in the United States. Author of more than ten books on economics and business management, including the critically acclaimed *The Rise of the Hispanic Market in the United States, Nafta's Second Decade,* and *The Dot-Com Debacle,* he is director of Hispanic Economics, which analyzes Hispanic consumer behavior. A contributor to Pacific News Service, his op-ed pieces appear in newspapers throughout the nation. He divides his time between New York and Mexico.

He can be reached at Hispanic-Workforce.com.

Vaso Perimenis Ekstein is a principal and consultant with Ekstein Consulting Services based in Miami, Florida, providing a wide range of human resources and technology consulting to businesses across the nation. She has worked in the banking and health care industries in human resources for eighteen years, providing leadership to help optimize employee retention, attraction, communication, productivity, and commitment to support organizational business objectives.

She has an undergraduate degree from the University of Miami in economics and a master of business administration degree from Nova Southeastern University, and holds a Senior Professional Human Resources (SPHR) certification. She can be reached at vaso@eksteinconsulting.com.

Introduction

A demographic sea change is moving across the American workplace, as unprecedented in scope as it was unforeseen. As recently as 1990, the U.S. Census believed that Hispanics would not overtake African Americans to become the nation's largest minority until 2020. It was an arresting development, therefore, when, in 2002, the U.S. Census reported that there were more Hispanics than blacks, and that the United States was the fastest-growing Spanish-speaking nation in the world. "Hispanics have edged past blacks as the nation's largest minority group, new figures released today by the Census Bureau showed. The Hispanic population in the United States is now roughly 37 million, while blacks number about 36.2 million," Lynette Clemetson declared in the *New York Times* in January 2003, documenting the federal government's official acceptance of the historic demographic developments in the United States in the first decade of the twenty-first century.[1]

Every year since then the Census Bureau, along with other federal agencies, has continued to document the structural changes in the American population, changes that herald the increasing proportion of Hispanics—and thus of Hispanic employees—in ways that, a mere generation ago, were unimaginable. Consider a few tantalizing facts:

- On average, Hispanics are almost a decade younger than the general population.

- More than a third of Hispanics are less than eighteen years old.

- Fertility rates of Hispanics are higher than the natural replacement level.

- More than 34 million Mexicans have a legal claim of some kind to immigrate to the United States.

- Hispanics who attain graduate degrees earn more than 15 percent more than their non-Hispanic counterparts.

These changes have not unfolded without comment. "It is a turning point in the nation's history, a symbolic benchmark of some significance," Roberto Suro, director of the Pew Hispanic Center, said of the emergence of Hispanics as the largest minority, displacing African Americans from their historic position. "If you consider how much of this nation's history is wrapped up in the interplay between black and white, this serves as an official announcement that we as Americans cannot think of race in that way any more."[2] Other voices have been raised in alarm. "The persistent inflow of Hispanic immigrants threatens to divide the United States into two peoples, two cultures, and two languages. Unlike past immigrant groups, Mexicans and other Hispanics have not assimilated into mainstream U.S. culture, forming instead their own political and linguistic enclaves—from Los Angeles to Miami—and rejecting the Anglo-Protestant values that built the American dream," Samuel Huntington of Harvard University wrote in the pages of *Foreign Affairs*.[3]

That sweeping demographic changes are transforming America's workforce is undeniable. Consider two facts:

- Hispanics in 2005 were 14 percent of the nation's population—but 22 percent of workers.

- If things continue on their present course, Hispanics in 2050 will represent 32 percent of the nation's population, but 55 percent of workers.[4]

These demographic changes, with Hispanics fast expanding throughout the American workforce, come at a time when there is an emerging literature documenting how human resource management (HRM) has a direct impact on an organization's performance. Empirical economic analysis for more than a decade has continued to demonstrate that companies with HRM strategies that involve paying higher wages relative to their competitors reap significant benefits in reduced absenteeism and employee turnover and increased productivity.[5]

One of the most compelling analyses about the strategic role HRM plays in the success of an organization was conducted by James Baron, Michael Hannan, and M. Diane Burton, who examined how the philosophical approaches of start-up founders in Silicon Valley affected the success of their enterprises.[6] In firms where the founders espoused and embraced a commitment-based employment model, which was defined, in part, by explicit commitment by management to the employees and endeavored to complement the firm's and employees' cultural worldview, productivity was higher and HRM conflicts less common.[7] The compelling lesson of this large-scale study demonstrates that an articulated, proactive use of HRM as a management tool is a successful strategy for managing employee relations, streamlining problem resolution, and nurturing a culture of mutual commitment and reciprocal loyalty.

In essence, when general management clearly articulated and defined the role of HRM, making human resource (HR) professionals an integral part of the organization's strategy for success, both profit and shareholder value were enhanced. Furthermore, a recognition that HRM consists of economic, social, and cultural components is an integral aspect of creating the proper framework for the successful administration of an organization's "human capital." This important distinction has gained currency only recently. "Human assets are hard to evaluate quantitatively, so they don't show up on the balance sheet," James Baron and David Kreps write. "But *whether or not the bean counters can assign dollar values to them, assets they are, and general managers must think of human resources as a form of capital.*"[8]

In this present decade, building on the foundation of a growing body of empirical studies and data, HR managers have matured as partners in the strategic management of their organizations, and HRM has become more fine-tuned as a science that employs an increasingly skilled corps of professionals. To a significant degree the newfound importance of HRM arises from management's belief that HRM has become an integrated *structural* system, not a random collection of disparate functions centered on payroll and labor law compliance functions. This approach, often referred to as *complementarities*, has required a seismic shift in HRM, which stands in contrast to the way HR professionals have historically seen themselves.[9]

"There are many reasons the HR department has been slow to change, not the least of which is the widespread belief that human resources is simply a fact of organizational life that has little or no effect on business performance," argues Edward Lawler of the University of Southern California.

> The time has come, however, to see beyond this limited view. Technology is driving a revolution in the way HR administration can be managed, giving HR executives new data-collection and analysis tools with which they can more easily demonstrate the importance of effective human capital management—to strategy and the bottom line. Furthermore, large administrative cost savings can also be realized by outsourcing activities that don't contribute to shareholder value. Companies that hone HR's contributions in both the human capital strategy and administrative realms can build a significant competitive advantage.[10]

It is in this pursuit of competitive advantage that this book explores the Hispanization of the nation's workforce and the emergence of HRM as a strategic management tool.

CHALLENGES AHEAD

The increase of Hispanics in the workforce and the emergence of HRM as a management tool constitute two of the most significant changes facing corporate America as the twenty-first century begins to unfold. How can HRM take its proper role as a tool for increasing productivity and profits? What does the explosion of Hispanics in the workforce mean? What are the characteristics of Hispanic employees that require dedicated strategies from HRM? How does America's increasingly bilingual consumer economy affect and inform the working environment? Is the performance achieved by Hispanic women with graduate degrees—who earn an average of $7,867 more than their non-Hispanic counterparts—indicative of how Hispanics in general will transform corporate America's productivity in the age of globalization? How can HRM cultivate Hispanic employees for the benefit of both employee and organization?

These questions have taken on a new urgency in recent years. "The number of Hispanic college graduates increased by 806,000 from approximately 3.6 million to 4.4 million. The 4.4 million includes more than 1.3 million with advanced degrees," Robert Jordan, president of International Demographics (which produces *The Media Audit*), reported in 2001. "The incomes of Hispanic college graduates and incomes of all college graduates are probably more comparable than most people would expect," Jordan adds.[11]

In the two-year period between 2002 and 2004 the Hispanic adult population in the seventy-nine largest metropolitan markets rose by 16 percent, while the number of Hispanic college graduates increased by 22 percent.[12] Not only are Hispanics increasing faster than the population as whole; they are accounting for a disproportionate number of college graduates. "The relationship between education, income and occupation stands out in the

TABLE 1
Hispanics:
The Fastest-Growing Demographic

Hispanic median age	26.7
National median age	35.9
No. of live births per 1,000, U.S. Hispanics, 2001	96.0
No. of live births per 1,000, national, 2001	64.2
Hispanic total fertility rate, 2001	2.4
National fertility rate, 2001	2.1
Natural replacement level	2.1

Sources: Centers for Disease Control and Prevention, Department of Health and Human Services, Table 3. Crude birth rates, fertility rates, and birth rates by age of mother, according to race and Hispanic origin; United States, selected years 1950–2001, U.S. Census Bureau, "Fertility of American Women, June 2002."

survey," Jordan notes, "and this relationship dispels any thought that the increasing affluence among young Hispanics is solely attributable to longer hours worked or multiple income households. . . . Overall, the research reveals a culturally diverse segment of our population which is growing rapidly."[13] See Table 1.

For HR professionals, it is revealing that, once they attain a college education, Hispanic employees often outperform their non-Hispanic colleagues. One segment—Hispanic women who hold graduate degrees—already has surpassed their counterparts in income level, according to Table 2.

TABLE 2
Once Hispanics Attain Graduate Degrees, They Excel

POPULATION	ANNUAL INCOME
Hispanic females with graduate degree, 2002	$58,623
Non-Hispanic females with graduate degree, 2002	$50,756

Source: U.S. Census Bureau, 2002, "Mean Annual Earnings by Education Level," Table A-3.

TABLE 3

Entries into the United States by Mexicans

Number of Mexicans who enter the United States every day illegally	1,200
Number of Mexican visitors who enter the United States every day in full compliance with immigration laws	28,835

Sources: For illegal immigrants, CNN, International Credit Monitor, and Department of Homeland Security; for legal visitors, figures provided by U.S. Department of Commerce's Office of Travel and Tourism Industries. See http://tinet.ita.doc.gov/view/f-2003-147-001/index.html.

Of equal interest is the seismic shift in the role Hispanics play throughout the American workforce. Many figures have been misrepresented or sensationalized by the media, but a generally agreed-upon estimate is that, on any given day, approximately 1,200 Hispanics enter the United States illegally. (No figure is available for a possibly corresponding question: How many illegal aliens leave the United States on any given day?) More instructive, however, are two subjects never discussed:

- How many Mexicans enter the United States every day in full compliance with all U.S. laws?

- How many Mexicans have some legal claim to residency in the United States?

The answers are compelling: Twenty-four times as many Mexicans enter the United States legally as illegally (see Table 3), and, under present immigration law, fully one in three Mexicans in Mexico—almost 34 million people—can make a *legal* claim to establish permanent residency in the United States. That few choose to exercise this right is another matter, but it underscores the demographics that today inform the evolution of the workforce in the United States.[14]

This book examines the characteristics of Hispanic employees and provides the management tools necessary to nurture and cultivate an organization's Hispanic workforce. HR professionals have redefined their role in the success of an organization. Now viewed as strategic players whose participation is an integral part of a firm's ability to maintain a sustainable competitive advantage, HRM is senior management's partner in developing and executing strategies. "HR professionals need a perspective that is compatible with and distinct from other business perspectives," Dave Ulrich and Wayne Brockbank write in the *Harvard Business Review*.

> That is, they must be able to understand and value the finance and sales perspectives, but they must also add their own point of view. Without such a unique and powerful perspective, they are redundant and fail in their aspirations as full business contributors. For example, an HR perspective that is both unique and powerful is one that establishes the linkages between employee commitment, customer attitudes, and investor returns. This unique view demonstrates a powerful connection between what is carried out by managers and employees inside the firm and what happens with customers and investors on the outside.[15]

STRUCTURE OF THE BOOK

This book enables HR professionals to understand Hispanic employees and to speak to the needs of their organization's Hispanic workforce. It is divided into five chapters, each analyzing how organizations can develop successful strategies for the proper and successful management of Hispanic employees.

Chapter 1, "Employee Selection: How to Find, Attract, and Select the Best Hispanic Candidates," addresses the continuing challenges of attracting Hispanic candidates. It provides insights into the cultural and linguistic obstacles that Hispanic candidates sometimes encounter and examines the reason their interview performance can be weaker than that of non-Hispanic candidates. The specific challenge this poses may require HRM to use nontraditional screening methods for identifying qualified candidates for the positions available. Similarly, because of cultural predispositions that are often at odds with mainstream American society, the Hispanic value system has different priorities that may require specific benefits to be presented in the total compensation package for a job offer to be attractive.

Chapter 2, "HR Policies: Why Employee Policies and Manuals Are Necessary," addresses the need to document the company's policies toward these employees, addressing the rights and obligations that pertain to the Hispanic staff. One area that has to be understood and properly documented is the political economy of unions in Hispanic thought. In some Hispanic societies, unions, rather than being antagonistic and adversarial, have functioned as organizations that advocate the workers' concerns and demands. In many countries, from Mexico to Argentina, unions are in fact government-sponsored organizations, a mechanism for pacifically resolving problems in the worker-employer relationship. How does the Hispanic experience with, understanding of, and relationship to unions inform the organization at a time when the U.S. labor force includes increasing numbers of Hispanic employees? Finally, what are the specific provisions that speak to Hispanic employees?

Chapter 3, "Performance Management: How to Evaluate the Performance of Hispanic Employees," builds the skills of HR professionals for developing quantitative tools for meaningful performance reviews of Hispanic employees. This is vital if a performance management system is to be implemented successfully.

While the bottom line constitutes the definitive measure of an organization's performance in a market economy, ascertaining how individual members of a team performed is more difficult. Conducting the performance appraisal is more challenging, given the cultural nuances that inform the Hispanic experience in the workforce. This is where HRM's role as a strategic player can shine.

Chapter 4, "Training and Development: How Successful Companies Nurture Their Hispanic Workforce," builds on the enhanced HRM role and value to the organization. HRM must adapt to the basic nature and needs of Hispanic employees as it takes its place as a strategic player that can deliver value to the organization. This chapter provides a road map for implementing a program that can nurture Hispanic employees within the organization. How is orientation different for Hispanic employees? What are the educational and professional needs of Hispanic employees as they build seniority? What is the proper HRM response to the increasing use of Spanish in the workplace as the United States becomes a bilingual consumer economy? And finally, how does the Hispanic employee population affect notions of race and diversity in the American workforce?

The last chapter, "Employee Relations and Retention: How to Keep Hispanic Employees Challenged and Satisfied," addresses the daily interactions in the workplace that speak to the concerns of Hispanic employees. It discusses issues that may affect their success within the organization. In the same way that Hispanics challenge traditional HRM strategies for dealing with diversity, linguistic obstacles may arise as an integral part of internal corporate communications. While salaried Hispanic employees are expected to be fluent in English, this may be an impractical expectation for some nonsalaried workers. Of equal concern are the changes that Hispanic value systems are imposing on an organization's benefit structure. How does Spanish inform the way an organization communicates internally? How do Hispanic employees want to be recognized for superior achievement? What do they expect in terms of balancing their professional and personal lives? These expectations spill over into other areas: how internal employee relations are managed, how management can demonstrate its commitment to Hispanic employees, and how the social responsibility commitments of the organization are evolving to reflect Hispanic sensibilities in terms of service and responsibility to the community. For HRM, these conditions can be improved upon through succinct questioning of Hispanic employees who leave the firm; exit interviews can be a valuable tool for improving the work environment.

Each chapter concludes with an "In Review" summary of the major points addressed in the discussion.

Employee Selection

HOW TO FIND, ATTRACT, AND SELECT THE BEST HISPANIC CANDIDATES

With the increasing presence of Hispanics in the workforce, identifying, attracting, and retaining Hispanic workers represents an enormous investment on the part of organizations. The operational and transactional costs associated with employee turnover represent, on average, about two years' annual salary.[1] It is imperative to get it as right as possible, simply in terms of a straightforward cost-benefit analysis. With the reasonable concern about the expenses—in time, money, and organizational morale—of disruptions or interruptions in human resources, HR professionals are under mounting pressure to fulfill both the mandate for "getting it right" and the practical necessity of an ever-more-diverse workforce to compete in our increasingly complex business and social environment.

"The employment relationship is about much more than the exchange of labor services for a paycheck," James Baron and David

Kreps argue in *Strategic Human Resources*. "It is an economic relation in part, but it is a potent social and psychological one as well. Effective human resource management depends on process and symbolism no less than on the content and financial value of company personnel policies and practices. Taking a purely economic perspective on employment can blind you to important forces at work in HRM."[2]

But this is one side of the challenge. The market itself is the other side: "Verizon Wireless announced last week that it will hire 200 bilingual employees in the Washington, D.C., area because so many of its customers now speak Spanish. It's not surprising: after increasing in number by 142 percent since 1980, Hispanics are now the largest minority in the United States, according to the U.S. Census Bureau," Todd Raphael reported in *Workforce Management*.[3]

THE MARKET AND DEMOGRAPHICS

The demographic and social makeup of the workforce an organization wants is market driven. The emergence of the United States as a *bilingual consumer economy* requires HRM to focus on how it can encourage Hispanic, or at least bilingual, candidates to apply, and to develop mechanisms for vetting these candidates. Verizon Wireless is playing catch-up: caught ill prepared for the dramatic changes in the demographics of a specific market, it found itself understaffed in bilingual employees for its customer service department. Other firms arranged to have more time for the methodological implementation of strategic plans: American Airlines and FedEx, anticipating the increased business that the North American Free Trade Agreement, or NAFTA, would fuel, were prepared to hire and train the hundreds of employees required to meet the substantial growth in their business with Mexican passengers and clients.[4]

These are compelling economic reasons for a diverse workforce, and they go hand in hand with social and legal mandates that encourage, if not require, that an organization's workforce resemble the demographics of the general population. The demographics of a firm's customers are the single most significant external factor driving diversity—and the way diversity is defined.[5] A successful HRM strategy is an integral approach, one in which the role of HR is expressed in an organization's mission statement. "For openness, flexibility, and creativity vis-à-vis employee needs to be germane to company process, they need to be incorporated into the mission and vision statements by which a company defines itself," Harriet Hankin, author of *The New Workforce,* explains. "I am often amazed at how thoughtful and reasonable employees are when entrusted with company-related strategy development."[6]

An integral, structured HRM policy designed to identify, attract, hire, and nurture Hispanic employees remains a challenge for many organizations. One factor is the speed with which Hispanics are settling throughout the country. Whereas in 1998, 47.8 percent of adult Hispanics in the top metropolitan areas lived in Los Angeles, New York, and Miami, by 2003 this figure had dropped to 41.2 percent, meaning that Hispanic populations in medium-sized cities—and away from the East and West coasts—were experiencing double-digit growth.[7]

"The metro markets of Boston, Denver, Atlanta, Orlando and Philadelphia now have adult Hispanic populations of more than 200,000," Robert Jordan of *The Media Audit* reports. "And some of these markets are experiencing explosive Hispanic growth. Between 2000 and 2003 Denver's Hispanic adult population increased from 209,000 to 312,000. During the same years, Boston's adult Hispanic population increased from 209,000 to 255,000."[8]

Large as it is—twenty-eight U.S. cities now include 100,000 or more adult Hispanics—the adult Hispanic population throughout the nation is small compared to the number of Hispanic youngsters expected to enter the workforce by 2020. The case for diversity is strengthened as broader perspectives about the changing nature of the consumer economy become apparent. In the same way that Verizon Wireless underestimated the explosive growth of the Hispanic consumer population in northern Virginia and the nation's capital, most organizations have only recently begun to address in earnest the need to expand recruitment of Hispanic employees, consider their alternatives to courting Hispanic employees, and create opportunities that nurture Hispanic employees throughout their ranks.

CHALLENGES OF ATTRACTING HISPANIC CANDIDATES

In an ideal world, demographics would correspond with employees' needs. This would facilitate HRM's ability to meet an organization's strategic objectives—but it is seldom the case. As a result, conflicts emerge: the strategic mission of an organization becomes difficult to achieve in the face of a dearth of qualified applicants in a specific market. Critics often point to disparate statistics as evidence of corporate failures. Taking a page from historic civil rights and advocacy campaigns, Hispanics have begun to ask: If we constitute 14 percent of the population, shouldn't we constitute 14 percent of management positions, and not just 5 percent, as is the case?[9]

That's a fair question, considering the fact that talent is randomly distributed throughout humanity. In an ideal world, opportunities would be made available to all, and the workforce of most organizations would naturally reflect national demographics. Professional associations and social activists alike point to "parity" as a way of trying to sensitize organizations to the aspirations of Hispanics and the obligations expected of socially responsible firms that are good corporate citizens. But for all its noble intentions, parity faces harsh realities.

Hispanics with college degrees, for instance, are not randomly distributed throughout the country: they are concentrated in one specific geographic region—Miami, Florida. A comparison of the educational levels of Hispanics in Miami, New York, and Los Angeles, for instance, reveals remarkable differences. In Miami more than a third of all adult Hispanics are college educated. The percentage of adult Hispanics holding college degrees falls dramatically in the New York metropolitan area, to only 22 percent. And a much larger drop occurs in the Los Angeles market, where the proportion of adult Hispanics who have graduated from college is less than 17 percent.[10] Thus the local labor pool itself constitutes the single most important challenge for organizations seeking to attract and recruit Hispanic workers in salaried positions. For HR professionals, the regional differences represent significant obstacles: HR officers in south Florida have a plethora of qualified candidates, while those in Los Angeles have to scramble to find suitable candidates for the positions available, and often these positions languish unfilled quarter after quarter.

Disparity Between Hispanic Education Levels and Opportunities

Hispanics continue to have the lowest overall education attainment level of any demographic group in the United States. "Rarely do we see the market-to-market difference we find in the study of Hispanic college graduates," Robert Jordan points out in a report for the research firm of International Demographics. "It's important to note that some of the markets with the greatest number of Hispanics have enormous differences in the percentage with a college education."[11]

Four out of five Hispanics in the United States are of Mexican or Central American ancestry. The remaining Hispanics are of Caribbean (mainly from Puerto Rico, the Dominican Republic, and Cuba) or South American origin. It is the Mexican and Central American component of U.S. Hispanics that skews the education figures down. In the 2000 census, slightly more than half of Hispanics of Mexican or Central American background reported not understanding English "fluently."[12] The disparities in education account for the continuing economic disenfranchisement of the majority of Hispanics in California, Texas, and the Southwest.[13] For HR professionals, it is necessary to understand the different circumstances that Hispanics face: a Cuban American doctor in Miami has very little in common with a Mexican American day laborer in the parking lot of a Home Depot in Los Angeles.

It is not surprising, then, to see how differences in education levels lead to sweeping disparities between the opportunities of Hispanics in Miami and those of Hispanics in Los Angeles. In Miami, where Hispanics populate all aspects of business life (constituting almost half of managers throughout all organizations in Miami-Dade County), they exceed their proportionate representation in demographic terms.[14] If Hispanics make up 14 percent of the nation's population, one can argue that they are overrepresented in Miami. By the same token, in some areas of the country, where Hispanics account for as little as 3.2 percent of the workforce, HR professionals encounter numerous challenges in their quest for proportionate representation.[15]

A general observation can be made about the U.S. Hispanic population: Hispanics residing east of the Mississippi have higher educational attainment levels than Hispanics residing west of the Mississippi. It is far easier to find candidates for middle- and upper-level positions in New York and Miami than it is in San Francisco or Los Angeles. The geographic discrepancies in Hispanic education levels are attributable to various socioeconomic and cultural factors. South Florida has witnessed waves of immigration from Cuba, a nation whose managerial and educated classes sought political asylum after the Cuban Revolution created a communist state. New York has witnessed a continuous movement back and forth by Puerto Ricans (who are U.S. citizens by virtue of Puerto Rico's commonwealth status) and immigrants from the Dominican Republic. Puerto Ricans and Dominicans in the New York metropolitan area are characterized by patterns traditional to the United States: families seeking better lives arrive, entering the labor and trade professions, sacrificing to give their children increased opportunities for higher education. The Los Angeles area continues to be at the forefront of illegal immigration, where scores of thousands of Mexican and Central American rural individuals, often lacking basic schooling in their own language, arrive in a place where they don't speak the language and have only their labor to sell.

"The difference in unemployment rates between Hispanics and the overall U.S. population is not surprising in light of the gap in educational attainment and English-language skills faced by many Hispanic workers," Andrea Lehman reports in *Hispanic Business*. "A higher rate of unemployment among youths, a group mostly still in school and with less education and experience, is also expected."[16] Not only is it to be expected; it is what is found, to the consternation of many societal interests.

Despite the disparities in education levels, however, Hispanics continue to enter the workforce and make impressive catch-up strides in their education. In 2004, for instance, adults with college degrees represented 20.9 percent of the Hispanic population, an increase from 19.8 percent in 2002 and 18.9 percent in 2000.[17] Expectations are increasing that Hispanics will be afforded greater career and employment opportunities as more and more Hispanics complete their college education. Policymakers, Hispanic activists, and social commentators alike are raising the bar on what is expected of corporate America.

Hiring Obstacles for HR

Organizations throughout the United States face societal pressure to become more diverse and to work to resolve the inequities that continue to characterize the American workforce. HR professionals who work in regional markets where the supply of qualified Hispanic candidates is meager often grow exasperated by the obstacles they encounter. More often than not, while social commentators question the commitment of corporate America to ameliorating the inequities that exist in the workforce, it is the absence of working relationships with institutions of higher learning, community agencies, and industry organizations that impede progress.

Consider the experience of one industry: journalism. The National Association of Hispanic Journalists, or NAHJ, a Washington, D.C.–based organization, recognizing that the cause of the problem is not lack of will but inability to attract Hispanic candidates, launched its Parity Project, designed to increase career opportunities for Hispanic writers, editors, and news anchors *and* contribute to greater diversity throughout the print, broadcast, and Internet media. For many media organizations serving local markets undergoing explosive growth in the Spanish-speaking segment, finding qualified bilingual employees is a challenge. At the NAHJ 2005 convention in Ft. Worth, Texas, scores of companies participated in a job fair, attempting to identify Hispanic journalists. From ESPN Deportes to the *New York Times*, recruiters and HR professionals met with candidates for the better part of a week.

"For us at Knight-Ridder," one recruiter noted, "finding staff for *El Nuevo Herald* [the Spanish-language sister publication of the *Miami Herald*] is no problem, but for the [San Jose, California] *Mercury News*, it's another story."[18] An officer at the Gannett organization expressed disappointment that he and his staff had been unable to identify the number of candidates they had hoped to find for the scores of positions earmarked for bilingual staff. "There are simply more positions available than there are qualified Spanish-speaking candidates."[19] This stands in sharp contrast to the familiar American experience when it comes to immigrants and language.[20]

U.S. Hispanics, through sheer demographics, have reached such a critical mass, however, that the country is in the throes of developing a bilingual consumer economy. The sweeping implications for HRM of this reality must be reflected in HRM strategies for the proper management of an organization's workforce. Indeed, the challenges confronting journalism are not unlike those that virtually all organizations throughout American society are encountering. The demand for creative ways of identifying Hispanic candidates is one reason the NAHJ's Parity Project works purposefully to build relationships. "The Parity Project has been a critical part of our effort to improve newsroom diversity," says John Temple, editor, president, and publisher of the *Rocky Mountain News*. "The partnership with NAHJ put a new emphasis on this issue and gave us help in recruiting and developing future employees that we would not have had otherwise."[21]

THREE MAJOR CHALLENGES

The NAHJ offers a clear illustration of relationships HRM needs to build with industry associations and educational institutions to overcome three challenges to attracting Hispanic employees: inadequate educational attainment among Hispanics, Hispanic resistance to traditional employment recruiting, and subtle biases about Hispanics within organizations.

Lack of Education

Awareness of the history of education in Mexico can help make this problem understandable.

Education in Mexico
After decades of neglect, Mexico's educational system emerged in much better shape during Vicente Fox's administration, 2000–2006. Standards increased—until recently, Mexican children could drop out of school after six years, and many in impoverished rural areas did not attend even that long. But with the fast-track development of the "e-Mexico" program (which intended, with Microsoft's participation, to wire Mexico by the end of 2006), education was the Fox administration's largest public works initiative.

One achievement of the Mexican Revolution, 1910–1917, was to provide free public education, in principle including higher education. Mexico's National Autonomous University, for instance, charged an annual tuition of $3 for students who satisfied the academic requirements. In theory this was ideal; millions of American families would be grateful if their children's college tuition vanished so effortlessly. In practice, however, Mexico encountered harsh economic limitations. If public universities are open to anyone meeting entrance requirements, classes are crowded and have long waiting lists. If universities cannot defray their expenses by charging tuition, they must acquiesce to politicians who authorize budgets. If professors are overwhelmed by the number of students in classes and by the constant struggle with school administrators over department budgets and union leaders about their paychecks, they become demoralized.

In Mexico's case, other factors have compromised public education. Throughout much of the twentieth century Mexico's population grew fantastically—from 20 million in 1900 to over 100 million in 2000. This growth strained the public education system as efforts were made to reach out to rural communities where the local residents didn't even speak Spanish well. The difficulty of finding educators who were proficient in one of dozens of Native American languages was another impediment. Constrained by the inability to finance modernization through tuition and subjected to harsh political realities, Mexico's public education system has fallen further and further behind, especially since the 1970s, when technology became part of education systems in other countries.

That Mexico's middle class supported the private schools to which it sent its children (and that other privileged Mexican families were loyal to the foreign universities where they sent their children) did not improve matters. Private universities in Mexico have computers and state-of-the-art facilities; Mexican alumni give generously to their alma maters, from Harvard University to the London School of Economics. This has aggravated the plight of Mexico's public universities. While private institutions of higher learning in Mexico have prospered from the generosity of their alumni, large public universities languish. Mexicans' donation of millions to foreign universities has become a status symbol, resulting in the frustrating paradox that Mexican philanthropists are more eager to help rich institutions abroad than show concern for the dire circumstances confronting Mexican students. That well-to-do Mexicans have no vested interest in improving the nation's public education system constitutes yet another obstacle that must be addressed.

To address decades of educational neglect, Fox launched the e-Mexico program, which seeks to hook up all of Mexico to the Internet, giving millions of people access to the technology. "This is the first time a Mexican president has put in black and white a government program to do something regarding technological development to help his country become more productive and competitive," Leonardo Ortiz, Microsoft's spokesman in Mexico City, said when a $6 million donation was announced on April 25, 2002. This was less than nine months after Microsoft announced a $60 million investment to train twenty thousand Mexican software programmers. "Microsoft says its donation will help Mexico foster its national software industry by training Mexican engineers," *New York Times* reporter Graham Gori wrote.[22]

Yet this has done little to address the needs of Mexico's very poor, the source of most Mexican immigration (legal and illegal) to the United States.[23] By every economic measure, the most materially disadvantaged group of people in Mexico is her Native American citizens—some 10 million indigenous people. Education programs that reach out to indigenous communities have proved successful in other parts of Latin America in recent years. In Guatemala, where the eBay Foundation has spearheaded efforts to help the indigenous Maya people of San Pedro La Laguna, similar results are forthcoming. "Our kids are getting three years of computer training. It's excellent," Emilio Battz, who runs the Colegio Bethel (Bethel School), said of eBay's efforts to help connect this rural community to the information superhighway. "I'm a [Maya], and we're typically very timid and think we're less important than those people with blue eyes and blond hair. Now that the children are learning new skills, they are seeing their own value."[24]

This culture of educational neglect informs the lives of Hispanics in the United States. As in Mexico, the ability of American Hispanics to pursue higher education is a question of cost. "Latino high school graduates enroll in college at a higher rate than non-Hispanic white students but are far less likely to earn a four-year degree—the single-most important key to higher earnings and leading jobs—a nonpartisan research group said here today," Diana Jean Schemo reports.[25] The report, issued by the Pew Hispanic Center, suggested that Latinos were held back by financial pressures, not a lack of interest in pursuing postsecondary education. Many enroll in two-year community colleges rather than four-year institutions, take partial course loads, and must work to supplement their families' income.[26]

Throughout the twentieth century, consecutive waves of Mexican migration have been propelled as much by the wage disparities between Mexico and the United States as by the inability of the Mexican economy to create sufficient jobs for its population. Upon arriving in the United States, by virtue of coming from underprivileged backgrounds, these immigrants, legal or otherwise, find themselves linguistically, culturally, and socially alienated, disenfranchised, and at odds in their new land. How does HRM prepare for these future workers of America?

Reality for HR and Workers in the United States
For the majority of recent immigrants who swell the ranks of U.S. Hispanics, the question of securing an education is a challenge. Consider the experience in Denison, a small town in Iowa. After an influx of immigrants from Mexico and Central America, the town sponsored classes to teach these new residents English. Soon after the program was launched, as Dale Maharidge writes

in the acclaimed book he named after the town, a "revelation was that many of the adults were either illiterate or only marginally literate in Spanish. These were not cosmopolitan ... urbanites from Mexico City or other major Latin metropolises. They were *campesinos*, meaning peasants, or country people."[27]

Hispanics, not unlike other ethnic groups, may be self-conscious about their level of educational attainment, particularly if they feel it is lacking. They often don't understand their educational options. Far too many are forced to leave school to provide an additional income for their families and are able to resume their studies only through tremendous sacrifice.

HRM might take these facts into consideration in providing learning opportunities to ensure the success and contribution of Hispanic employees to the organization. A positive vehicle for securing the interest of competent future Hispanic workers is internship programs.

Citigroup offers one of the most successful internship programs in existence. Through its Citigroup Foundation, promising minority high school students are identified, supported through scholarships, and, once they are enrolled in college, given the opportunity to participate in summer internships at various divisions. In this way future employees are identified, acculturated to the firm's way of doing business, and allowed to gain the experience and confidence that will bring them success as they complete their studies and embark on their professional careers.

Hispanic Resistance to Traditional Employment Recruiting

If level of educational attainment limits the pool of potential Hispanic employees west of the Mississippi, HRM encounters another limit for the entire nation: the challenge of overcoming Hispanic resistance to the recruiting methods generally employed by corporate America. "Once the firm decides what types of workers it wants, both in terms of their average qualities and the amount of dispersion sought around those averages, it must find ways to select among applicants," Baron and Kreps report. "But this formulation—the firm chooses from a set of applicants—doesn't do justice to an important part of the process, namely *encouraging desirable people to apply*."[28]

Cultural and acculturation factors undermine the usual recruitment process where Hispanics are concerned. Consider the three fundamental recruitment tools organizations throughout the United States use to identify, screen, and hire employees: applicant self-selection, co-worker referrals, and staffing agencies and search firms. Then read the discussion on using an employment brand to attract Hispanic candidates.

Applicant Self-Selection

This refers to the actions an organization takes to tell the general public about the career opportunities it offers, its corporate culture, its participation in civic and community endeavors, its workplace conditions, and its responsiveness to the needs of Hispanic workers. Applicant self-selection remains an underperforming way to identify Hispanic candidates, provided efforts to diffuse a firm's reputation are conducted exclusively in English. However, it is possible to overcome this problem. Procter & Gamble is one example of a firm that has cultivated a Hispanic-friendly workplace environment and is held in high esteem by Hispanics. Although Hispanic women total about 500 employees out of P&G's 38,000-strong workforce, recruiting for more Hispanic women has become a priority for the firm. With the naming of Graciela Eleta de

Cacho as vice president for Procter & Gamble's Multicultural Development Organization in North America, making her P&G's highest-ranking Hispanic woman, a more aggressive campaign is under way to get the word out to Hispanics through Spanish-language media.

Eleta de Cacho, whose responsibilities consist of the development and execution of marketing and retail strategies aimed at the Hispanic and African American market in the United States and Puerto Rico, has been at the forefront of taking P&G's stellar reputation among Hispanics and making it into a recruitment tool by focusing on Hispanic media outlets in both English and Spanish, letting U.S. Hispanics know about P&G's career opportunities, attractive salaries, and workplace environment sensitive to Hispanic culture. Taking to heart P&G's mission statement, "We attract and recruit the finest people in the world. We build our organization from within, promoting and rewarding people without regard to any difference unrelated to performance. We act on the conviction that the men and women of Procter & Gamble will always be our most important asset," P&G consistently makes the ranks in *Hispanic Magazine*'s "Hispanic 100" best companies for Hispanics.

Co-worker Referrals

Referrals are a preferred way of identifying candidates, and this is particularly true of Hispanics because loyalty to a company or brand is high, ranking with loyalty to family in some marketing studies. Nonetheless, companies using this system often run into difficulty. First, the positive side: A study by the University of North Carolina, Chapel Hill, indicates that Hispanic workers are approximately 50 percent more likely to use contacts, friends, or relatives to find a job than whites or other minority groups are.[29] Employee referral programs offer several advantages:

- They bring in quality candidates. Current employees are well situated to determine if someone they know has the qualifications to perform the duties of the job and also if that person would be happy in the open position.

- They prescreen candidates for cultural fit. The informal communication between an existing employee and a potential one serves as a prescreening method for locating a match for the requirements of the job, workplace environment, and culture.

- They involve employees in the recruiting process. A current employee often feels a moral responsibility to both the employer and the potential candidate; the current employee's reputation may be at risk if the candidate is not able to perform the job or if the candidate is unhappy and leaves.

- They provide resulting hires with a support system from their first day on the job. Hispanic employees are likely to be happy working with the friend or relative who recommended them. This also fosters teamwork.

- They reduce overall costs of hiring. Search costs are greatly diminished if existing employees can identify potential new hires.

The value of co-worker referrals is so great that most organizations have an incentive package, in terms of bonuses or other benefits for referrals (paid vacation, additional time off).

Thus an employee referral program can be an effective recruitment sourcing strategy since Hispanic workers tend to find jobs through networks of family and friends. In today's tight labor market, encouraging existing staff to act as ambassadors and recruiters for your organization is inexpensive, efficient, and effective.

For example, Angela Greenfeather, recruiting operations program coordinator of Sabre in Fort Worth, Texas, reports the company's employee referral program generated more than 7,000 résumés in the first twenty-four months. Sabre awards cash (from $100 to $1,000 based on the position) to the referring employee. In just over two years, the program has paid out more than $450,000 while saving Sabre almost $1,000,000 in recruiting expenses.[30] At Baptist Health South Florida, a health care organization in Miami, the employee referral program was the source of 42 percent of hires. Most referral bonuses are paid in two parts: upon hire and then after the recruit's first ninety days of employment. Many companies also offer annual raffles and super prizes such as trips, cruises, and the like. Furthermore, depending on staffing shortages, companies can offer special deals throughout the year for a defined period of time, targeting certain jobs.

On the negative side, the limit of this HRM tool is self-evident: so few people in the United States socialize with those outside their race or ethnic group that an organization needs to have *some* Hispanic employees before it will get internal referrals for other Hispanics as candidates. This may not be a problem for organizations in the agricultural, food processing, service, and construction industries, which, in some places, rely disproportionately on Hispanic manual laborers, but when an organization attempts to identify Hispanics for managerial positions, co-worker referrals are a limited, and limiting, HRM tool.[31] Once a few Hispanics are hired throughout an organization, however, brand recognition throughout the community of potential employees follows. "Referrals have been generating our biggest pocket of diverse employees," reports Ayesha Khan, a staffing specialist at the GE Medical Systems facility in Waukesha, Wisconsin. "We make the program very visible."[32]

Unlike with the GE facility, some HR groups undersell their referral programs. Employees who don't know about them can't use them. Even those who know about them may forget or ignore them. If recruitment of Hispanic employees is a priority, nothing is more important than broadcasting your referral program. Consider some of these practical ways to get the word out about the importance of the employee referral award program.[33]

- Mention the program and its awards in every companywide publication.

- Post flyers on bulletin boards in area stores, on campuses, or in other areas likely to attract Hispanic employees.

- Send periodic companywide e-mail messages reminding employees of the program.

- Stress the importance of the program to department heads. Ask managers to bring up the program in meetings.

Review your current referral bonus program. Is it up-to-date? Does it offer enough incentive to make it worth an employee's while to recruit on the company's behalf? If what you're offering seems too small for the economic climate, think about increasing it. If new funds aren't available to add to the program, think about adjusting your existing recruiting budget. Remember: Employee referral programs are the most cost-effective recruitment strategy, so they are well worth funding.

Staffing Agencies and Search Firms

The third tool offers mixed results, driven by geography. In Miami, search firms are a magnificent resource for identifying world-class candidates for positions at all levels. In New York, they provide a respectable roster of Hispanic candidates. But west of the Mississippi, their utility diminishes greatly.

In addition, although search firms specialize in a variety of fields and industries, their superior technology for identifying candidates is skewed toward the technical fields: engineers, computer programmers, and accountants, for example. When it comes to identifying Hispanic managers outside the major urban centers on the eastern seaboard, search firms are of limited use.

What to Do
The challenge for HR professionals, then, is to identify Hispanic candidates outside the realm of traditional recruiting methods. The emphasis on campus recruiting to identify future employees, the widespread use of internship programs to nurture potential managers—and spread the organization's reputation as part of a branding campaign on campuses—and the use of mentoring programs for acculturating Hispanic employees once hired are the foundation upon which attracting Hispanic employees can develop. Of course, demographics will drive Hispanic recruitment: When one in five available workers is Hispanic, recruiters will see more Hispanics simply because they constitute the available labor force. In terms of competitive advantage, however, firms such as Procter & Gamble will maintain an edge as Hispanics see them as *preferred* employers.

Once the recruiting process begins, it generates its own momentum: campus and internship programs lead to identifying and hiring Hispanics, and as their ranks grow within an organization, the reputation—or brand—of the firm is enhanced within the Hispanic community. Through mentoring and the identification of role models Hispanics in the organization feel secure and thrive. These trends complement each other, and Hispanics begin to self-select themselves for positions, co-worker referrals increase, and search organizations find that candidates identify that firm as a place where they would like their résumés to be considered.

The Hispanic Labor Pool and Employment Brands

Organizations manage two interrelated brands—a product or service brand in the product market and an employment brand in the labor market. The product and employment brands are related and mutually supportive. A strong product brand can play a major role in the health of the employment brand. The employment brand can in turn be instrumental in attracting and retaining employees who can add value to the company and its services or products, reinforcing the product brand.

Creating an effective employment brand is an important part of the employment sourcing strategic plan for any organization. With the increasing numbers of Hispanics throughout the workforce, HR practitioners have an opportunity to avail themselves of existing employees for recruitment purposes. A firm's employment brand, in many ways, is the labor market's perception of a company's employment value proposition. It can also be thought of as the internalized sum of impressions your organization makes on an applicant.[34] The employment brand attracts the type of employees necessary to build and support the company's products and services. It also helps to retain talent, reducing the cost of turnover.

Although the benefits of attracting Hispanic workers are clear, HR professionals are having difficulty tapping into that labor pool. If Hispanics are not attracted by traditional recruiting efforts, it may be because they often don't believe that traditional methods will help them get a job, says Abe Tomas Hughes, chairman of the board of the Hispanic Alliance for Career Enhancement (HACE). This lack of appreciation may be due to lack of understanding regarding how these methods work.[35] The director of recruiting services at one of the most prominent electronic job boards for Hispanic professionals provides the following advice regarding employment branding for Hispanics.[36]

1. Hispanics typically do not respond well to cool or trendy descriptions of work or work environments.

2. Terms such as *young, dynamic,* and *entrepreneurial* and statements such as "define your own job" do not resonate as well with the Hispanic community as with other segments of American culture.

3. Hispanics typically seek out job opportunities that are clearly solid and have defined paths.

4. Job titles hold a great deal of weight with Hispanics, especially when designed in a manner that provides a sense of movement toward higher positions.

Hispanics often find jobs through networks of friends and family. As a result, employers wishing to attract Hispanic workers must take a long-term approach that establishes a word-of-mouth reputation that accurately reflects what employment with the company may offer to this particular segment of the workforce.

Edwin Garcia, CEO of the National Society of Hispanic MBAs (NSHMBA) in Dallas, says the biggest recruitment concern for organizations is to "cultivate a positive employer image within the Hispanic community." Hispanics tend to be brand conscious and loyal when it comes to purchasing decisions, so organizations with a strong employment brand will benefit.

Establishing a brand requires the following steps:

1. Understand the Hispanic culture. Reaching the right people is impossible without knowing who they are.

2. Show that the organization offers opportunities for advancement. Talented workers need to know that they will have genuine chances for advancement regardless of their ethnicity, culture, or accent.

3. Get involved in the Hispanic community. This goes a long way in building trust.

Understanding the Hispanic culture is vital to creating the right employment brand. Before understanding can occur, it is vital to recognize that the global label of "Hispanic" cannot be used as the sole basis for creating the canvas for the employment brand. Hispanics are not a homogeneous group. As mentioned earlier in this chapter, the values of Mexican Americans will differ from those of Cuban Americans. Recruiters must understand these differences if they wish to create the proper connections and relationships with Hispanic job candidates. For example, when Walgreens planned to place employment ads on radio stations targeting Hispanic workers, the director of recruitment realized that using the same ad for different radio stations would prove to be ineffective. Instead, Walgreens customized the ads to target Hispanic subgroups, a lesson learned from HACE, an organization that can help educate companies on the Hispanic community.

Hispanics are proud of their heritage but they want to be hired based on their merits and credentials. Having talented Hispanics in upper-level positions to serve as role models and reflect a culture of inclusion sends an important message to current and potential workers.

Building trust within the community is also a big part of branding. Many companies, such as Hewitt Associates and Caterpillar, have developed strategies that reach out to schools to build a pipeline of future Hispanic talent. Caterpillar formed a partnership with Texas A&M University because of the school's reputation for producing outstanding engineering students.[37] Participating in or sponsoring local cultural events is also a great way to tap into the Hispanic community.

Subtle Biases Against Hispanics

Corporate America has made great progress in creating an inclusive workplace environment. Business and the military are the two areas of American life that are most integrated, most welcoming of the sweeping diversity of peoples that make up the American population, and most active in creating opportunities. With clearly articulated visions advocating diversity and written policies outlining acceptable and unacceptable behavior in the workplace, strides continue to be made.

Discrimination Based on What the Candidate Lacks

These diversity achievements in the United States continue to raise the standards by which discrimination is judged. With the surging numbers of Hispanics in the workforce, several factors that constitute subliminal and subtle biases and prejudices are emerging as a challenge for HR professionals. "When Anglo men apply for a job and have an interview, the discussion afterward centers on what the white man 'brings' to the job," Ana Guzman, an executive vice president at Austin Community College in Texas, observes. "For the Hispanic applicant, the discussion is on what he is lacking."[38]

Oftentimes the emphasis on what someone is lacking rather than what someone brings to an organization reflects the subliminal concerns of those making the decisions. This is a natural human instinct, where we can empathize with those who are similar to ourselves. If applicants look like us, or went to the same school we did, or are members of the same fraternity or sorority we are, or have a career trajectory similar to ours, or have a lifestyle that resembles our own, we may be biased in their favor. If they look like us, then our life experiences are likely to be the same—living life as a male is different from living life as a female; being white in the United States is a different experience from being black; the fully abled have a different perspective on life from that of those who are handicapped, and so on.

Discrimination Based on Race

Race may not be an issue for Miami Cubans—the majority are Caucasian—but it may be an issue for other Caribbean Hispanics (Puerto Ricans and Dominicans, primarily) and for Mexican and Central American Hispanics, most of whom are of mixed European (Caucasian) and indigenous ancestry. In an exhaustive examination of this issue, M. Bendick Jr., of Geneva, Switzerland, asked, "Do immigrants and ethnic minorities suffer from substantial discrimination in the labour market?"[39] The answer was instructive:

> Some commentators in the United States developed this line of reasoning into a broader concept sometimes labeled "managing diversity." This concept argues that discrimination in the United States labor market today reflects less the circumstances of specific minority groups than the inability of employers (who are primarily non-disabled, non-elderly, White males) to deal comfortably with employees and job applicants who are "different" from themselves in any way. Under this line of reasoning, the problems of discrimination experienced by racial and ethnic minority groups such as Blacks and Hispanics are closely allied to those experienced by women, older workers, persons with disabilities, and others.... The results of U.S. testing studies seem broadly consistent with this line of reasoning.[40]

As individuals, we generally like people who like us and people who are like us. In the second half of the twentieth century this undeniable fact of human psychology impeded the progress of women (men were reluctant to open the doors of opportunity to women) and the integration of the workplace (whites were reluctant to give blacks the same privileges they themselves enjoyed). While gender and race have long been recognized as obstacles to overcome for the sake of creating an inclusive and diverse workplace, some of the discrimination Hispanics encounter can be more subtle in nature, centering on the question of language. "Another factor that may be limiting Hispanics in the workplace is that non-Hispanic employees and managers may equate poor English-language skill with less education or lower intelligence," Carla Joinson reports. "This, coupled with real statistics that show Hispanics lagging in education, may color perceptions about the capabilities of an individual Hispanic worker."[41]

Discrimination Based on Accent

This form of discrimination has some roots in social and cultural questions that inform the American mentality. Consider how geographic differences affect how native English speakers may be regarded. In the United States, those who speak with a southern drawl may be regarded as slow and not particularly intelligent. The bias against southerners, of course, is a relic of the Civil War, when all things southern were often disparaged and held in contempt. More than 150 years after that war, the continuing bias against the southern accent is testament to the lingering power of cultural biases. A more intriguing aspect of the American mentality is the high esteem in which it sometimes holds those who speak with a British accent. Marketing executives have long exploited this cultural bias by using spokespersons who have—or affect—that accent in order to associate their goods and services with class, high social status, and intimate exclusivity.

Recognizing the role of language in discrimination, the Equal Employment Opportunity Commission warns employers: "Because linguistic characteristics are a component of national origin, employers should carefully scrutinize employment decisions that are based on accent to ensure that they do not violate Title VII."[42] There are clear exceptions—circumstances under which employers can use their discretion to accommodate the question of accent—but these are rare.

In the United States, English spoken with a foreign accent is almost uniformly frowned upon.[43] English spoken with a Spanish accent is not always welcome, and many Hispanic speakers may be subjected to prejudice because of this accent. The accent bias against Hispanics is not dissimilar to the kind of prejudice that youngsters who stutter or have another speech impediment endure. Both groups can be subjected to ridicule, and speaking English with a Spanish accent is, like stuttering, incorrectly associated with lower intelligence. One has only to recall, for instance, the running joke of Ricky Ricardo's accent on *I Love Lucy* to understand how, on a cultural level, American society finds people who speak English with a Spanish accent a laughing matter.[44]

In the real world, the effect of accents on hiring and promotion decisions cannot be dismissed out of hand. "There was an incredibly strong statistical correlation between judging someone cultured, intelligent, competent, etc., and placing them into prestigious jobs and their lack of a readily identified accent," Dianne Markley, director of marketing at the University of North Texas at Denton, reported of the findings of "U.S. Regional Accent Discrimination in the Hiring Process: A Language Attitude Study."[45] Such studies are validated with crushing personal experiences. "I also knew that it was far harder to bend one's tongue to accommodate the American ear than to assimilate," Andrew Lam, a Vietnamese American, writes. "My uncle [who spoke with a heavy accent], for instance, was not rejected for lacking qualifications or intelligence. It was his unruly tongue that gave his foreignness away, pronouncing him interminably alien and, unfortunately, unemployable. . . . 'Speak like Connie Chung and you're okay. Talk like me and you end up running a grocery store.'"[46]

Hispanic candidates often agonize over their accents and see their speech as a career obstacle, much as stutterers may be self-conscious about speaking up in meetings, let alone in public, the prospect of which can cause tremendous anxiety. HR professionals need to sensitize line managers about accent as an impediment to identifying suitable candidates for employment. In much the same way that a generation ago there were many "firsts" with women and blacks—the first woman partner at this law firm, the first black architect at that design firm—it is now Hispanics' turn to break through and make many "firsts." That speaking English with a Spanish accent has often held back worthy candidates is a past injustice that can be better addressed with the increase of Hispanics in the workforce.

Other Forms of Discrimination
Other biases work against Hispanics, to be sure, including stereotypes that lead people to believe Hispanic employees are unprofessional about time management and that they are informal in compartmentalizing their work and personal lives, allowing family obligations to interfere with job performance. Each of these observations relies on cultural differences between the predominantly Protestant work ethic of American business and the predominantly Catholic sensibilities of Hispanics.[47]

This is part of American history. Founded by Protestants in the eighteenth century, the United States has looked with suspicion and distrust on non-Protestants. Consider the controversial anti-Hispanic argument put forth by Samuel Huntington of Harvard University in *Foreign Policy* magazine in the spring of 2004:

> America was created by 17th- and 18th-century settlers who were overwhelmingly white, British, and Protestant. Their values, institutions, and culture provided the foundation for and shaped the development of the United States in the following centuries. They initially defined America in terms of race, eth-

nicity, culture, and religion. Then, in the 18th century, they also had to define America ideologically to justify independence from their home country, which was also white, British, and Protestant. Thomas Jefferson set forth this "creed" . . . in the Declaration of Independence, and ever since, its principles have been . . . an essential component of U.S. identity.

Examining the "challenge" that Hispanics (Catholics) pose to America (Protestant), Huntington continues:

> By the latter years of the 19th century, however, the ethnic component had been broadened . . . [and U.S.] religious identity was being redefined more broadly from Protestant to Christian. With World War II . . . , ethnicity virtually disappeared as a defining component of national identity. So did race. . . . As a result, American identity is now defined in terms of culture and creed. Most Americans see the creed as the crucial element of their national identity. The creed, however, was the product of the distinct Anglo-Protestant culture of the founding settlers. Key elements of that culture include the English language; Christianity; religious commitment; English concepts of the rule of law, including the responsibility of rulers and the rights of individuals; and dissenting Protestant values of individualism, the work ethic, and the belief that humans have the ability and the duty to try to create a heaven on earth, a "city on a hill."[48]

Had this been written in the nineteenth century and titled "The Catholic Challenge" rather than "The Hispanic Challenge," it might have seemed just as apt, given historical and cultural realities. HR specialists need a conscientious plan to address the realities of these subtle forms of racism and discrimination in hiring and promoting practices. In the American workplace, discrimination against Catholics lingers, and it is a question of liability should HRM not recognize the problem and ensure that programs and procedures address these issues.

Turning to the popular views of Hispanics and time management, the cultural differences in how time is perceived and the nature of punctuality have more to do with social class than ethnicity. The majority of U.S. Hispanics are immigrants from rural communities or the children of parents with an agrarian background. Their more informal attitude toward time is consistent with that of country people everywhere; the sense of immediacy and urgency are urban phenomena, born of a lifestyle in which the idea that "time is money" governs city life. Manual laborers in many human societies have a different perspective on punctuality, the importance of schedules, and the need to meet deadlines. For HR professionals, however, the impact remains the same: Hourly Hispanic employees are often not familiar with the role of time management as a crucial aspect of the American workplace.

A similar criticism involving family may also affect hiring decisions. Hispanics are often described as *clannish,* a characterization that can be used for many groups of people; humans have lived in family groups consisting of extended family members for most of the history of the species. The "nuclear family" is an American invention that came into existence at the end of World War II. A household consisting of a family with only two adults and their two children living under the same roof is an aberration; only people in the United States have thought of such a situation as an ideal one—and then only since the 1950s. In fact, less than a quarter of all American households conform to this model.[49]

Hispanics, as a rule, continue to live in households where an elder parent or an adult sibling or even a close cousin is living with the "nuclear family," often not only to share housing expenses but also to provide a wider support group for raising children. Hispanics, who can avail themselves of grandparents or adult siblings for child care assistance, often view the use of babysitters—

wherein unrelated strangers are paid to look after one's children—as strange behavior, bordering on child endangerment. The practical consideration for HRM, of course, is that Hispanic employees will—and do—request personal time when adult siblings, elderly parents, and grand-aunts or grand-uncles are ill or need help. Corporate America has a very narrow definition of "family," usually meaning a spouse or dependent child, and Hispanics are sensitive to what they perceive as "cultural discrimination" for an organization's reluctance to accept, validate, and accommodate a more generous and general definition of *family*.

NUANCES OF INTERVIEWING HISPANICS

A profile of the Hispanic candidate pool is emerging, one characterized by individuals who have had to overcome obstacles, who are normally from an underprivileged background and strangers to the norms that mainstream America takes for granted growing up, and who are, if not insecure, then at least very sensitive about their linguistic and cultural literacy. Here is where different objectives are in order for HRM. Foremost is recognizing the breathtaking diversity among Hispanics. Their races, ethnicities, creeds, education attainment levels, and life experiences span the spectrum of humanity. What they have in common, along with language (despite regional accents and inflections), social values, and historical experiences that arise from originating in Europe and colonialism in the New World, is the humbling experience of being a minority in the United States.

Hispanic immigration to the United States has proved a tremendous benefit to the nation's economy. Unlike other groups—black or white—that are U.S. born and live in poverty for generations, Hispanics land on their feet and contribute productively. Consider how Galbraith describes the way lack of jobs has trapped generations of Americans in cycles of poverty that far outstrip the ability of local governments to provide basic services:

> The poor in the United States, while none could doubt their degradation and misery, were once largely invisible—poor blacks were hidden away on the farms and plantations of the rural South with primitive food, clothing and shelter, little in the way of education and no civil rights. Many poor whites were unseen on the hills and in the hollows of Appalachia. Poverty was not a problem when distant, out of sight. Only as economic, political and social change brought the needy to the cities did welfare become a public concern, the poor now living next to and in deep contrast with the relatively affluent.[50]

In comparison, Hispanic immigration is revitalizing urban centers with daunting speed. "New York has always been the quintessential immigrant metropolis, a place of dreams and magic, opportunity and hardship," Kenneth Jackson, author of *Crabgrass Frontier: The Suburbanization of America,* argues. "And everywhere we look, newcomers are giving life to neighborhoods that otherwise would be in decline. Twenty years ago, the South Bronx was full of abandoned buildings; today, it is thriving. Similarly, since 1975 the borough of Queens has become the most ethnically diverse place in the world."[51]

As Hispanic population growth accelerates throughout this century, with Hispanics becoming the majority in 2100, these trends suggest that the emergence of a bilingual consumer economy will be one with revitalized urban centers, integrated and expanded families, and spectacularly diverse communities. There is always danger in making predictions based on current trends, since trends always change. But consider one riveting development that no one anticipated: A decade after the implementation of NAFTA, less English and more Spanish is spoken in North America!

"In 1962 in Mexico, total [TV] programming was mostly national (59 percent), with a sizable amount from the U.S. (38 percent), little (3 percent) international and no regional programming," Joseph Straubhaar, Consuelo Campbell, and Kristina Cahoon report. English, however, failed to "dominate" Mexico during the three decades that followed. In fact, "By 1991, total television programming was 66.6 percent national, 24.4 percent U.S., 7 percent international, and 2 percent regional."[52] English-language television programming continues to decline in Mexico—and in California, the Southwest, Texas, Florida, and New York as well. As Univision and Telemundo increase their market share throughout the United States, these two Spanish-language television networks are changing how language and the media function.

In NAFTA's first decade, while American programming—particularly cable—has entered Mexico, language exchange has become a two-way street. Consider the proliferation of Mexican television programming in the United States. While "U.S. programming has not really declined much in the NAFTA markets, as it has in some other parts of the world . . . other intra-NAFTA production and flow has grown: more from Mexico (and Puerto Rico) into the Hispanic U.S.; more production within Quebec coupled with a continuing presence of English-Canadian material; and a seemingly stable balance in broadcast television between English-Canadian and U.S. programs in Calgary," Straubhaar, Campbell, and Cahoon write. "This supports our argument that globalization is a complex phenomenon that needs to be examined at four separate levels: a largely U.S. global layer, varied cultural-linguistic markets (including Anglophone, Francophone and Latin American within NAFTA), continuing strong national-level production (particularly within the U.S. and Mexico within NAFTA); and, particularly in the cases of Quebec and, to lesser degree, U.S. Hispanics, a strong subnational layer, built upon language and cultural differences within the nation."[53]

This notwithstanding, by virtue of being a Hispanic in the United States, one is apart from the mainstream. This informs the perspectives of Hispanic employees, often in ways that are not immediately clear to Anglophone America. Consider the Hispanic cultural predisposition to focus on family. While this observation, if not criticism, has been levied against Hispanics as evidence of their predisposition not to commit fully to their job, often resisting long-distance travel or overtime work if it interferes with family obligations, another aspect is not immediately apparent. The Hispanic focus on family togetherness often limits the educational choices college-age Hispanic youth are able to make. With strong family pressure to remain close to home, Hispanic youth encounter enormous pressure to select colleges and universities in their hometowns.

This may even make economic sense; living at home offers students considerable cost savings in terms of housing and transportation. But other costs pile up instead: young Hispanic adults do not participate in the mainstream American experience of moving away to college, living on their own (on campus or in student housing), participating in the social activities associated with independent living (joining fraternities, sororities, professional associations, and the like). For example, two young men from the same class of the University of Miami, with the same degree and grade point averages, will strike an interviewer quite differently if one is a native Miamian who lived at home and focused on his studies while the other grew up in Chicago, participated in the campus's Greek community, and belonged to the American Institute of Architecture Students. Hispanic parental impulse to protect—and not let go of—their child can create sheltered young adults who are outside the mainstream American experience and are thus at a competitive disadvantage as they enter the workforce. Hispanic youth often develop "gaps of experience" that may haunt them as they move through their professional careers.

These are the nuances HR staffers must be aware of as they identify Hispanic candidates. Line managers must be made sensitive to the point that an absence of mainstream experience often results from cultural differences and is not a reflection on a candidate's initiative. This is not an easy task, for line managers are human and largely unaware of the subliminal influences on their perceptions and assessments. In the same way that humans often assume incorrectly that people who stutter are less intelligent than those who speak with normal fluency, line managers tend to like those who have experiences similar to their own: "So, you went to school 1,500 miles from home? I couldn't wait to get out of my hometown as well!" "Well, I see there's a possibility of a Sigma Chi posse in this department!"

It is up to HRM to adjust feedback to reflect gaps in the interview process. Ana Guzman at Austin Community College reports that in postinterview discussions the question of what Hispanic candidates lack is oftentimes a reflection of the inability of line managers to connect with individuals whose experience seems, relative to their own history, to be "incomplete." To factor in these cultural differences, along with others, HRM needs to be familiar with the cultural differences that inform how Hispanic candidates interview.

Interviewing Hispanic Candidates for Management Positions

To compensate for not being part of the American mainstream, Hispanics use various defense mechanisms, many of which make an interview a difficult situation. Often unsure of their command of English, Hispanic candidates, however qualified they may be for the position, are apt to be self-conscious and hesitant in interviews. What line managers interpret as being intimidated, shy, or passive may not truly reflect the candidate's character. A Hispanic marketing executive who is charismatic, well-spoken, and aggressive in Spanish, well capable of developing a marketing campaign that zeroes in on the Hispanic consumer market and hits the bull's-eye, can appear bashful when speaking exclusively in English in an interview situation. And even a Hispanic executive who speaks English with great confidence and authority may do so with an accent that Anglophone line managers find distracting. To improve the consistency of results, HRM can create formal scripts to ensure that communication is tailored for both hourly and salaried audiences. Working out the questions in advance helps develop the information needed for accurate assessment of managerial, employee, or upper management candidates' qualifications for the position.

Hispanics, not unlike far too many other employees, often do not understand corporate benefits. They are reluctant to ask about benefits and salaries because they may not understand U.S. business practices or fear appearing uninformed. HRM must recognize these difficulties and would do well to have meetings or seminars where benefits are discussed once a year. Formality can be broken down by offering light refreshments—coffee, tea, mineral water, fruit and cookies—at these town hall–style meetings. This would encourage employees to raise their hands and ask about issues that affect everyone who works for the firm.

Interviewing Hispanic Candidates for Hourly Positions

The majority of Hispanics entering the workforce in the United States are blue-collar workers or hourly employees, or both. The retail, food service, construction, and hospitality industries have disproportionate percentages of Hispanic employees, and many positions require no more than a high school diploma, if that. Working-class Hispanics have, as a group, not only a lower level of educational attainment but also a weaker command of English. Many are more marginalized from mainstream American society and, as a consequence, are not acculturated to the business norms of organizations throughout corporate America. This poses obstacles to their hiring and promotion. More often than not, differing cultural values limit their ability to prosper in the United States, which is a concern even though, as a group, Hispanics have a strong work ethic and feel a firm commitment to fulfill their duties on the job.

That Hispanic laborers can often prove enigmatic to their Anglophone managers and supervisors creates another set of challenges for HR professionals. What has been dismissed as "Latino" thinking or "Third World" mentality is nothing less than the workplace confrontation between Western perceptions and the indigenous (Native American) worldview. It is possible that the bias Samuel Huntington alludes to also affects the way HRM operates: "The persistence of Mexican immigration into the United States reduces the incentives for cultural assimilation. Mexican Americans no longer think of themselves as members of a small minority who must accommodate the dominant group and adopt its culture. As their numbers increase, they become more committed to their own ethnic identity and culture. Sustained numerical expansion promotes cultural consolidation and leads Mexican Americans not to minimize but to glory in the differences between their culture and U.S. culture."[54]

Many Hispanic workers of indigenous ancestry know that they are seen as belonging to a group of people who resist "cultural assimilation." This is often interpreted as a lack of ambition and is expressed in various generalizations about how Hispanic employees handle themselves in their work environment. Those who find Hispanics difficult to understand and work with say things like this:

- What motivates them as workers? Are they building a new life in the United States, or are they sending money to their family in their home country, where they plan to retire?
- Why are they reluctant to look you directly in the eye? Is it out of respect, or fear?
- Why are they reluctant to call managers by their first names, or to speak up at all?
- Why do they say they understand directions when they don't? Is it from ignorance or pride?
- Why don't they speak up when there is a problem?
- Why are they often reluctant to wear safety equipment?
- Why are they often uninterested in the organization's benefit plans?

The traditional answers HR professionals—and union officials—have offered to explain these cultural differences vary, but they are all born of issues identified here: lack of educational attainment by Hispanics, as well as the immigration of large numbers of country people from Latin America. In addition, cultural traditions about respect, loyalty, subservience, status, and power inform the way recent immigrants from Mexico and Central America conduct themselves. That their deference is seen as backwardness by mainstream American society only complicates things, and it frustrates managers who have a job to do: operating a factory floor, managing a warehouse, providing housekeeping for a hotel, making sure the lunch hour is served properly at a restaurant, and so on.

HR specialists, however, must act as liaison, bridging management's needs and the realities of the hourly workers. Indeed, for many recent immigrants from Mexico and Central America, the immediate concern is to make a living.[55] Oftentimes they are prepared to live lives of deprivation in the United States so they can send money back to their families in Latin America. Remittances to Mexico alone came to more than $17 billion in 2004, a sum that exceeds the revenue Mexico generates from tourism.[56] Hispanics seeking hourly work often arrive in the United States with the idea and the expectation that they won't settle down and establish roots. Many return to their homelands after a few years in the United States.

This is a familiar pattern in American history. "Before 1900 an estimated 78 percent of Italian immigrants were men. Many of them traveled to America in the early spring, worked until late fall, and then returned to the warmer climates of their southern European homes for the winter. Overall, 20 percent to 30 percent of Italian immigrants returned to Italy permanently," Steven Mintz, professor of history at the University of Houston, writes in *Digital History*.[57] Many others, of course, do settle down as months become years, and years become a lifetime.

That they become U.S. residents de facto and not by intent colors how they see themselves and their place in the American workplace. That their acculturation is different from earlier immigrants' is a factor of globalization and modernity: "Adapting to life in a new country is in some ways more complex now than a century ago, when immigrants typically broke most ties with their native lands," Donatella Lorch argued in the *New York Times* a decade ago, adding, "Home-country ideas are reinforced by Spanish-language cable television channels, newspapers and radio talk shows and several new Spanish-language women's magazines published in the United States. And because many of their native countries are relatively close, many immigrants can see friends and relatives regularly. Even the Internet helps some keep in touch."[58] And the pattern Lorch reported is only stronger today.

Although many commentators point to what they see as the "cult of fatalism" in Native American thought, or the "rootlessness" of Hispanic immigrants, the answers to the questions posed at the beginning of this section are, for the majority of Hispanic workers in the United States, culturally straightforward:

- **What motivates them as workers?** They are usually motivated by the desire to earn a living to provide for their families, most of whom are back in their homelands.

- **Why are they reluctant to look you directly in the eye?** It is a sign of respect in indigenous societies throughout the Americas never to make direct eye contact with a higher-status person.

- **Why are they reluctant to call managers by their first names?** They use surnames out of respect for authority figures; the use of first names is seen as too informal, and embarrassing.

- **Why do they say they understand directions when they don't?** Out of insecurity about their level of education, or fluency in English, they don't wish to appear ignorant by acknowledging a failure to understand what they are being instructed to do or how they are being instructed to perform their duties.

- **Why don't they speak up when there is a problem?** They generally remain silent out of insecurity about their mastery of English, or because they are unsure of their right to bring a problem to the attention of managers.

- **Why are they often reluctant to wear safety equipment?** Coming from countries where safety standards are more lax than those in the United States, many Hispanic laborers are experienced in performing their jobs without safety equipment. Additionally, most are not familiar with the proper use of such equipment and are embarrassed to admit their ignorance.

- **Why are they often uninterested in the organization's benefit plans?** They don't see themselves as remaining in the United States long enough to make use of benefit plans. Also, since they come from countries, such as Mexico, Guatemala, El Salvador, and Honduras, with nationalized programs for health care, housing, and retirement, they mistakenly assume that the United States has similar social welfare programs, making a company's benefit plans superfluous.

Once they establish residency in the United States, and they gain experience working in corporate America, most Hispanic immigrants who remain in the United States find that their worldview changes. Economists refer to "demonstration effects" to understand how workers' ideas, perceptions, and preferences change over time. Globalization itself is a factor in the streamlining of how the workplace functions. A decade into NAFTA, for instance, the views of many Mexican peasants have changed to reflect a more corporate attitude about labor. "I used to think the whole world was like my village," Antonio Ek, a Maya worker, explains. "But when I went to Cancún I saw things I had never seen before. I saw airplanes and high-rise hotels. There were so many kinds of different people, so many wealthy people from all over the world.

The stores were like dreams, selling everything you could imagine. It made me realize just how much there is in the world, and I understood how many different kinds of people there are in different countries. It also made me feel good that they would make the effort to come and visit my homeland, and that they liked it here."[59]

Whether they are applying for salaried or nonsalaried positions, Hispanic candidates all face subtle biases that impede their hiring and promotion. These biases often appear to be substantiated by inferior assessments—assessments reached after interviews conducted without attending to the candidates' culture and background. Hispanic candidates tend to share insecurities about their educational attainment levels, and to be self-conscious about the accents and cultural norms that separate them from the life experiences of mainstream Americans. All this tends to undermine how Hispanic candidates handle the interview process. HRM must sensitize and train line managers to be aware of these peripheral distractions that color how otherwise qualified candidates are assessed.

Table 4 presents a set of questions that are appropriate for Hispanic candidates. It can serve as the basis for individual organizations to develop their own lines of discussion to elicit more candid responses about these candidates' abilities, objectives, and fit with the organization. Although not exhaustive, it can open up more insightful discussions. To be sure, interviewers are legally required to ask every candidate questions about employment status: "Are you legally entitled to work in the United States? If you are not a citizen or a permanent resident, what is your visa status?" But attention to a Hispanic candidate's background should not stop there. Note that all interview questions need to adhere to a strict level of professionalism, and they must be job related. Develop questions based on the specific job requirements of the position.[60]

TABLE 4
Sample Interview Questions: Strategic Approach for Hispanics

- Expand on your experience (in field or specific area or as it relates to the job at hand).
- In what ways do you feel your previous employment will help you in performing the job that we are discussing?
- What experiences have you had away from work that have responsibilities similar to those of the job I have just described?
- How well do you handle supervision of subordinates?
- In what ways have you been required to demonstrate leadership in the past?
- Tell me about a particularly tough problem you had to deal with in that job.
- What kinds of decisions were you required to make on that job?
- What kinds of decisions were most difficult for you?
- How much contact did you have with your supervisor on a day-to-day basis?
- How did you feel about the people with whom you worked?
- How do your fellow employees treat you?
- This job requires initiative and willingness to work without close supervision. What have you done that demonstrates your ability to handle these requirements?
- What are your career goals and how does this job relate to them?
- What are some of the things you are looking for in this job?
- What is there about being a [job title] that appeals to you?
- What are you looking for in a job change at this time?
- What do you hope to find in this job that you do not have in your present job?
- Why do you think you would like to work here?
- In what ways do you believe you can make a contribution to this office?
- What part of the job I have just described sounds most interesting to you?
- What aspects of this job do you not like?
- What do you consider to be some of your significant job [or education and training] accomplishments?
- Tell me what you enjoyed most about your last [or present] job.
- What types of job assignments do you enjoy the most?
- What was an unpleasant feature of the job?

TABLE 4 cont'd

- What, if anything, is there about your present job that makes it a bit difficult for you?
- What, if anything, was there about your last job that made it a bit difficult for you?
- When you were in school, what types of classes did you like best? Why?
- What things, related to this job, do you feel you learned most about in school?
- How would you describe yourself on the job?
- If you had a choice, what would be the most ideal job for you?
- What plans do you have for self-improvement?
- Do you have any hopes or plans for continued study?
- What would your last [or current] supervisor tell me are your weakest areas?
- What are your greatest strengths?
- Think of an example when you had too many things to do at once and tell me how you went about accomplishing the tasks.
- Discuss your abilities as a team player.
- What are your short- and long-range objectives? How do you think this position will help you accomplish them?
- What responsibilities give you the most professional satisfaction?
- What is the most important decision that you have ever made?
- What methods of communication do you use to keep your boss informed? Your team members?
- Select a job you have had and describe the paperwork you were required to complete. What specific things did you do to ensure your accuracy?
- Describe a high-pressure situation you had to handle at work. Tell me what happened, who was involved, and what you did in terms of problem solving.
- Getting the job done may necessitate unusual persistence or dedication to results, especially in the face of obstacles or distractions. Tell us about a time in which you were able to be very persistent in order to reach goals. Be specific.
- What do you consider as your greatest weakness? What do you need to do to overcome this weakness?
- Explain to us what makes you the best candidate for this position.
- Do you have any questions for me at this time?

Preemployment Screening and Testing

HRM often uses preemployment testing to assess the skills of nonsalaried employees. Testing for quantitative skills (vocabulary, spelling, mathematics, problem solving) and for character traits (personal integrity, reliability, work ethic) is standard in many organizations. In addition, testing for illegal substances is widespread throughout the United States. That said, given the specific characteristics of Hispanic candidates, preemployment testing can be misleading: English-language competency test scores may be low, and Spanish-language skills—which might make an employee especially valuable with the United States fast becoming a bilingual consumer economy—are rarely assessed.

To compensate for these shortcomings, HRM is well advised to use probationary periods as a screening device. A get-acquainted period can be a valid way to assess someone's skill levels and determine the quality of performance on the job, while helping the company develop an environment that can accommodate the nation's changing demographics. A probationary period gives newcomers to the company the benefit of internal screening, resembling the internal labor markets that traditionally provide opportunities for promotion from within. When complemented with mentoring and role model programs, probationary periods give HRM a powerful tool, one that can replace unreliable preemployment testing with prepromotion (or predismissal, if it turns out that way) evaluations of people who have become known quantities.

IBM under Lou Gerstner launched a program that used mentoring as a mechanism for identifying minority candidates for management positions. "Sustaining change requires that diversity become an integrated part of the company's management practices. This was a priority for Gerstner, who told me: 'If you were to go back and look at ten years' worth of executive committee discussions, you would find two subjects, and only two, that appeared on every one of the agendas. One was the financial performance, led by our CFO. The second was a discussion of management changes, promotions, moves, and so on, led by our HR person,'" David A. Thomas wrote in "Diversity as Strategy," in the *Harvard Business Review*.

> In my interviews, among the most frequently mentioned diversity-related HR practice was the five-minute drill, which began with Gerstner's top team and has cascaded down from the chairman to two levels down from CEO. The five-minute drill takes place during the discussion of management talent at the corporate and business unit levels. During meetings of the senior team, executives are expected at any moment to be able to discuss any high-potential manager. According to interviewees, an explicit effort is made to ensure that minorities and females are discussed along with white males. The result has been to make the executives more accountable for spotting and grooming high-potential minority managers both in their own areas and across the business. Now that it's been made explicit that IBM executives need to watch for female and minority talent, they are more open to considering and promoting these individuals when looking to fill executive jobs. Managing diversity is also one of the core competencies used to assess managers' performance, and it's included in the mandatory training and orientation of new managers.[61]

IBM's innovative program, which developed the skill sets of promising candidates throughout the ranks, was closely tied to the rapid empowerment and growing numbers of minority managers. Where HRM encouraged mentoring and role model programs, minority candidates exceeded expectations as their managerial skills and know-how grew. "It allows them to add to their professional competence, establish credibility in the firm, develop confidence in their ability to succeed, and strengthen their relationships with colleagues and supervisors," David

Thomas reports. "Minority managers do, in fact, have to be more deeply grounded and better prepared than their white peers if they are to become top executives because they are promoted only after proving themselves again and again."[62]

To be sure, questions linger about the widespread use of probationary periods, especially with regard to the way to deal with employees who do not meet expectations during the period and the still more difficult phenomenon of workers who perform exceptionally well during the probationary period itself but fail to produce similar results after it. Discharging unsuccessful candidates is fraught with legal considerations, many of which are related to discrimination statutes governing wrongful discharge. Courts have ruled that despite clear written stipulation that a position has a probationary period attached, employees still have legal recourse to protest dismissal.

MAKING AN ATTRACTIVE OFFER

Apart from competitive salaries and benefit packages, what do Hispanic employees want from their employer? (That they see their co-workers and colleagues as an informal extended family is of great influence.) What makes one job offer more inviting than another? (Hispanics consistently rate job satisfaction as more important than Caucasians or African Americans do.)[63] Why are nonpecuniary considerations almost as important to Hispanic candidates in surprising ways? (Hispanics turn down offers that require relocating more often than non-Hispanics.)

For Hispanic candidates, the opinions of friends and families matter greatly, and so does a firm's leadership brand. All offers should be in writing as well as verbal, and language should extol the pride of joining that firm. At the same time, the anticipated value and contribution the employee makes must be stated explicitly. One point that must be considered is that in many Latin American and European countries concepts surrounding the idea of noncompetition differ from those current in the United States. As a result, if a position requires a noncompete clause, this should be a separate document, similar to a nondisclosure agreement.

The entire process must reflect such nuances in communication. HRM has tremendous leverage in making an offer attractive to the Hispanic candidate simply by communicating that the interviewee is welcome and valued—in writing.

According to the Corporate Leadership Council, efforts to create a compelling employment offer for ethnic minorities fall into five principal categories:[64]

- **Positive organizationwide image**—employers must foster a culture that values diversity through practices and policies that promote mutual respect.

- **Clear concern for equality**—employer practices ranging from recruiting to performance management and disciplinary action must demonstrate equal respect for all ethnic groups.

- **Career development options**—employers must ensure that ethnic minority employees have equal access to desirable management positions and access to resources needed to assist them in attaining those positions.

- **Fair hiring practices**—employers must ensure that minority candidates have equal opportunity to be hired into desirable positions.

- **Fair management practices**—management practices must reflect commitment to diversity; management should recognize the contributions and ideas of all employees and make efforts to communicate effectively with employees who do not speak English as their first language.

When encouraging Hispanic candidates to become long-term employees committed to the organization, it is useful to remember that Hispanics have certain concerns that often go unaddressed by employers. A successful strategy for addressing these concerns is to create committees or teams that can reach out to Hispanic employees. P&G's Hispanic Employee Steering Team, for example, works as a source of support and networking for employees. The Steering Team at P&G not only works to create a sense of belonging for Hispanic employees but also educates them about company benefits. This is important because Hispanics tend to participate in profit sharing and 401(k) plans to a lesser degree than non-Hispanic employees do: a little over 29 percent of Hispanic workers contributed to employer-sponsored savings plans in 2004—compared with 53 percent for non-Hispanic whites and 46 percent for African Americans. The lower participation rate is attributed, in part, to the numbers of first-generation U.S. Hispanic workers, who are the least likely to save of all ethnic groups. P&G strives to increase Hispanic participation in the company-sponsored plans. Another mission of the Steering Team is to inform Hispanics of P&G's specific benefits, such as reimbursing employees up to $500 for child care expenses when they travel on business, or allowing new mothers the option of taking up to a year off (with eight weeks paid).

Organizations throughout corporate America need to determine precisely what the priorities of their Hispanic employees happen to be. As with P&G, HRM can best assess and analyze their employees' wants and needs through the creation of employee network associations.

Most blue-collar Hispanic employees have other categories of express wants and needs on the job. Raised with the cultural sense that their employers are part of an extended family—in Spanish *patron* means "boss" but also includes the English notion of being a patron—Hispanic workers often expect their employers to act according to two closely linked concepts: *simpatía* and *confianza*.

Simpatía is defined as an intrinsic value that favors collectivism and group cohesion. With its origins in Native American thought, which values a communal approach to problem solving, this behavioral and philosophical ideal has been successfully used to unionize workers and enlist extraordinary cooperation from Hispanics during crises. *Confianza* means confidence or trust—and more. It embodies the concept of an emotional bond. Marketing executives understand this idea very well: in branding, creating an emotional connection to the product is more important than creating an intellectual one. The idea that Hispanic workers can have *confianza* in their supervisors solidifies the bond between employees and the organization.

But how can HRM convey to Hispanic workers that they have *simpatía* for their concerns and are worthy of their *confianza*?

If the purpose of HRM is to nurture the relationship between employers and employees, being aware of and supporting the Hispanic worker's longings and desires is central to its effectiveness. Since 80 percent of U.S. Hispanics are of Mexican and Central American background, recognition of their values is important. In the same way that socially responsible corporate citizens become involved in issues that concern specific groups of employees, HRM needs to entice Hispanics by making corporate community involvement speak to their concerns. If organizations make known their support for causes dear to other groups of employees, from the March of Dimes to AIDS research, then similar overtures can and should be extended to Hispanics.

A simple investment in social capital for Hispanics is to offer an optional holiday. An analysis conducted by Hispanic Economics of the attitudes of blue-collar workers throughout the United States who are of Mexican or Central American descent confirms that, for instance, most would welcome the option to work one existing holiday in exchange for taking December 12 off with pay.[65] This day is of such cultural importance that it could conceivably be either a floating holiday or a permitted use of an existing sick day. HR professionals, moreover, need to understand that more important than having one holiday substitute for another holiday is demonstrating that the organization values its Hispanic employees and their Hispanic identity.

IN REVIEW

- Attracting Hispanic candidates is a challenge because they often do not respond to traditional recruiting methods and because qualified candidates are rare in many parts of the country.
  - Lack of educational attainment, exacerbated for many by the state of education in Mexico and other locales, remains a challenge for Hispanics and reduces their opportunities for appropriate jobs in the United States.
  - HRM policies should recognize that Hispanic employees can, and need to, play a central role in the recruitment of suitable candidates, both for hiring purposes and for nurturing bonds of loyalty.
  - Organizations need to establish their organization's credibility within the Hispanic community and nurture their brand among Hispanic workers if they wish to increase the numbers of Hispanic candidates who come forward as a result of applicant self-selection, co-worker referral, and staffing agency efforts.
  - Subtle biases work against the hiring and promotion of Hispanics; these arise from reactions to English spoken with a Spanish accent and from the distance between the life experience of Hispanics and that of people in the American mainstream.

- Those responsible for interviewing Hispanics must be aware of the cultural distinctions that make Hispanics appear relatively weak as candidates.

- Anglophone line managers and HR professionals often mistake the way Hispanics show respect for passivity and intimidation.

- The use of formal scripts when conducting interviews results in a more accurate assessment of a candidate's qualifications for the position.

- Blue-collar candidates may appear particularly passive, fatalistic, or shiftless as a result of cultural manifestations of how Hispanics of indigenous ancestry defer to authority.

- Preemployment screening and testing currently does not reflect the cross-cultural realities of the life experience of U.S. Hispanics.

  - Apart from testing for illegal substances, traditional preemployment screening and testing are not as effective for Hispanic candidates as they are for non-Hispanic candidates.

  - HRM should use probationary periods as valid screens to assess the skills and job performance of Hispanics.

- Hispanics are more inclined than non-Hispanics to want job offers to address their value systems and their familial responsibilities.

  - Hispanics expect a more paternalistic relationship with employers, wherein they bond with the organization and see their colleagues and managers as an extended family, and in which their HR professionals respond to their wider concerns and needs.

  - Social expectations, which may hold higher priority than salary for some Hispanic employees, may include a willingness on the part of the organization to be flexible in family-related benefits, including time off and holidays.

HR Policies

WHY EMPLOYEE POLICIES AND MANUALS ARE NECESSARY

HRM policies are evolving to reflect the changing demographics of the American workplace. This change is consistent with the process by which HR professionals are becoming strategic partners for their organizations. What does strategic partnership mean for today's HR professionals?

WORKING AS A STRATEGIC PARTNER

Strategic partnership is composed of several evolving functions for HR professionals: business expert, change agent, consultant, and knowledge manager. "In our view, the most potent action HR managers can take to ensure their strategic contribution is to develop a measurement system that convincingly showcases HR's impact on business performance," Brian Becker, Mark Huselid, and David Ulrich argue. "To design such a measurement system, HR managers must adopt a dramatically different perspective, one that focuses on how human resources can play a central role in implementing the firm's strategy. With a properly developed strategic HR architecture, managers throughout the firm can understand exactly *how people can create value and how to measure the value-creation process.*"[1]

This is sound business practice. As the nation moves toward becoming a bilingual consumer economy, diversity is the key to achieving a sustainable competitive advantage—and delivering profits, quarter after quarter. "Consumers are now putting more emphasis on corporate citizenship," explains Bill Picture of IWF Group, a Los Angeles–based advertising and marketing firm that specializes in helping companies reach the Asian American market. "They want to see themselves reflected in corporate culture. And case studies show that [multicultural] ad campaigns are generating a lot of new business, and driving incremental share growth."[2]

Table 5 compares the traditional role of HR with the new emphasis from HR and how each factor contributes to the ongoing development of HRM.

HRM policies, as they apply to Hispanic workers, are evolving to reflect the way HR professionals are becoming business experts, change agents, and knowledge managers for their organizations' top leadership. In this chapter we examine how the increasing number of Hispanics in the workforce is influencing language in the workplace and employee relations, how management is rethinking its traditional relationships with unions, and some specific addenda the employee manual needs to include for the Hispanic employee population. Each of these policy areas requires forward-thinking HR initiatives to enhance a firm's responsiveness to the emerging needs of its workforce and to enable

TABLE 5
Changing Role of HRM

TRADITIONAL ROLE OF HR	NEW EMPHASIS FROM HR	DEVELOPMENT OF HRM
Employee champion	Employee advocate (EA) or human capital (HC) developer	Organization recognizes employees are critical to success. EA focuses on the needs of current employees; HC developer focuses on how the organization and employees prepare for future challenges and needs.
Administrative authority	Functional authority	Management recognizes HR functions are central to the organization. Some HR functions are provided through administrative efficiency (using technological advances such as online payroll and benefits functions), while others are best delivered through policies, workshops, and arbitration, expanding the "functional expert" role.
Change agent	Strategic partner	HR professionals as strategic partners carry out multiple roles: business expert, knowledge manager, and internal consultant. What was once considered being a "change agent" has evolved into a more complex function. As demographics and bilinguals have transformed the workplace, HR professionals are now strategic partners critical to the organization's success.
Change agent	Leader	The evolving roles for HRM translate to HR leadership. The enhanced HRM function has far-reaching implications, including monitoring workplace harmony, collaborating with line managers, participating in the execution of proper corporate governance, and ensuring that the organization conducts itself as a responsible corporate citizen in the community in which it operates.

management to achieve its strategic goals. Specifically, in the same way that society at large is coming to terms with the implications of an ever-larger Hispanic population, Hispanophiles are increasingly championing changes to HRM.

LANGUAGE IN THE WORKPLACE

Employee manuals currently in use by most organizations accomplish their missions adequately. The one glaring omission can be proper documentation of language in the workplace. While "English only" policies have historically been enforced, Hispanics now have a share of the workforce that makes such language rules impossible to enforce. And a multilingual policy can be a competitive advantage; recall Verizon's desperate search to recruit, hire, and train Spanish-speaking customer service representatives for the Washington, D.C., and northern Virginia market. There are also, given the state of the world, life-safety issues: New York City is one metropolitan region that, cognizant of public safety concerns, offers Spanish-language courses to police officers, first responders, and medical emergency staff.

U.S. society is naturally experiencing a lag between its increasingly multilingual nature and recognition of the development's implications for the work environment. Consider the experience of "Private Bank," a division dedicated to meeting the needs of high-net-worth clients of a major financial institution in New York. As is often the case with institutions that cater to the wealth management needs of high-net-worth individuals, Private Bank has clients scattered around the globe, and it has dedicated staffs that specialize in key markets. Wealthy individuals in Brazil expect to be able to call their Private Banker in New York or Miami and speak Portuguese. Similarly, Mexican and Argentinean clients expect to speak Spanish when dealing with their Private

Bankers. For an institution, this requires the recruitment and staffing of professionals who are fluent in the languages to which they are assigned. Meandering through the offices of such banks, it's not uncommon to come upon the "Brazil desk" or the "Mexico team," a group of professionals whose clients are in a specific market or speak a specific language.

In such a work environment, one is apt to to hear English, Spanish, Portuguese, and French being spoken as a matter of course. The question then arises as to how to manage acceptable and unacceptable speech. In the case in question (where the identity of the bank is withheld at the request of individuals involved), it turned out that some employees conducted themselves impeccably while speaking in English but not when speaking in Spanish. In this case study, the lone female trader working in the department that handled trading transactions for Latin American clients was surrounded by male colleagues who, as is often the case among brokers, created a fraternitylike atmosphere, one in which sexual comments and inappropriate innuendo (in Spanish) peppered the back-and-forth of the trading desk.

Over time, this created a hostile work environment. The lone female trader felt humiliated and uncomfortable, finding the comments directed at her boorish and offensive. Without an explicit policy statement—and *a vocabulary of what is unacceptable speech in Spanish*—HR was unable to investigate the situation properly, let alone offer a solution. When asked if a particular kind of language was used in interviews conducted in English, forthright answers in the negative were truthful. Absent the binding inclusion of Spanish, there was no satisfactory legal recourse for either the aggrieved employee or HRM. The inability to remedy the situation in a manner that adequately addressed the creation of a hostile work environment in a language other than English was seen as a major failure of HRM, and the HR professionals' reputation among employees at the Private Bank was adversely affected. The resolution, if it can be called that, came when the female trader resigned from the department.

This failure of employee manuals to reflect the linguistic realities of the American workplace is a challenge for society at large. Consider the public airwaves. While the Federal Communications Commission, or FCC, has made a celebrated case of scrutinizing the radio broadcasts of Howard Stern, often levying enormous fines for his obscene language, a double standard is in operation. Why should one "shock jock" be admonished if his obscenity is spoken in English, while another is overlooked, simply because his offensive material is broadcast in Spanish?

"In terms of English- and Spanish-language broadcast, there is a clear discrepancy on how much scrutiny the indecency problem is given," U.S. Representative Peter Deutsch, a member of the House Energy and Commerce Subcommittee on Telecommunications and the Internet, which oversees the FCC, is on the record as stating. "The bottom line is that the FCC just doesn't have enough people to translate Spanish."[3]

Lawmakers are not the only ones aware of the crisis. The media carry numerous reports of the social consequences of the growing linguistic schism in society. "Spanish-language shock jocks seem to have a de facto grant of immunity from the FCC," Joseph Contreras complained in *Newsweek*. "Only one of its 20 staff investigators speaks Spanish, and none of the nine radio and TV stations fined in the last 15 months for violating the agency's indecency standards was a Spanish-language broadcaster. After Janet Jackson's Super Bowl breast-baring stunt, the FCC and its chairman, Michael Powell, began cracking down on the likes of Howard Stern, whose talk show has been dropped by six of the radio giant Clear Channel's stations; this month Clear Channel was fined $495,000 for Stern's blue-tinged broadcasts, and has agreed to pay $755,000 for similar trespasses by Bubba the Love Sponge. Now some Hispanic media watchdogs accuse the agency of neglecting their community's segment of the industry—which has grown from 347 Spanish-language radio stations in 1993 to 626 last year."[4]

Voices in the Hispanic community are expressing concern about the degradation in society at large when vulgarity is allowed to spread throughout Hispanic culture in the United States. "The standard by which we judge radio has been shattered. The level of acrimony that is there, the crude language, it's inappropriate for public hearing," Raul Yzaguirre, then president of the Washington-based National Council of La Raza, said, voicing the growing frustration of the failure of government to regulate the public airwaves in both languages. "Spanish-language radio is raunchier than English. And there is no accountability whatsoever."[5]

HRM's mission, in essence, is precisely to exact accountability in the workplace. The challenges confronting U.S. society reverberate throughout corporate America, and it is the HR professional who is at the forefront of finding creative solutions. The way Spanish is spoken in the workplace—an inevitable fact of twenty-first-century life—can contribute to the creation of a hostile work environment. HR professionals must develop and implement strategies for creating employee manuals that establish a clear understanding of the problem and its urgency, document policies for dealing with inappropriate speech in a language other than English, and have the investigative and arbitration tools to resolve complaints and offer solutions should a situation arise.

EMPLOYEE RELATIONS

Employee relations (ER) is a broad term used to refer to the general management and planning of activities related to developing, maintaining, and improving employee relationships by communicating with employees and processing concerns, grievances, and disputes. Issues associated with ER vary across companies but normally include discipline, compliance, employment law, performance management, conflict resolution, corporate culture, communication, union negotiations, and employee assistance. It is imperative that the employee manual cover these areas in detail, and in both English and Spanish. ER activities are those whose objective is to create an atmosphere of trust, respect, and cooperation and are an indispensable part of HRM.

With our changing society becoming more focused on tangibles, keeping organizations focused on the intangibles that make up employee relations may be difficult. Relationships—especially employment relationships—are constantly evolving, partially due to changing business needs and laws and regulations that bear on this relationship. The current trend is for managers to focus more and more on the bottom line, which is more tangible and a lot easier to manage than employee relationships.

Far too many employees at many organizations, meanwhile, do not believe that they have an advocate in management. Current thinking of most human resource professionals is that HR *should be* an advocate for employees while remaining a strategic partner to management. Obviously, this is a difficult role at best, but it is a necessary role. HRM must be involved in assisting operations staff to achieve their goals. HRM must also serve as a legitimate employee advocate. But what is a legitimate employee advocate?

Here are some actions and beliefs that employees expect from an advocate:

- Work toward fair treatment of employees.
- Help resolve employee problems.
- Try to improve employee morale.

- Believe that employees should be treated with respect and dignity and work toward that end.

ER issues arise because of barriers that inhibit full employee participation and compliance with organizational policies. These barriers may come from organizational or personal factors, including the following, all worth reviewing:[6]

Communication—Ongoing two-way communication is the most important component in employee relations with Hispanics, but supervisors should be aware of language barriers to communication. This is especially important when dealing with Hispanic employees who are less likely to ask questions if they do not understand what is being communicated because they do not want to admit they don't understand. This is particularly crucial for hourly employees who may require an interpreter to communicate properly with their immediate supervisor and who may try to make do on their own even if they are not fluent in English. Thus, translating written materials into Spanish is a possible solution. But employers should understand that some immigrants may not know how to read or write well in Spanish, either. If this is the case, using a translator is an option. It may seem like an easy solution to ask someone who speaks Spanish to translate. However, this may not be the best choice since some people paraphrase or omit words. In addition, using a third party to interpret reprimands or discuss personal issues may put that person in an awkward position.

Trust—The old saying "Someone who does not trust cannot be trusted" should be taken seriously. If employees do not trust a manager, the flow of upward communication will be compromised. If managers do not trust employees, the downward flow of communication will be affected. As discussed, managers can build their credibility with Hispanic workers by demonstrating that they are people of *confianza* who have the employees' interests in mind. For Hispanic employees, trust is built on proper dignity and respect, a foundation of Hispanic culture. Managers can build good working relationships by remembering to use measures like these:

- Saying "please" and "thank you"
- Treating others as equals
- Maintaining a positive attitude[7]
- Speaking with employees in Spanish (at least common words and phrases)

Hispanics respond very well when the actions of managers and supervisors demonstrate real interest and respect.[8]

Ethics—If employees do not support or do not understand the ethics of a manager, they will indirectly question the manager's motives. This may be stressful for employees and may hinder performance. However, Hispanic employees are less likely than members of other groups to question manager motives or decisions because of the importance of hierarchy and roles to them. HR professionals and managers need to understand this cultural attribute when dealing with employee relations issues. Be aware, though, that the whole question of ethics is crucial, particularly since, because of immigration status or difficulties in their home countries, Hispanic employees tend to be ambivalent about bending the rules. What mainstream Americans call scofflaws and halfway admire, for instance, are seen as perpetrators of major ethical breaches by Hispanics.

Fairness—Fairness simply means that all employees are treated the same under similar circumstances. No favoritism should be shown. No one likes to be second best. This does not mean that superior performance should not be rewarded. To employees, fairness also means comparable (fair) wages and benefits. Hispanic immigrants, many of whom come from countries where the powerful are showered with privileges, are sensitive to being treated justly, whether in earning a year-end bonus or in receiving the same gift as everyone else at a company-sponsored event.

Feelings—Managers need to be sensitive to employee feelings. Acknowledgment and concern for employee feelings about work issues are an important part of establishing a relationship. American managers sometimes deal with Hispanics as a group rather than as individuals. They must be aware of this tendency and express individual interest in the Hispanics who report to them. It can help to kindle personal relationships by talking with people about family and friends. Managers should make time each day for personal interactions.[9]

Perceptions and beliefs—In employee relations, perceptions are more important than reality. Employees will act on what they perceive or believe. It is important that employees be properly informed and told the truth, even when it may be uncomfortable for management or employees. Employee beliefs (whether true or not) and uncertainties will affect performance. Good communication will ensure that employee beliefs are related to reality in the organization.

Expectations—Employees need to know what to expect from managers. No one likes surprises unless they are good surprises. Knowing the expectations of managers will greatly reduce stress for Hispanic employees, who often have unclear expectations of what is reasonable in terms of promotion or recognition for work they have performed.

Again, because of the cultural importance placed on roles, Hispanic workers may be less likely to question supervisors if they do not understand instructions because they want to please the boss. Language barriers can create even more apprehension and misunderstanding. Therefore, managers must make sure expectations are clear.[10]

Conflict resolution—Conflicts arise in all organizations, but they should be managed in such a way that undue stress does not affect employees or performance. For Hispanic employees to participate in the resolution process, companies must build trust and credibility by listening and acting on what they have to say. When conflicts do arise, Hispanics favor arbitrators for conflict resolution. Use this means when possible because it is a familiar mechanism for them. See Chapter 5 for further discussion of conflict in the workplace.

Career counseling and development—Career counseling and career development in the form of training opportunities of any kind communicate to Hispanics that the organization cares about their career and future.

All these attributes provide the foundation for a performance management model that is a continual process of managing effective performance and quality.

HISPANICS AND UNIONS

Hispanic workers are fueling the resurgence in organized labor in the United States simply by their numbers in the trades and service industries. As recently as the mid-1990s (during the height of the dot-com mania), there was a growing consensus that organized labor's best days were behind it. "Years of negative publicity about corruption in the big Teamsters Union and other unions have hurt the labor movement," the U.S. State Department stated in its *Outline of the U.S. Economy,* voicing the conventional wisdom on the state of organized labor:

> Even unions' past successes in boosting wages and benefits and improving the work environment have worked against further gains by making newer, younger workers conclude they no longer need unions to press their causes. Union arguments that they give workers a voice in almost all aspects of their jobs, including work-site safety and work grievances, are often ignored. The kind of independent-minded young workers who sparked the dramatic rise of high-technology computer firms have little interest in belonging to organizations that they believe quash independence.[11]

This appraisal was accurate enough, particularly at the time it was written. The triumph of the individual envisioned by the Internet's founders—with everyone the star of a personal Web site—spoke to the American character. Indeed, what distinguishes the United States from other Western nations is the ideal of independence. Americans romanticize the individual, whether it be George Washington standing up and telling his father he cannot tell a lie, or John Wayne portraying the ideal of the American cowboy riding off alone into the sunset, or Rosa Parks standing up by sitting down on a bus in Alabama, or, in our own times, the dot-com entrepreneur rising to renown from obscurity, and the notion that one gets what one deserves suffuses their thought. The United States rejects the European embrace of a communal approach to society's political economy.

American society, in essence, may be out of step with the rest of the world when it comes to understanding management-labor relations. "Organized labor has gained a questionable reputation in global competition," Jim Heskett reports. "Europe, where it is arguably the strongest these days, appears not to be competitive in many global industries in which labor costs are still important. Germany, in particular, where workers and union members routinely occupy seats on boards of the largest companies (through a process called 'co-determination'), recently has lagged behind other European countries in its ability to increase its productivity, grow its economy, and compete globally."[12]

This shared evolution in the way management and organized labor work together is not part of the American experience. The more antagonistic relationship in the United States has as its origins the conflict between innate American values that champion individualism, the nineteenth-century idea that socialism was an alien ideology imported from corrupt Europe, and the role of investigative journalists such as Sinclair Lewis (author of *The Jungle*, an exposé of conditions endured by workers in Chicago). In this climate of acrimony, organized labor has sought to establish its hold on American thought. This is how James Baron and David Kreps summarize the legal rights of employees to have a voice:

> In the United States, nonsupervisory employees are entitled to organize themselves into a union. A single union may represent all or most nonsupervisory employees in a single firm—this is typical in so-called *industrial union* settings like automobile assembly (the United Auto Workers). Or workers may be organized into several unions on the basis of the types of work they do. In newspaper publishing, for example, the typesetters, printers, paper handlers, mailers, and journalists each have their own craft union. But whichever form it takes, employees are entitled to organize. If enough employees request (through a very precise procedure), the National Labor Relations Board (NLRB) will hold a certification election in which all eligible workers can

vote for or against union representation. Management can campaign against the union, but its election-related activities are circumscribed by law. And if a majority of the eligible workers vote for union representation, management is required by law to bargain in good faith with the union over a host of issues. The covered workers—the technical term is the *bargaining unit*—can subsequently decertify the union as their bargaining agent, in an NLRB-supervised decertification election.[13]

What is often overlooked, in fact, is that the Wagner Act, signed into law by Franklin D. Roosevelt, begins by stating, "The denial by some employers of the right of employees to organize and the refusal by some employers to accept the procedure of collective bargaining lead to strikes and other forms of industrial strife." The primary responsibility belongs to management to facilitate the creation of the "workers' voice" through representation, something management is often reluctant to do.

This American standoff, in which issues are politicized—Republicans backing management and Democrats supporting labor—has been used to establish clear social, political, and economic divisions within American society, often to the detriment of the interests of all parties. For many Hispanics, such adversarial stances are unfamiliar and culturally incomprehensible. Recent labor history in the United States, however, shows a pattern that Hispanic influence is changing in fundamental ways.

"In the 1980s and 1990s, many employers developed new ways to organize their work forces," the U.S. State Department also says in *Outline of the U.S. Economy*, summing up the past two decades' experience of management-labor relations.

> In some companies, employees were grouped into small teams and given considerable autonomy to accomplish tasks assigned them. While management set the goals for the work teams and monitored their progress and results, team members decided

among themselves how to do their work and how to adjust their strategies as customer needs and conditions changed. Many other employers balked at abandoning traditional management-directed work, however, and others found the transition difficult. Rulings by the National Labor Relations Board that many work teams used by nonunion employers were illegal management-dominated "unions" were often a deterrent to change. Employers also had to manage increasingly diverse work forces in the 1980s and 1990s. New ethnic groups—especially Hispanics and immigrants from various Asian countries—joined the labor force in growing numbers, and more and more women entered traditionally male-dominated jobs. A growing number of employees filed lawsuits charging that employers discriminated against them on the basis of race, gender, age, or physical disability. The caseload at the federal Equal Employment Opportunity Commission, where such allegations are first lodged, climbed to more than 16,000 in 1998 from some 6,900 in 1991, and lawsuits clogged the courts. The legal actions had a mixed track record in court. Many cases were rebuffed as frivolous, but courts also recognized a wide range of legal protections against hiring, promotion, demotion, and firing abuses. In 1998, for example, U.S. Supreme Court rulings held that employers must ensure that managers are trained to avoid sexual harassment of workers and to inform workers of their rights.[14]

The relationship between management and labor has historically been different in the Hispanic experience. Whereas in the United States labor unions have been independent movements that seek to bargain collectively on behalf of their members, in many Hispanic societies, unions are quasi government agencies that seek to manage tension and conflict through arbitration and peaceful resolution. This reflects the sensibilities of indigenous philosophy, where communal resolutions to social conflicts are deemed superior outcomes. It is intrinsic in the Hispanic cultural outlook to organize labor not to confront management but to solve problems. In an approach closely linked intellectually to the concept of *simpatía,* Hispanics tend to see unions as a way to achieve group cohesion and use the persuasion of collectivism to achieve common goals.

To most Hispanics, union leaders are authority figures, to be respected once they earn workers' trust. They can earn *confianza* through honesty and building relationships with the members. Union leaders who empathize with the needs of Hispanic parents, for instance, find tremendous loyalty. When we examine the charismatic appeal of Cesar Chavez, an early Hispanic labor organizer, we find an extraordinary effort on his part to attend to the human needs of his followers, his way of establishing his authenticity with them and nurturing an emotional bond. "For more than three decades Cesar led the first successful farm workers union in American history, achieving dignity, respect, fair wages, medical coverage, pension benefits, and humane living conditions, as well as countless other rights and protections for hundreds of thousands of farm workers," says the official biography of Cesar Chavez on his foundation's Web site. "Against previously insurmountable odds, he led successful strikes and boycotts that resulted in the first industry-wide labor contracts in the history of American agriculture. His union's efforts brought about the passage of the groundbreaking 1975 California Agricultural Labor Relations Act to protect farm workers. Today, it remains the only law in the nation that protects the farm workers' right to unionize."[15]

Among Hispanics, *dignity* and *respect* are code words for the demands of union leaders. In the Hispanic experience, unions are a way to engage management in constructive conversation and reciprocal dialogue, and not to create an us-versus-them paradigm. This dialogue is designed to guarantee that management treats all employees with dignity and respect. Understanding these concepts can allow HR professionals to fulfill their roles as change agents and knowledge managers by understanding the needs and wants of their Hispanic employees and developing strategies for addressing issues that Hispanics prefer to manage through collective approaches, whether it be a union or an employee committee.

This is all consistent with the emerging role of HR professionals as strategic partners in an organization. "The evidence is unmistakable: HR's emerging strategic potential hinges on the increasingly central role of intangible assets and intellectual capital in today's economy," Brian Becker, Mark Huselid, and David Ulrich explain. They continue,

> Sustained, superior business performance requires a firm to continually hone its competitive edge. Traditionally, this effort took the form of industry-level barriers to entry, patent protections, and governmental regulations. But technological change, rapid innovation, and deregulation have largely eliminated those barriers. Because enduring, superior performance now requires flexibility, innovation, and speed to market, competitive advantage today stems primarily from the internal resources and capabilities of individual organizations—including a firm's ability to develop and retain a capable and committed workforce. As the key enabler of human capital, HR is in a prime position to leverage many other intangibles as well, such as goodwill, research and development, and advertising.[16]

HR professionals have an important function to perform in connection with the increasing participation of Hispanics in the American labor union movement. The sentiment throughout corporate America, in the face of global competition and the widespread impact international trading blocs such as the European Union and China are having on our economy, is shifting toward recognition that management and labor—managers and Hispanic workers—need to create partnerships, often partnerships where unions may play a central role.

The foregoing information addresses the specific realities of Hispanics of Mexican and Central American origin, which represent almost 80 percent of all U.S. Hispanics. HR specialists need to realize, of course, that such general discussions always involve exceptions. Cubans, the most educated and successful group of Hispanics in the United States, are very sophisticated in employment issues. And other groups, such as Puerto Ricans (who are U.S. citizens by birth) and Dominicans (who have lived in the United States for many generations), are more aware of their legal rights and employer obligations. Cubans, Puerto Ricans, and Dominicans are familiar with U.S. labor laws, including federal minimum wage and OSHA and FMLA regulations. They are also familiar with their rights to avail themselves of recourse to the Equal Employment Opportunity Commission (EEOC) and various state and local agencies with jurisdiction over labor practices and working conditions.

Profile of a Successful Company

Costco has won publicity raves through collaboration with its union, The American Rights at Work organization reports. "The excellent compensation of Costco's union-represented employees is a testament to the company's belief that treating employees well is good for business. A 2004 *BusinessWeek* study confirmed the wisdom of this approach. Costco's corporate philosophy that workers should share in the profits they generate is the key to its high rate of employee retention—a cornerstone of productivity."[17]

An indispensable part of Costco's success—along with that of other notable firms, including Cingular Wireless, Harley-Davidson, and Kaiser Permanente—is a proactive HRM that plays the role of "strategic partner," facilitating interactions between management and employees. The adversarial stance that has historically characterized management-labor relations is fundamentally different when Hispanic cultural values are introduced into the workplace. HRM must understand what drives Hispanic workers' admiration for unions and collective bargaining before it can build the tools for developing the language, fine-tuning the strategies, and acting as liaison between managers and staff. This is the more urgent mission of HR professionals at organizations with significant numbers of blue-collar workers, for one simple reason: one mechanism for compensating for the inability to speak English fluently among Hispanics is to have their union representative speak on their behalf.

Criteria for Success

HR professionals identify certain basic principles as integral to the success of healthy management-employee relations. Example 1 lists some of the criteria HR professionals use to refine their approaches to managing the Hispanic workers in blue-collar industries, where unions can often articulate the concerns and needs of workers. These principles are consistent with concepts generally accepted by HR practitioners. "Giving workers a voice via a union has broader consequences," Baron and Kreps explain in *Strategic Human Resources*. "Most importantly, perhaps, it shifts management's attention from the desires of younger workers to the desires of older workers. In designing HR policies and practices, management will naturally be concerned with whether those policies and practices appeal to workers. Yet workers are not unanimous in what they want. Which workers will be the focus of management's concerns?"[18]

Hispanics, through shared cultural values, diminish the dilemma Baron and Kreps describe simply because younger His-

---
EXAMPLE 1

American Rights at Work Strategies for HR

Successful partnerships between employers and unions share commendable labor relations strategies that balance profitability with workers' rights:

- Collaborating as equal partners with workers and their unions to craft innovative strategies on compensation, performance, and productivity to meet business goals and address challenges
- Providing sustainable wages or progressive increases and worker-friendly benefits
- Creating new jobs and implementing employee retention strategies
- Protecting workers' safety and health
- Fostering diversity and inclusion in the workforce
- Offering training and professional development opportunities
- Contributing positively to the broader community

Source: American Rights at Work (www.americanrightsatwork.org).

panic workers are more inclined to want the same things as older Hispanic workers, compared to younger and older non-Hispanic workers. By virtue of being outside mainstream American society, confronting the same language and educational challenges, and sharing a worldview, Hispanic workers of all ages empathize with one another in ways that defy easy characterization. For these reasons, where blue-collar Hispanic workers are concerned, allowing their voice to be empowered through unions is useful, because it enables savvy HR practitioners to duplicate the experience of Costco and avoid the HRM failures at other firms. Allowing Hispanic workers input signals management's *confianza* in them, deepening the bonds of loyalty and mutual respect between employer and employee.

The Role of Communication

When workplace issues arise, bilingual union officials tend to speak in rapid-fire Spanish slang with Hispanic workers and then summarize the "issues" or "points" in a few sentences in English. Management naturally worries whether much is lost in translation. Are the details lost in greater, more general, complaints? Consider the case of a high-tech assembly plant in the San Francisco Bay Area. Whereas the union representative spoke of a "degrading" environment in which "a climate of hostility" existed that "subjected" the assembly line workers to "humiliation on a daily basis," what the employees, mostly women from Mexico, El Salvador, and Honduras, had raised as an issue was the fact that the restrooms were locked and they were embarrassed at having to ask the floor manager (a male) for the key every time they wanted to use the restroom. (Management had put locks on the restrooms as a safety measure, mindful of incidents that had occurred in previous months late at night.) The solution, issuing the entire staff their own keys to the restroom, was a simple enough matter, but one that could not be communicated directly by workers to managers. Here we can see how a simple thing can escalate into a major problem, one fraught with recriminations and hard feelings, and all because of language difficulties and cultural sensibilities. (Compared to non-Hispanic women, Hispanic women tend to be more embarrassed about discussing bodily functions with men who are not family members.)

Absent HR professionals who, if not bilingual, at least have a working knowledge of Spanish, misunderstandings—management's concern for the safety of assembly line employees being interpreted as a sign of disrespect and the humiliating imposition of authority on them—can escalate unpleasantly. What is of greater concern, of course, is that a linguistic schism can be used by union officials to advance their own agenda—which might not be in the interest of either union members or management—by virtue of having a monopoly on communications between managers and workers. HR practitioners, in fact, now find themselves an instrumental part of management efforts to maintain stable labor relations.

As Baron and Kreps explain in *Strategic Human Resources,*

> Management that has sought overall cooperative labor-management relations may see some benefits in centralizing labor relations, or at least insisting that national units coordinate with corporate HQ on these matters, as they may be able to leverage a reputation for good relations achieved in one part of the company to achieve similar relations elsewhere (for instance, in a new part of the world the company plans to enter or in a separate enterprise the company plans to acquire).[19]

In these efforts, HR professionals are the vital liaison, and many organizations are already reaping the benefits of this forward-thinking approach. In fact, with HRM's emergence as a strategic partner between management and labor, stunning successes are being scored by major organizations throughout corporate America. The following "Labor Day List" recognizes organizations whose HRM plays a strategic role in cultivating management-employee partnerships that lead to success in the marketplace:[20]

- Addus Healthcare, Inc., SEIU (Palatine, Illinois)
    - This nationally recognized provider of health care staffing is improving living standards for its in-home health care aides while advocating for higher wages throughout the industry.
- Brightside Academy, AFSCME (Pittsburgh, Pennsylvania)
    - By collaborating with its child care workers' union to increase wages, benefits, and training, this early education provider reduces staff turnover and improves care for kids.

- Catholic Healthcare West, AFSCME, CNA, CHEU, ESC, IBT, LIUNA, SEIU, UNITE HERE (San Francisco, California)
  - The largest nonprofit hospital care provider in California has improved working conditions by partnering with employees and their unions to advance patient care.
- Cingular Wireless, CWA (Atlanta, Georgia)
  - This telecommunications leader reaps the benefits of respecting workers' rights and collaborating with employees.
- Costco Wholesale Corporation, IBT (Issaquah, Washington)
  - By providing wages and benefits above industry standards, this retail membership warehouse chain demonstrates that treating employees well is good for business.
- Douglas County School District, ATU, AFT (Castle Rock, Colorado)
  - A partnership between the fourth-largest school district in Colorado, its employees, and their unions has resulted in improved instructor training and higher student achievement.
- Edward Kraemer & Sons, Inc., IW, IUOE, LIUNA, OPCMIA, UBC (Plain, Wisconsin)
  - This national contractor and construction aggregates supplier boasts a strong commitment to safety, diversity, and collaboration with its workforce.
- Harley-Davidson Motor Company, IAM, USW (Milwaukee, Wisconsin)
  - This leading motorcycle manufacturer partners with its employees' unions at every level, which boosts productivity and quality—and keeps jobs in America.

- Kaiser Permanente, AFSCME, AFT, IFPTE, KPNAA, OPEIU, SEIU, UFCW, USW (Oakland, California)
  - America's leading integrated health care organization believes that partnering with employees and their unions empowers workers and provides patients with higher-quality care.

ADDENDA FOR HISPANIC EMPLOYEES

Employee manuals need to cover three points to reflect emerging Hispanic sensibilities in the workplace. These provisions address time off for holidays, language in the workplace, and an emerging form of racial discrimination.

Holidays

Hispanic employees often want official recognition of holidays not celebrated by other groups of employees. For example, as noted in Chapter 5, the vast majority of U.S. Hispanics regard December 12 as a more cherished holiday than Thanksgiving. If, in certain work environments, one national holiday can be exchanged for another, HR practitioners may ameliorate issues that have the potential for escalating into ill will between rank-and-file workers and management. Refer to Appendix 2 for a complete month-by-month list of important Hispanic dates and events.

Language in the Workplace

The second matter is the question of the use of language in the workplace. The question is no longer one of permitting Spanish to be spoken in the workplace; it now involves ensuring that Spanish spoken in the workplace is not inappropriate, to avoid creating a hostile work environment. This section of the employee manual provides, in both English and Spanish, an acceptable code of conduct that is binding on all employees to avoid creating a hostile work environment in either language. Explicit documentation of this stance should be incorporated into a code of ethics (see Example 2) and a definition of workplace responsibilities (see Example 3) that all employees and outside consultants working for the organization should be required to sign. Without a firm position on this point, problems will continue to arise as Spanish use proliferates throughout the United States in the decades ahead.

The code of ethics and workplace responsibilities, while designed to acculturate Hispanic workers to the norms and expectations of the American workplace, are appropriate for all employees throughout every organization.[21]

Backlash Against Hispanic Employees

The third provision is very sensitive, particularly since it evokes a strong and passionate response among some other groups of employees. It speaks to the emerging backlash against Hispanics in U.S. society—and especially that from one specific constituency: African Americans. The U.S. workplace, not unlike its society at large, has spent the greater part of the past half-century striving to overcome the socioeconomic and sociopolitical obstacles imposed by segregation. In the workplace, in fact, integration has made greater strides than in U.S. society as a whole: while Americans of different races work together without issues, Americans of different races or ethnicities do not socialize to a comparable degree.

Discussion of integration and race relations, however, has defined *race* in terms of black and white. With Hispanic employment

---EXAMPLE 2---
Code of Ethics

ENGLISH

We have a responsibility to OUR CLIENTS.
We must put our clients first, provide superior advice, products, and services, and always act with the highest level of integrity.

We have a responsibility to EACH OTHER.
We must provide outstanding people the best opportunity to realize their potential. We must treat our teammates with respect, champion our remarkable diversity, share the responsibility for our successes, and accept accountability for our failures.

We have a responsibility to OUR ORGANIZATION.
We must put the firm's long-term interests ahead of each unit's short-term gains and provide superior results for our shareholders. We must respect the local culture and take an active role in the communities where we work and live. We must honor those who came before us and extend our legacy for those who will come after us.

SPANISH

Tenemos una responsabilidad con NUESTROS CLIENTES.
Nuestros clientes deben ser lo primero, debemos proporcionarles asesoramiento, productos y servicios de calidad superior y siempre actuar con los más altos niveles de integridad.

Tenemos una responsabilidad LOS UNOS CON LOS OTROS.
A fin de que las personas sobresalientes desarrollen su potencial, debemos brindarles las mejores oportunidades. Debemos tratar con respeto a nuestros compañeros de trabajo, fomentar nuestra extraordinaria diversidad, compartir nuestros éxitos y aceptar la responsabilidad de nuestros fracasos.

Tenemos una responsabilidad con NUESTRA FRANQUICIA.
Debemos anteponer los intereses a largo plazo de la empresa por encima de las ganancias a corto plazo de cada unidad y generar resultados superiores para nuestros accionistas. Debemos respetar la cultura local y participar activamente en las comunidades en las que trabajamos y vivimos. Debemos honrar a aquellos que nos precedieron y extender nuestro legado para aquellos que vendrán después de nosotros.

EXAMPLE 3
Workplace Responsibilities

ENGLISH

Fair Employment Practices and Diversity
The Firm believes that diversity in our staff is critical to our success as a global organization, and we seek to recruit, develop, and retain the most talented people from a diverse candidate pool. Advancement at The Firm is based on talent and performance. We are fully committed to equal employment opportunity and compliance with the letter and spirit of the full range of fair employment practices and nondiscrimination laws. In addition, retaliation against individuals for raising claims of discrimination or harassment is prohibited.

Discrimination and Harassment
The Firm values a work environment where diversity is embraced, and where our employees' differences are valued and respected. We prohibit sexual or any other kind of discrimination, harassment, or intimidation, whether committed by or against a supervisor, co-worker, customer, vendor, or visitor. Discrimination and harassment, whether based on a person's race, gender, gender identity or expression, color, creed, religion, national origin, citizenship, age, disability, marital status, sexual orientation, ancestry, veteran status, or socioeconomic status, are repugnant and completely inconsistent with our tradition of providing a respectful, professional, and dignified workplace.

SPANISH

Prácticas laborales justas y diversidad
La Empresa considera que la diversidad en la composición del personal es esencial para nuestro éxito como organización mundial, por lo que tratamos de contratar, desarrollar y retener a las personas más talentosas de un conjunto de candidatos integrado por diversos grupos demográficos. En la Empresa, el crecimiento profesional se basa en el talento y el desempeño. Estamos plenamente comprometidos con el ofrecimiento de iguales oportunidades de empleo, así como con el cumplimiento del espíritu y la letra de toda la gama de leyes sobre no discriminación y de prácticas laborales justas. Además, queda terminantemente prohibido tomar medidas de represalia contra cualquier persona por presentar un alegato de discriminación o acoso.

Discriminación y acoso
La Empresa valora un ambiente de trabajo donde se dé cabida a la diversidad, y en el que se valoren y respeten las diferencias de nuestros empleados. Prohibimos la discriminación por motivos de sexo o por cualquier otro motivo, el acoso o la intimidación, bien sea por parte o en contra de un supervisor, colega, cliente, proveedor o visitante. La discriminación y el acoso, bien sea por motivo de raza, sexo, identidad o expresión sexual, color, credo, religión, origen nacional, ciudadanía, edad, incapacidad, estado civil, orientación sexual, ascendencia, condición de veterano o situación socioeconómica, constituyen prácticas repugnantes, y son totalmente incompatibles con nuestra tradición de proporcionar un centro de trabajo donde impere el respeto, el profesionalismo y la dignidad.

EXAMPLE 3 cont'd

ENGLISH

Discrimination and Harassment
Never use the Firm's systems to transmit or receive electronic images or text of a sexual nature or containing ethnic slurs, racial epithets, or any other material of a harassing, offensive, or lewd nature. If you believe you are being subjected to discrimination or harassment, or if you observe or receive complaint regarding such behavior, you should report it to your supervisor or senior business manager, or to your human resources representative. The Firm will promptly investigate all allegations of harassment or discrimination and will take appropriate corrective action to the fullest extent permitted by local law. Retaliation against individuals for raising claims of harassment or discrimination is prohibited.

Drug-Free Workplace
To meet our responsibilities to employees, customers, and investors, the Firm must maintain a healthy and productive work environment. Misusing controlled substances or selling, manufacturing, distributing, possessing, using, or being under the influence of illegal drugs on the job is prohibited.

SPANISH

Discriminación y acoso
Usted no deberá nunca utilizar los sistemas de la Empresa para transmitir o recibir imágenes o textos electrónicos de contenido sexual, o que contengan comentarios o epítetos despectivos sobre el origen étnico o racial de una persona, o cualquier otro material de índole lasciva, ofensiva u hostigante. Si usted considera que está siendo objeto de discriminación o acoso, o si observa o recibe una queja con respecto a cualquier conducta de este tipo, deberá reportarlo a su supervisor o gerente comercial [superior], o a su representante de recursos humanos. La Empresa investigará de inmediato todos los alegatos de acoso o discriminación, y tomará las medidas correctivas pertinentes con todo el rigor que permitan las leyes locales. Queda terminantemente prohibido tomar medidas de represalia contra cualquier persona por presentar una queja de acoso o discriminación.

Centro de trabajo libre de drogas
A fin de que podamos satisfacer nuestras responsabilidades con respecto a los empleados, clientes e inversionistas, la Empresa deberá mantener un ambiente de trabajo saludable y productivo. Quedan prohibidos el consumo indebido de sustancias controladas, así como la venta, fabricación, distribución, posesión o utilización de drogas ilegales, al igual que el hecho de encontrarse bajo los efectos de las mismas en el centro de trabajo.proporcionar un centro de trabajo donde impere el respeto, el profesionalismo y la dignidad.

EXAMPLE 3 cont'd

ENGLISH	SPANISH
Safety in the Workplace The safety of people in the workplace is a primary concern of the Firm. Each of us must comply with all applicable health and safety policies. We maintain compliance with all local and international laws, and internal guidelines have been developed to help maintain secure and healthy work surroundings. Questions about these laws and guidelines should be directed to your supervisor, or to Human Resources.	**Seguridad en el centro de trabajo** La seguridad de los empleados en el centro de trabajo es preocupación primordial de La Empresa. Cada uno de nosotros deberá cumplir con la totalidad de las políticas pertinentes en cuanto a salud y seguridad. Acatamos todas las leyes locales e internacionales, y hemos desarrollado pautas internas, a fin de ayudar a mantener un medio laboral seguro y saludable. Toda pregunta referente a estas pautas y leyes deberá dirigirse a su supervisor, o al Departamento de Recursos Humanos.

increasing, what is now occurring is not so much a conflict between Caucasians and Hispanics (who can be of any race) as one between black and brown. Some African Americans have issues with Hispanics, and these issues spill over from the greater society into the workplace.[22]

HR professionals cannot do anything about the nation's changing workplace demographics, but they must be aware of emerging issues that can create a hostile work environment for the Hispanic employee. HRM would do well to develop workshops and seminars that address the development of hostility in the workplace between African American and Hispanic employees.

The following lists summarize what employees and managers need to learn about eliminating hostility in the workplace. They can be used as a basis for a workshop.

Each employee must be taught:

- The causes of workplace harassment and disrespect
- Why almost all harassment and disrespect are unintentional
- The legal definitions of harassment
- The meaning of the firm's harassment policy and procedure
- How to apply the company policy to specific case examples
- The manager's duty to identify and prevent harassment
- How to communicate acceptable boundaries for speech and actions
- How to listen to others with care and respect
- How to create positive synergy with fellow employees in the workplace

Each manager should be expected to:

- Inform management of the issues and principles that are shared with their subordinates, in order to allow management to act consistently with policies, program recommendations, and legal requirements
- Report to management on current legal trends that affect their policies
- Secure direction from management to ensure that the firm's compliance program fits with the stated goals and objectives
- Monitor information from HRM that can be shared with managers, to facilitate management buy-in and enhance the program's credibility with all employees

- Alert management to issues and concerns raised during ongoing feedback sessions

- Share ideas for innovative ways to address the issues raised and instances that occur in the normal course of the workday

How does HRM deal with this? How can the tools used to train generations of Caucasians about being sensitive to and inclusive of African Americans in the workplace be modified to address the growing challenge of "black on brown" and other kinds of bias and bigotry? How can HR professionals recognize the problem, identify approaches to address it and similar concerns, and implement solutions without themselves being called racially insensitive for pointing out that any recognizable group, by virtue of being human, is as capable of being prejudiced as any other group of people?

The existence of "black on brown" hostility in the workplace may well be a subject to address as a phenomenon in the employee manual, if for no other reason than to assure Hispanic employees that management recognizes and validates this as a problem. In the same way that management recognized the prevalence of sexism and misogyny and took steps to develop policies in writing that addressed the concern of female employees who were (and are) subjected to a backlash by male staff members, the same is required for the issue of Hispanophobia, along with recognition that it may be present among other groups of employees who themselves have been subjected to discrimination, exclusion, and disenfranchisement. Table 6 shows the challenges and solutions for successful HRM.

Recall that Costco has successfully embraced unions and has used union representation as a way to bridge the cultural, linguistic, and social barriers between management and Hispanic workers, which shows how, in the twenty-first century, unions can in

TABLE 6
Challenges and Solutions for HRM

OLD CHALLENGE	NEW CHALLENGE	HRM STRATEGY
Side with management on question of union	Serve as arbiter between management and Hispanic workers	HR professionals recognize that when Hispanic workers speak of unions what they mean is the creation of successful partnerships between management and employees, a partnership that embodies the Hispanic values of *simpatía* and *confianza* and is not inherently adversarial in nature.
Monolingual workplace	Bilingual workplace	HR professionals recognize the need for workshops and seminars to assuage the anxiety and apprehension monolingual (English-speaking) employees have as Spanish enters the workplace with increasing authority.
Management obligations	Employee responsibilities	HR professionals have a strategic role to play in ensuring Hispanic workers are instructed through workshops and seminars in and knowledgeable of the codes of ethics and workplace responsibilities that govern the American workplace, with a special emphasis on zero tolerance for hostile speech in Spanish and for conduct that can be deemed sexist or disrespectful of sexual orientation of co-workers.
Black versus white	Black versus brown	HR professionals must be sensitive to and aware of the emerging tension between African American and Hispanic employees, a tension that reflects the larger sociological phenomenon of Hispanic presence in American society. The anxieties of African American workers have to be addressed through support groups, seminars, and classroom instruction, lest hostility emerge in the workplace.

fact be management's partner in creating a stable, productive, and profitable enterprise. It is HRM at Costco that is the liaison between management and the union, balancing the competing needs of management and workers, a strategy that handsomely meets the challenges confronting the company. Costco's superior HRM delivers exceptional value to the organization.

IN REVIEW

- Employee manuals must reflect the fact that, as the nation moves toward becoming a bilingual consumer economy, Spanish in the workplace is inevitable.
  - HRM needs to establish and document policies to the effect that Spanish in the workplace must conform to the rules that apply to English in the workplace.
  - HR professionals need to understand that written and spoken Spanish in the workplace can contribute to and constitute a hostile work environment.
  - Codes of conduct can be used effectively to ensure that Spanish will not be used in ways that create a hostile work environment.

- Organized labor in the United States is benefiting from the emergence of a Hispanic workforce.
  - Hispanic cultural values embrace a communal approach to problem solving and Hispanic societies have a strong tradition of officially sanctioned unions.
  - Hispanic workers often use labor unions to speak on their behalf to management to compensate for lack of fluency in English.
  - Hispanic workers see labor unions as organizations not for confronting management but for articulating their concerns and interests, mechanisms for ensuring that their dignity is recognized and that they are as individuals respected by their managers and supervisors.

- There is a backlash against Hispanics in the United States, one that intrudes into the American workplace.
  - As race relations in the United States shift focus from "black on white," the phenomenon of "black on brown" is emerging as a social problem for the nation.
  - HRM must recognize this as an issue in the same way that it recognizes both racial discrimination and sexism as impediments to a healthy work environment.
  - Employee manuals must affirm and validate the concern Hispanic employees have for the subtle biases they encounter as a direct consequence of the transformation of the nation's demographics.

3

Performance Management

HOW TO EVALUATE THE PERFORMANCE OF HISPANIC EMPLOYEES

Organizations encounter challenges when evaluating Hispanic employees. The cultural divide tends to reduce the objectivity of performance evaluations. Oftentimes, the remedy is for those conducting the evaluation to understand the nuances that inform how duties are executed. "Empirical research on performance evaluation suggests that the most important ingredient in programs that are successful is that those being evaluated see the system as equitable and in line with the general culture and strategy of the organization," James Baron and David Kreps write in *Strategic Human Resources*. "It is also important from the perspective of those being evaluated that the system support the individual's social and organizational roles, that it neither denigrate the individual nor create role conflict, and that it respect the individual's privacy and dignity."[1]

The act of judging or evaluating other people is a natural and inescapable part of our lives, both professionally and privately. When we are introduced for the first time, we automatically form an impression based the other's appearance, voice, and personality traits. Right or wrong, these first impressions can be lasting ones. At times, we base our evaluations of other people on more substantial evidence—the way they perform their jobs or interact with their co-workers and superiors.

If you are a manager, your working day involves a series of appraisals. Line managers, for example, may begin by making rounds of various activities for which they are responsible, checking the status of major projects. Managers often chat briefly with staff to find out how they are and what they are doing. The way work is delegated is also based on what managers know about individual employees. If you have visitors during the day, you may do a quick mental assessment of them and adjust your speech and actions accordingly. If employees are due for a salary review, you decide whether or not their performance merits more money. These are standard activities for any manager or supervisor, and yet each involves a deliberate act of appraisal. Performance management is not an occasional or chance occurrence—it is an integral part of a manager's job. These judgments may determine who gets a job, who is given an opportunity for additional training or promotion, who is transferred, and who is reprimanded or terminated. All this is to say that performance management occurs continually on both a formal and an informal basis.

THE CONTINUAL PROCESS OF PERFORMANCE MANAGEMENT

A successful performance management system is a continual process of managing effective performance and quality. It consists of five parts, and it is a living process, in that it is ongoing and evolving as the organization's needs change over time. It involves

- Clarifying performance expectations and setting goals
- Delegating
- Training and development
- Coaching and counseling
- Performance appraisal

A performance management system serves a strategic purpose for HRM, as shown in the following list. Hispanic increases in the workforce add a new level of complexity to the difficult task of performance reviewing. Global competition since the mid-1990s—with the implementation of NAFTA and the introduction of a single currency, the euro, for the European Union—has intensified the pressure on HR professionals to develop adequate performance management systems that respond to both heightened diversity within organizations and increasingly fierce competition in the marketplace. Line managers charged with getting more out of the resources they have turn to HRM for the development of performance review techniques that can maximize their department's—and organization's—productivity. In turn, this often translates into pressure on HR professionals, line managers, and individual employees alike.

The performance management system:

- Conducts performance planning
- Provides employees with an incentive to improve performance by evaluating strengths and weaknesses in relation to future career opportunities and development

- Improves communication between staff and managers. The continual feedback process is designed to open communication channels that have been blocked by misunderstandings and personality conflicts. It allows employees to express concern about performance-related issues.

- Functions as an effective counseling tool. Coaching or counseling is a necessary factor in getting employees to improve their performance, and the annual appraisal provides a perfect opportunity.

- Assesses the status of an organization's staffing needs. It helps managers make decisions regarding transfers, promotions, and terminations. It helps identify employees who are out of place in their present position.

- Links employee performance with overall success of company objectives and values

- Demonstrates commitment to treating all employees fairly and with dignity and respect

"When the workforce is demographically diverse, the potential for bias in subjective evaluations is greater (where the biases run along race, gender, age, and disability lines)," Baron and Kreps argue. "Objective measures of performance may be less biased, as long as the objective measures are *valid* indicators of performance. Yet we should also worry about biases in so-called objective performance measures."[2]

Management depends on HRM to involve line managers as champions of performance management activities and must hold managers accountable for performance improvement by building performance management–related goals into managers' own performance expectations. The Corporate Leadership Council 2002 Performance Management Survey, for instance, interviewed

19,000 individuals at thirty-four organizations to understand how this can best be accomplished. Managers' poor track records in honoring performance management commitments stems from five problems that are shared by most of the council's members: inadequate manager focus, insufficient manager skills in key performance management tasks, narrowly defined ownership of performance management, disconnect between performance management and business strategy, and failure to execute in support of goal realization.

Organizations, in no uncertain terms, should devote a significant amount of their attention to developing and implementing a viable, supportive performance management system. The performance appraisal process is not the sole province of HR; it is the prime responsibility of all line managers. The HRM responsibility includes program design, training of assessors, procedural implementation, review and maintenance, evaluation, and monitoring of the process. But how do performance management systems reflect the changes ushered in by the increasing presence of Hispanics in the workplace?

HRM's strategic role in helping management is clear: It must refine performance evaluation systems to reflect the cultural nuances that Hispanic employees bring to the workplace, and it must be a strategic partner in the analysis of performance reviews. A fundamental value HRM can deliver is the development and presentation of seminars and workshops that can train evaluators on how to do their jobs more accurately. As it is, many evaluators find performance evaluation an unpleasant task, one fraught with potential pitfalls and approached with misgivings. This is bad enough when the evaluator is of the same race, age, and gender as the person being evaluated. When the cultural differences between Hispanics and mainstream American society are thrown into this equation, the entire evaluation process becomes more time-consuming and uncomfortable for all parties—

TABLE 7

Cultural Considerations for Hispanic Employee Evaluation

- *Hispanics culturally tend to take significant pride in their work and to be invested emotionally in their professions.* As a consequence, they have a tendency to be more sensitive to criticism than members of other groups that find it easier to distinguish between criticism of their work and criticism of themselves as individuals.

- *Hispanic employees are often unwilling to sacrifice family considerations for work,* meaning they are reluctant to agree to travel, incur extended separations, or accept definitions of *family* that include only nuclear family members and adult parents; balancing the family-versus-work dynamic informs how Hispanics view the totality of their performance.

- *Hispanic culture has a more generous view of time,* one in which a sense of urgency is not equated with impatience; there is a more methodical approach to delivering correctly rather than promptly, a trait that may not be conducive to meeting organizations' expectations.

- *Hispanic culture places a value on long-term planning and long-term goals.* This can lead to conflict with management that seeks to deliver results for shareholders for the immediate quarter.

---

and less accurate. HRM can address these concerns through seminars for line managers and other evaluators that examine the four areas where Hispanic employees are often—characteristically but incorrectly—found to be lacking. Table 7 describes these issues and the proper discussion to be explored during a training session.

IMPLEMENTING A PERFORMANCE MANAGEMENT SYSTEM

How and when to introduce a new performance management system requires careful thought. Here are some ways to implement a new process:[3]

Give advance notice—People do not always like change. Line managers, not unlike other employees, often need help to prepare for change, especially when it affects their jobs and potentially their pay. It may take six months to a year to develop and implement a new performance management system. It is important to let managers and employees know that change is in the works. If they find out about the new system just before it is implemented, it likely will meet with more resistance, part of the natural suspicion employees have toward the introduction of changes about which they were not informed well in advance.

Create a task force—Performance appraisal is not an HR tool or program; it is one designed to ensure maximum capability and productivity of the organization. A major component of the process is to increase the line's sense of ownership for performance management by giving it a greater role in the design and management of the system. A task force can include subject matter experts, managers, and nonmanagement employees. The members of this task force need to be visible and to speak up in meetings about the value of effective reviews and the design of the new system. The Private Bank, for instance, with operations throughout Latin America, has different criteria for evaluating Private Bankers based in Mexico and those based in Brazil, and each of these groups faces different criteria than do those based in Miami.

Use focus groups—Employees are the primary customers of the performance management system, and it is important to ask them what kind of feedback they want. One way to collect this information is to meet with employees in small groups. HRM can share various approaches with them, including the sample forms in this book. Employee feedback will help HR design a system that meets their needs. This was precisely the approach taken by Philip

Morris, the cigarette manufacturer, when it decided to move its headquarters from New York to Richmond, Virginia. The firm needed to maintain a workforce that was fluent in the cultural differences among consumers, and that need was made more difficult to satisfy by its relocation from the culturally diverse urban center of New York to the more homogeneous communities that make up the greater Richmond area.

Understand organizational strategies and goals—The strategic objective of a responsive performance management system must be to support organizational goals and values. It is critical that these components be understood and incorporated into any performance management system, specifically as it needs to address the ongoing redirection in how HRM carries out its evolving role as management's strategic partner.

Start with a pilot project—Once HRM develops a preliminary model, and if time permits, pilot-test the new system in one or two divisions. If the performance management system was developed to reflect the sensibilities of the Hispanic employee, line managers who either are Hispanic or have experience supervising Hispanic employees should be recruited. This will allow HRM to benefit from the feedback of knowledgeable and experienced line managers. It is more advisable to introduce changes on a small scale than to have to rework the system across the entire organization. Here are a couple of ways to pilot the program:

- HRM can conduct performance evaluations concurrently under the current and proposed systems. Compensation, however, will be based on results from the current system. This way, employees will not feel penalized if the review under the new system is perceived to be anything less than that under the current program.

- HRM can also introduce the new system and advise employees that their evaluations will be based on the new process.

With either approach, it is important to build in an evaluation of the new system. After the pilot, discussions and interactive work sessions with managers and employees are necessary to elicit thoughts, perceptions, and feedback about the new system.

Articulate the purpose and goal of the project—Any changes to a performance management system require a culture change. This is an instance in which HRM's role as a change agent is transformed into that of a leader. An integral aspect of the success of this initiative is to secure the support of the organization's workforce. Change as a concept must be linked to the broader objective of market signaling, one in which employees and potential employees alike respond to the particular signals the organization is sending about itself. As HRM fulfills its leadership role, it must be prepared to articulate clear reasons for change as well as goals and the purpose of the new plan. The message that introduces the new system should make sense to managers and employees. The system most likely will not work if the HR team is the only group convinced it is well planned.

An indispensable part of this task is to articulate clearly the how and the why of changes. Consider, for instance, how Hispanic employees are affecting the nature of training. Historically, training has been used as a bargaining chip by management. By providing, authorizing, or subsidizing training, management has signaled its good-faith intentions for that employee's future at the organization. For Hispanics, on the other hand, training is seen not as a commitment to the future but as a manifestation of *confianza*, a means through which management validates its commitment to the *present*. HR professionals must be ready to answer some tough questions from line managers.

Here is where the cultural, educational, and psychological aspects of the Hispanic employee come together to make a real difference. Because Hispanics lag in educational achievement, they tend to place great value on workshops, seminars, and on-the-job training programs. These courses may substitute for formal education for them, and in the same way that diplomas document achievements, "certificates of completion," whether for perfect attendance in a calendar year or for completing a seminar, are highly valued. An organization's pilot project should give weight to the psychological role training plays and present answers up front to typical questions.

Managers' Concerns About Performance Management Systems

- When will the new system go into effect?
- Will I still be able to use the supplemental form that I developed for my department?
- What can I say to employees who claim that the new program penalizes them financially?
- Do I have to fill out every section of the form? What if I think something does not apply to my employee?

Employees' Concerns About Performance Management Systems

- Will this change the timing or amount of my pay increase?
- What happens if I disagree with the comments my manager writes on my review?

- Why does the organization keep changing the program?
- Why do three people sign the review before I see it?
- Why are you so worried about what happens right this quarter? It looks like you don't care about long-term planning or long-term goals.

If issues arise during the pilot or focus groups, it is better to take a little longer to correct flaws or incorporate recommended changes than to implement a system with known defects.

Presenting the Results to Senior Leadership

When the results of the pilot are known and revisions have been made, it is time to approach top management about organization-wide implementation. In preparation for this meeting, have the following data available:

- A concise description of the goals of the new system
- A description of the implementation plan
- The tangible results of pilots and focus groups
- A draft of an open letter the CEO can send to all employees introducing the program
- A set of recommendations on next steps

Introducing the System to Managers and Employees

Most organizations focus on training managers to understand the new system, assuming that employees are passive participants in the performance review process. This may be one of the biggest mistakes made in performance management. Employees, and certainly Hispanic employees, should have the opportunity to learn about the system and their role in it. They cannot be effective participants if they do not know how the system works.

HRM's training goals will serve as a guide in planning your program. An effective program will accomplish the following four goals:

- Introduce participants to an idea, concept, or skill
- Let participants experiment with the idea, concept, or skill
- Provide helpful feedback on how well participants are using the new idea, concept, or skill
- Provide tools for participants to use when they leave the program

Training Managers

A successful training program for managers includes a number of elements:

Introduction—The program should start with an overview of what managers hope to accomplish and how you plan to help them accomplish it. List your training goals and briefly explain the types of exercises and activities the group will be involved in.

Opening exercise—It is useful to open the training with an exercise to help group members get to know one another and to start focusing on performance management. One way to do this is to ask participants to share their own experiences with performance reviews. For instance, a manager might ask half of the room to work in pairs to discuss the most effective review they ever received and the other half to talk about the least effective one they ever received. When the groups have finished sharing, ask a few of them to share their stories. Managers can use these stories to highlight some of the key points that will be covered in class.

Awareness of legal issues—Providing an overview of the legal issues related to performance reviews is important for managers. They do not need to know everything about the law that a labor attorney knows—or even as much as an HR professional—but they do need to know when they may be in an area that could create problems and where to get advice. Your program should give them this information. For example, to mitigate legal liability and possible discrimination claims, reviews should

- Have specific performance standards that are communicated to employees in advance of the review period
- Include objective data
- Be standardized and formal

Cultural awareness—Reviews based on traits associated with culture should be avoided. Managers should be trained to

- Identify common cultural stereotypes
- Learn research-based characteristics of various cultures
- Identify the advantages and necessity of a diverse workforce
- Understand basic cultural competencies for the workplace
- Develop skills for interacting with individuals from different cultures in the workplace

Working with the new form—At this point, HR practitioners can introduce HR's new form. Once line managers have been instructed in how to perform and write a review, HR professionals can have them work together to complete some or all of HR's new forms to review an imaginary employee.

Training Employees

More and more companies are training their managers on how to conduct performance reviews, but few train their employees on what to expect and how they can participate. Hispanic employees must be taught the definitions of terms, what ratings mean, how to receive feedback, what to expect from their managers in terms of feedback, and where to turn if they are not receiving the feedback they need.[4]

Most important, Hispanic employees need to understand they are not passive listeners in the performance review process. To ensure effective communication and continuous feedback, managers should help employees understand that they play an active role in determining their performance ratings. Hispanic employees may feel that the performance evaluation meeting is where they should be polite and sit and listen, but they should prepare themselves to contribute to their evaluation. To help increase their active participation in the process, managers can have them:

- Review their job description
- Review goals set during the last performance evaluation meeting
- Complete a self-assessment
- Gather materials and self-assessments and bring them to the interview
- Bring a list of training programs or sessions attended during the year

Employees should know that if they aren't getting enough feedback, they should ask to receive more. They can ask questions like "How am I doing?"

The objective is to create a performance management system that is equitable, forms a level playing field, and neutralizes the cultural impact on workplace norms and standards. Table 8 outlines the stated objectives and strategies for achieving these goals. When employees are comfortable asking "How am I doing?" they are validating HRM's success in creating a productive and inclusive workplace environment.

NUANCES OF PERFORMANCE APPRAISAL OF HISPANIC EMPLOYEES

Cultural differences influence—and often distort—the performance appraisal process, a concern many HR professionals have recognized ever since the American workplace began the process of integration and diversity building more than a quarter century ago. With the growing numbers of Hispanic workers, these concerns have increased. The U.S. labor force includes more and more individuals with cultural and social backgrounds that differ from those of the traditional mainstream. How will this diversity affect the performance evaluations used by companies to make important decisions?

Effect of Culture on Performance Ratings

In the mainstream culture, subordinates tend to evaluate themselves more favorably than do supervisors. Leniency in self-ratings is consistent with the notion that people view themselves in a positive light. The tendency to have a positive self-image is common among people whose culture stresses individual

TABLE 8
HRM's Role in Culturally Equitable Performance Appraisal

OBJECTIVE	HRM STRATEGY
Create level playing field	■ Implement an organizationwide effort to have every employee, outside consultant working on-site, and temporary worker sign the code of ethics. ■ Implement an organizationwide effort to have every employee, outside consultant working on site, and temporary worker sign the workplace responsibilities form. ■ Acknowledge that sensitivity and cultural awareness training workshops and seminars must be on a *voluntary* basis, since making these mandatory creates a backlash that is counterproductive.
Culture versus workplace norms	■ Acknowledge the importance of an individual's cultural identity and his or her self-perception. ■ Identify core values of the employee's self-image and how culture influences this self-image. ■ Identify strategies for managing cultural differences specific to the values and worldviews of the Hispanic employees. ■ Identify strategies for managing cultural conflicts between Hispanic and African American employees.
Implement diversity awareness as part of performance management system	■ Acknowledge the benefits of thoughtful planning in developing awareness and diversity programs as part of the performance management system. ■ Introduce active and innovative recruitment strategies to appeal to Hispanic candidates. ■ Identify mentors and leaders who can spearhead diversity implementation programs. ■ Monitor workplace environment prior to awareness training to assemble information for comparative purposes.

TABLE 8 cont'd

OBJECTIVE	HRM STRATEGY
Assess employee and corporate awareness	• Acknowledge the benefit of diversity audits *before* they are integrated into the performance management system. • Perform diversity audits that are compatible with your industry and workplace environment. • Use feedback to measure the effectiveness of your multicultural awareness training sessions and seminars. • Assess management commitment to diversity as workshops and seminars are developed.

achievement and self-promotion. In comparison, collectivist cultures encourage interpersonal harmony, solidarity, and interdependence with other group members. They do not draw attention to individual achievement.

As noted in Chapter 1, Hispanics of indigenous ancestry tend to see themselves primarily as part of a larger community, a perspective that is often read as lack of ambition by those reared in mainstream American society. Understanding people from various cultures through psychology is a relatively new field of inquiry, but one that has tremendous implications on how HR practitioners can perform evaluations. "Throughout the 1950s and 1960s when cross-cultural psychology was in its infancy, evaluation results were very strange," points out William Lambert, an authority on cross-cultural psychology at Cornell University. He continues,

> The tests showed a tremendous gap in the scores of Westerners and people from other cultures.... How could such disparities among people possibly exist? One knew instinctively that there

was something very amiss—not with people, but with our method of testing them. But when we approached cross-cultural psychology from a different perspective—assume the human mind is the same across cultures—then psychologists began to make progress in understanding how culture affects human development and why societies are structured the way they are. This approach has added tremendous rigor to the discipline and it helped completely change the way we understand the world.[5]

What is important to remember, however, is that Hispanics are a subset of groups researchers have compared and contrasted with the larger society that constitutes the North American culture area. An international team of researchers reviewing how management and employees interact with their colleagues, subordinates, and supervisors examined the performance ratings of more than nine hundred supervisor-subordinate pairs. The ratings of people working in Taiwan were compared to those of Americans. When Chinese workers evaluated their own job performance, they gave themselves lower ratings than they got from their supervisors. The ratings were also lower than what American workers gave to themselves. This study concluded that the use of self-evaluation can create a bias against Chinese employees.[6] Similar findings hold true for Hispanics of Mexican and Central American background, who are further from the mainstream than Hispanics of Cuban, Puerto Rican, or Dominican origin.[7]

Implications of Cultural Differences for HRM

Cultural differences within the workforce raise critical issues for HR practitioners. Concepts such as formal appraisals and rewards based on individual performance have proven difficult to implement and to make work effectively in some parts of the world.

TABLE 9
Contrasting Cultural Profiles

EASTERN AND SOUTHERN CULTURES	WESTERN AND NORTHERN CULTURES
Characteristics of cultures: Collectivist, hierarchical, particularistic, ascribed status, person focused, external control, intuitive and holistic, high power distance	**Characteristics of cultures:** Individualistic, egalitarian, universalistic, achieved status, task focused, internal control, analytical and reductionist, low power distance
Countries with cultures that favor this profile: Japan, China, Egypt, Indonesia, Turkey, Brazil, Venezuela, South Korea, France, Greece, Italy, Spain	**Countries with cultures that favor this profile:** United States, United Kingdom, Canada, Australia

Some of the reasons for the difficulty are relatively obvious. For example, the notion of differentiating at the individual level for purposes of pay administration is not universally accepted. But even where pay differences based on individual performance are acceptable, the manner in which performance is defined, appraised, and communicated will have a significant impact on motivation level and on attitudes about appropriateness. Principles such as making rewards contingent on contribution may be increasingly adopted on a global basis, but local strategies may shape the way these principles are applied.[8] Table 9 shows fundamental differences among workers of various backgrounds and constitutes a foundation on which differences between workers of various cultures can be addressed.

The characteristics identified in Table 9 are based on cultural research described by Fons Trompenaars and Charles Hampden-Turner in *Managing People Across Cultures*,[9] and by Geert

Hofstede in *Cultures and Organizations*.[10] These researchers identified cultural differences between countries by measuring the extent to which the characteristics existed in samples of the national populations. Both sets of researchers used cultural "dimensions" to describe contrasts across national borders.

The characteristics discussed are based on the following contrasts, which HRM should incorporate into its performance appraisal process:

- *Collectivistic* (group and society oriented) versus *individualistic* (self-oriented)

- *Particularistic* (circumstances or involved individuals cause the actions to change) versus *universalistic* (one set of rules is applied to everyone in all situations)

- *Ascriptive or ascribed status* (how people are treated depends on who they are) versus *achieved status* (all status is earned through achievements)

- *Outer directed* (person not in control; external forces govern outcomes) versus *inner directed* (can-do attitude caused by the belief that people control results)

- *High power distance* (hierarchy and authority are prominent) versus *low power distance* (less differentiation by level and more democratic processes)

Cultural and social backgrounds have an undeniable impact on the effectiveness of performance appraisal methods and processes. In mainstream business cultures, performance evaluation generally aims to

- *Translate* organizational goals into individual job objectives
- *Communicate* management's expectations regarding employee performance

- *Provide feedback* to the employee about job performance in light of management's objectives

- *Coach* the employee on how to achieve job objectives and requirements

- *Diagnose* the employee's strengths and weaknesses

- *Determine development* activities that might help the employee make better use of skills and improve performance on the current job

The highly individualistic cultures fitting the Western and Northern profile favor individual appraisals that involve direct and specific feedback. Measuring individual performance and tying consequences to the appraisal will be more acceptable in cultures that are *individualistic* than in cultures that are *collectivistic*. Employees from countries such as the United States, the United Kingdom, Canada, Denmark, the Netherlands, and Australia tend to be more individualistic in their orientation than employees from Egypt, Mexico, India, Japan, France, and Venezuela, who are more likely to prefer performance to be measured at an aggregated level, since they believe results require collective effort.

Evaluating individuals based on what they accomplish rather than who they are will be more acceptable in cultures that are *achievement oriented* than in cultures that are *ascription oriented*. Employees from countries such as the United States, Australia, Canada, the United Kingdom, and the Netherlands are more likely to accept evaluation based on what people have accomplished than are employees from countries such as Egypt, Japan, China, Russia, Mexico, and France, who are more likely to believe the status and qualifications of the individual should be a consideration in evaluating performance.[11]

A Third Culture

This is all instructive, as background. For HR professionals, however, a more defined approach for the Hispanic employee is in order. Over the past quarter-century, Baptist Health South Florida hospitals have been pioneers in the integration of Hispanic employees and the development of a bilingual workplace. The successful evolution of Baptist Health South Florida—from a monolingual organization whose clients were primarily non-Hispanic Americans into a bilingual institution, more than half of whose customers are either U.S. Hispanics or Latin Americans—is the result of pioneering programs developed and executed by HRM.

The stated strategic objective has been to create and implement a "third culture" for the Hispanic workforce that includes elements of the two other corporate cultures: salaried employees and nonsalaried workers. The "third culture" concept refers to the process by which line managers are sensitized to ways to critique an employee's performance without creating conflict. So many conflicts arise over supervision that many small- and medium-sized firms avail themselves of the growing industry of cultural liaisons that specialize in helping non-Hispanic managers communicate with Hispanic workers. "My class is similar to the book *Men Are from Mars, Women Are from Venus*," says Jennifer Thomas, a Spanish-language and leadership consultant, with amusement. "The Hispanic culture is great. The U.S. culture is great. But problems may arise when the two groups interact." A consultant to the landscaping industry, Thomas argues that "lack of communication can really hit the owner's profits. It can lead to time wasted, mistakes, and a lot of rework. For example, one employer said he sent someone to prune the shrubs, and the workers misunderstood and spent seven hours pruning the trees." Apart from providing an in-depth orientation to Hispanic workers on the English-language vocabulary used in the landscaping business, Thomas also delves into the area of cultural differences. "Americans tend to 'tell it like it is,' while the Hispanic culture is more sensitive," she explains. "Americans may take constructive criticism, but the Hispanics may see it as more of an insult."[12]

HRM throughout the United States increasingly recognizes the importance of outside consultants in helping design and construct a responsive and effective set of tools managers can use in creating a successful work environment, particularly with the "third culture" issues identified in Table 10. "Saving face," "managing deadlines," "risk aversion," and "personalismo" are issues that together can create a communications and expectations breakdown. HR professionals need to help non-Hispanic managers become aware of, and sensitive to, these issues so they can avoid having their meaning lost in translation when communicating with Hispanic workers.

Of the many ways to overcome these obstacles, one of the more effective is through the establishment of communal, which is to say group-based, incentives. For mainstream workers—where the Protestant work ethic and the principles of individualism are part of the cultural bedrock—such an approach is open to strong criticism. "Group-based performance measures raise important issues of legitimacy," Baron and Kreps explain in *Strategic Human Resources*. "If there is homogeneity within groups and heterogeneity between groups in terms of abilities, individuals 'stuck' in a group with mediocre or poor performers may see injustice. On the other hand, if within-group heterogeneity is high, high-fliers in a group may be upset at having to 'carry' their colleagues who are less able, ambitious, or energetic, particularly if group-based rewards are divided equally."[13]

HR practitioners, then, need to understand the Hispanic impulse to approach problem solving and job performance from a communal perspective, at least in nonmanagerial positions, and

TABLE 10
"Third Culture" for Hispanics

OBJECTIVE	HRM STRATEGY
Saving face	Hispanics invest tremendous pride in their work and are reluctant to admit to mistakes or errors, believing that doing so is a reflection on their personal dignity. HR professionals must train line managers to preface critical comments by distinguishing between the Hispanic employee and the task at hand, whether it is a report or something on the production line.
Managing deadlines	Acknowledge the importance of time and the expectations people have for it. For Hispanics in professional and management positions, this is not an issue. For Hispanic workers in manual and hourly positions, however, there is often a conflict between their expectations and what their employers demand. Hispanics tend to want to deliver a product that is 100 percent perfect, rather than meet a deadline.
Risk aversion	Hispanics tend to be conservative with their capital, or *patrimonio* (patrimony). With experiences in societies plagued by extreme boom-and-bust economic cycles, many are reluctant to engage in financial planning or to see the value of company-sponsored 401(k) plans. As a consequence, HRM must reach out to Hispanic employees to help them understand their benefits fully and make informed decisions.
"Personalismo"	Hispanics develop fierce loyalties in the workplace as well as in their personal lives. Managers who demonstrate respect and concern for Hispanic staffs can expect loyalty "beyond the call of duty."

communal perspective, at least in nonmanagerial positions, and to embrace the opportunity to work in a cohesive unit where individual talents can contribute to a larger group objective rather than to individual ambitions. Many Hispanics prefer this because

ers better understand as "teamwork." This kind of incentive program, in fact, works not unlike team negotiating. "Teams stimulate more discussion and more information sharing than individuals do, particularly concerning issues, interests, and priorities," Elizabeth Mannix argues. "Teams also feel more powerful and more advantaged than solo negotiators. Even under highly stressful situations, as when they're accountable to constituents, team negotiators feel less competitive and pressured than do solo negotiators.... With greater numbers comes a sense of security."[14] It is this sense of security that is appealing for a group, particularly when they are working toward a common goal or reward.

CONDUCTING PERFORMANCE APPRAISALS

As discussed in Chapter 1, the growth of the Hispanic workforce varies by region. It is most noticeable on the East and West coasts, along with Texas, the Southwest, and the greater Chicago metropolitan area. Organizations throughout the United States have responded with varying degrees of success to the explosive increase of Spanish-speaking consumers and participants in the U.S. workforce.

As noted in this chapter, south Florida is the nation's leader in both integrating Hispanic employees and courting Spanish-speaking consumers. Baptist Health South Florida is one of the pioneering organizations in this effort which, more than a decade in the making, has transformed the way Baptist Health South Florida sees itself as an enterprise and understands the community in which it operates. The transition has allowed it to manage breathtaking diversity in the workplace.

HRM has been, and remains, central to the success of this endeavor. With a team of highly professional HR practitioners,

Baptist Health South Florida has developed a series of tools that have proved instrumental in evaluating, nurturing, and promoting Hispanic talent within its ranks and attracting capable Hispanics from the greater community. "Baptist [Hospital] is one of the more respected employers in south Florida, and with good reason," states Alex Penelas, former mayor of Miami-Dade. "They exemplify the very best in our community."[15]

A Three-Part Approach to Evaluation

Evaluating the performance of Hispanic employees is enhanced by use of a three-part approach that consists of preparing well before the evaluation, conducting the interview with attention to cultural needs, and then reviewing the results. Oftentimes, as we have seen, Hispanics are cognizant of their accents, which creates anxiety and leads to inarticulate or incomplete responses in oral interviews. Of similar concern, their cultural predisposition to be modest can on occasion result in self-deprecating analysis of their own work or reluctance to speak up and point out their achievements.

One such three-part interview process evolved over time as Baptist Health South Florida made the transition from monolingual to bilingual (see Figure 1). It has helped overcome barriers—and employee resistance—to the process of integrating Hispanics and the Spanish language into all levels of the organization, particularly in the hospitals that serve the Miami-Dade area. Developed originally to integrate Hispanic employees, it has proved so successful that it is now used to evaluate all employees. Review the suggestions that follow and use them as guides in planning or training.

FIGURE 1
A New Approach

Preinterview	Interview	Postinterview
• Review goals and documentation • Give employee adequate notice • Ask employee for self-appraisal • Set aside sufficient time by arranging a meeting with employee • Arrange for privacy and no interruptions	• Put employee at ease • Ask for self-appraisal and *listen* • Compare self-appraisal with your evaluation • Discuss discrepancies • If goals/expectations met, praise specific accomplishments • If not met, have employee suggest ways to improve • Identify next year's goals	• Make final preparation of forms, including those relating to money issues • Give to employee to add comments • Have employee sign off and take a copy • Identify when you will meet again to discuss performance (3 months, 6 months, 9 months)

Source: Baptist Health South Florida Human Resources.

Preinterview

- Schedule the meeting in advance. Allot an uninterrupted time, at least thirty minutes, in a confidential setting. At the time the interview is set, determine the language in which it will be conducted. (Note that arranging for sufficient time is particularly important if there is to be an interpreter present.)

- Determine language comfort. If you know the employee does not feel comfortable speaking in English, offer the opportunity to conduct the interview in Spanish. It is appropriate to ask, "Would you like to conduct this interview in English or Spanish?" or "Our policy is to conduct interviews in English—will you require an interpreter?" If needed, obtain a translator who has signed a confidentiality agreement in advance. Ensure that the employee has approved the use of a translator.

- Review goals, documentation, and job description, making sure to document each point in writing.

- Ask the employee for a self-appraisal. Give consideration to individual employee comfort with this. Although it works well most of the time, some Hispanics view disagreeing with the superior as inappropriate. Be aware of this and, if needed, skip this step.

Interview

- Build rapport; put the employee at ease. It may be helpful to point out the numbers of Hispanics who have been, or are, employed by the firm. Offer food, water, or coffee to facilitate the meeting. This hospitable act is looked upon favorably in Hispanic cultures.

- Briefly explain the purpose and value of performance evaluation. Let the employee know it is something that managers value and take seriously and that you hope the employee will, also.

- Ask for self-appraisal (if applicable) and listen carefully to the employee's response. It is especially important to give full attention since this is one of the rare opportunities employees have to speak directly about their jobs, work environment, and performance.

- Listen as much as you talk, and perhaps more.

- Compare the employee's self-appraisal with your evaluation (if applicable).

- Use specific examples. When identifying areas that need improvement, make sure deficiencies and goals are identified in writing.

- Discuss discrepancies (between expectations and current realities). Be aware that Hispanics tend to be hesitant to question the status quo for fear of recrimination. This means that it may be difficult for Hispanics to discuss discrepancies and performance.

- Praise specific accomplishments if goals and expectations have been met. This is extremely important for Hispanics as it demonstrates respect for their contributions.

- Have the employee suggest ways to improve if goals have not been met. What is agreed on should be in writing. Because continuing education is important to Hispanic employees, you should create a development plan.

- Identify next year's goals jointly. Be sure these are in writing.

- End on a positive note.

Postinterview

- Make final preparation of forms, including those dealing with money. Document specifics.

- Give the performance evaluation to the employee to add comments.

- Have the employee sign off and get a copy of the forms. All finished forms should include both manager's and employee's signatures.

- Set follow-up meetings to monitor performance and to provide feedback at three months, six months, and nine months into the new year.

- Honor the commitments agreed on.

Use this process as is or adapt it to the particular needs of your workplace.

Rater Error Effect on Evaluation

Another important topic worth mentioning in relation to performance appraisal training is rater error. Every rater is subject to making some common types of errors, and research has shown that the best antidote is to identify each type and to talk about how to avoid it or minimize its impact.

Here are some of the most common errors:

- **Bias**—Allowing personal likes and dislikes on nonperformance-related factors to influence employee ratings

- **Halo effect**—Tendency to let one favorable or unfavorable trait affect judgment; employee can do no wrong or no right

- **Leniency**—Giving higher ratings than deserved (may occur more with employees the rater knows well or likes more)

- **Strictness**—Giving lower ratings than deserved; being overly critical or demanding (may occur more with employees the rater knows less well or likes less)

- **Central tendency**—Rating in the center or average; often given to avoid confronting more extreme (positive or negative) earned ratings or when rater is less informed on employee performance

- **Recency**—Overemphasis on isolated or recent events

HR practitioners should be aware of these errors in making performance evaluations and make special efforts to view them through a cultural lens, which can be applied to each of the six areas.

Assessment of Cultural Effectiveness in Performance Evaluation

HRM, as the strategic partner in executing the organization's performance management process, needs to address issues before they turn into problems. This includes design, administration, and evaluation of effective performance appraisal systems. HR professionals can take an active role in assessing the cultural efficacy of performance appraisals.

One of the best places to start is with a review of completed evaluations. Although most managers are trained in how to conduct evaluations properly, HR staff should assume an audit role. Having a third party review evaluations can ensure consistency in application of standards, identify any potential issues arising from unreasonable expectations, and flag subjective ratings based on personal traits or characteristics.

If performance evaluation information and ratings are maintained online, aggregating data and creating reports correlating performance ratings and race may also provide indications of problems with the appraisal process. These can include rating biases, lack of training or understanding regarding completion of the evaluation or of performance standards, or other employee relations issues.

Identify the cultural composition of the workforce. Without stereotyping people based on their national or ethnic origin, undertake a concerted effort to understand their views about performance management. This may take the form of a survey, a set of focus groups, or another data-gathering method.

Potential issues identified will provide the HR professional with the basis for further communication or for system refinement and lead to decisions regarding how much accommodation will be made to people holding different views. Here are the objectives an organization seeks to meet through its various employee review processes:

Primary Objectives

- Improve job matching throughout the organization
- Communicate values, objectives, and priorities of the organization to employees
- Develop a management tool for use in training and career development
- Document pay increases and promotions
- Provide documented reason for staff retention or reduction

Secondary Objectives

- Generate feedback to improve recruitment and hiring
- Provide the feedback necessary for the organization's self-improvement
- Validate HRM practices
- Document processes in place for legal purposes
- Provide source of feedback to evaluators

Regardless of how cultural differences are addressed, they must be addressed. A process, such as performance appraisal, that deals with issues such as a person's worth to the organization can be charged with emotion and can have a significant impact on employee relations. Organizations must, of course, ensure performance is appropriately defined, measured, and rewarded. Appraisals must be based on an in-depth understanding of cultural differences if HR professionals are to make an organization's performance better. Here are some questions evaluators need to ask themselves before they interview Hispanic employees:

- What is the organizational environment that this department needs to create so that our Hispanic employees value our firm over our competitors?

- What tools do Hispanic employees need so that they can understand, respond to, and meet the short-term and long-term goals of our department?

- How do we invest in our Hispanic employees so as to deliver business results?

- How do we work with HR to deliver maximum value to Hispanic employees in seminars, workshops, and classroom situations?

- How does this department create a strategy that sets an agenda for how we will help our Hispanic employees—and, by inference, our company—succeed in the marketplace?

- How do we communicate to HR professionals what we need in order to have the strategies, tools, and support to accomplish our goals?

- How can we deliver value to our Hispanic employees so they can return even greater value to this department?

IN REVIEW

- The implementation of a performance management system needs to reflect the issues involved in evaluating Hispanic workers.

  - HRM must understand that Hispanics generally share a cultural tendency to invest tremendous passion in their jobs, on occasion taking constructive criticism as a personal affront.

  - Performance can be affected by tendencies to be meticulous and perfect, which can conflict with time management issues centered on delivering results on a quarterly basis.

  - HRM can overcome these issues by giving sufficient notice of the goals of the performance management system, creating a task force to debrief employees, and using focus groups to articulate the purposes, goals, and time frames involved.

  - HRM is more successful if it tailors communication for different audiences: managers, employees, and upper management.

  - HRM, through pilot programs and targeted training, can overcome the conflict between cultural and workplace expectations, creating a level playing field for both evaluators and employees being evaluated.

- HR must understand the nuances of conducting performance appraisals of Hispanic employees.

- HRM needs to understand that cultural differences underlie people's philosophical approaches to life and work, specifically the individualistic American approach versus the collectivistic Hispanic tendency.

- HRM must factor in how this results in Hispanic employees' reluctance to boast about their individual achievement in deference to their team or department.

- HRM must compensate for the tendency of anxiety about fluency in English, or about speaking with an accent, to affect the way a Hispanic employee performs in an oral evaluation.

- HRM can compensate for these issues by incorporating the concepts in the "third culture" for Hispanics, a strategy to correct for the Hispanic tendency to be modest and shy about professional and career achievements.

- When conducting performance appraisals, HRM should incorporate the principles of the "new approach," which emphasizes the preinterview, interview, and postinterview preparedness and so facilitates a more thorough and accurate evaluation.

  - HRM must articulate goals of performance appraisals well before the actual evaluation takes place.

  - HRM must help evaluators identify potential areas of bias or cultural misunderstanding that can hinder the evaluation process.

  - HRM must document the primary objectives of the evaluation and assist evaluators in preparing questions to ask themselves before conducting the appraisal.

4

Training and Development

HOW SUCCESSFUL COMPANIES NURTURE THEIR HISPANIC WORKFORCE

Hispanics are entering the American workplace in a wave unprecedented in scope. The only comparable event in living memory was women entering the labor market en masse in World War II, more than half a century ago. Organizations throughout the American economy have been unprepared for this historic influx of employees who are linguistically and culturally different from other workers.

Some firms have been unable to come to terms with the realities of the new American labor market. When every employee has to be replaced each year, on average, what we are seeing is the failure of an organization's leadership, HRM, and attitudes toward developing workers, which may also include union representation for them.

In contrast to those of companies with constant high turnover, Costco's approach—and savvy HRM—has resulted in high profits and a stable and loyal employee population—a model in its industry. Costco's approach to its sizable Hispanic workforce is a sound business practice, since low employee turnover, fierce loyalty to the firm, and what amounts to an army of bilingual ambassadors to the Spanish-speaking community continue to give Costco a distinct competitive advantage vis-à-vis others in its industry. The how and the why of Costco's success form the basis of what HR practitioners need to understand in order to adopt strategies, policies, and initiatives that foster the loyalty of Hispanic employees and nurture their development within the firm. It is this sense of conviviality, mutual respect, and shared purpose that serves as a role model for other industries.

The Parity Project launched by the National Association of Hispanic Journalists, briefly described in Chapter 1, seeks to create opportunities for Hispanic journalists, writers, editors, and news anchors throughout the nation's media outlets. "The Parity Project involves NAHJ's work with selected English-language news organizations that serve large [Hispanic] communities, but that do not have a representative percentage of [Hispanic] journalists in their newsrooms," the NAHJ states, clearly in tune with the successful strategies employed by other industry organizations working toward parallel ideals.[1]

This makes sense, particularly since research confirms that Hispanics, not unlike other minorities, need nurturing if they are to flourish in the corporate environment. Writing in the *Harvard Business Review*, Judith Ross explains this phenomenon:

> [David] Thomas and [John] Gabarro discovered that the successful African-American, Asian-American, and native-born Hispanic executives in their study participated in a separate tournament in which they moved at a significantly slower rate than their white counterparts as they ascended to middle management, moved more quickly from middle to upper management as they passed plateauing fast-starters, and finally marched in step with whites who were heading for the executive suite.

Thomas explains that the early career period of minority executives, despite its relative lag, contributes significantly to the fact that they eventually become outstanding performers.[2]

CREATING THE ENVIRONMENT

As with all other company initiatives, the success of training and development for Hispanic employees depends on the commitment of upper management. A general attitude of helping Hispanics succeed in the company and become loyal, contributing workers must be established at the top. (The importance of corporate role models is briefly discussed in Chapter 1.)

According to a survey by Korn/Ferry International, senior management's commitment to diversity is one of the organizational attributes that matters most to Hispanic professionals.[3] To ensure that managers are taking steps to exhibit commitment to retaining Hispanic employees, organizations should hold managers accountable for retaining as well as developing a diverse workforce.

It follows, then, that HR practitioners also have a strategic role to play in nurturing Hispanic employees. Considering that, as Joseph Baccarro reports in "The Hidden Cost of Employee Turnover," replacing an employee approximates two years' annual salary, it is important that HR practitioners work to ensure that Hispanic employees' professional development within the organization is successful.[4] In relation to this, Table 11 summarizes the "perspectives" HRM gives management in this role. As has been the case with women, African Americans, and Asian Americans, Hispanics operate under the pressure of having to prove themselves, working doubly hard to dispel misgivings about what they lack as much as delivering on what they bring to the organization's table.

TABLE 11
HRM's Role in Developing Hispanic Talent

HRM STRATEGIC ROLE	IMPLICATIONS FOR HISPANIC EMPLOYEE
Employee perspective	HRM can focus on identifying and nurturing exceptional Hispanic employees.
Compensation perspective	In addition to bonus and merit pay, HRM can develop benefits that are tailored to the needs of Hispanic employees.
Alignment perspective	HRM can leverage its skills in nurturing and developing Hispanic talent to validate its strategic partnership with management.
High-performance perspective	HRM becomes an instrument through which the larger organization's goals can be met with greater efficiency.

TRAINING AND DEVELOPMENT FROM DAY ONE

Keep in mind that employee training begins with orientation. The process of orientation and socialization, often referred to as *onboarding,* includes all the company actions that support new-hire assimilation. Onboarding goals include assurance that the fit is good by appropriate skills evaluation; acclimation to the job, people, and workplace; proper training and orientation; separation of mismatched employees; and increased retention of the right employees. All of these add up to increasing the likelihood that new employees' socialization will be successful.

The onboarding process actually begins before the new employee starts work. The following seven steps can serve as a checklist.

Step 1: Prearrival

Preparation is often not so much forgotten as simply not given adequate attention to ensure the first day's success.

- Inform the staff that a new employee will be joining the department.
- Provide some background information (name, work experience, start date).
- Make sure the work station is ready, neat, and clean.
- Prepare a tentative schedule of first-day and first-week activities, including daily and weekly check-ins for employee questions and feedback.
- Have work ready and waiting for the employee.

Step 2: Welcome to New Employee

Before plunging into training, it is good to take some time to get acquainted with the new employee. A good opportunity for this is with a company tour highlighting those areas that will be part of the new work experience. HR specialists might keep in mind that, culturally, this sort of personal attention is greatly valued by Hispanic employees.

Most important, introduce the new employee to as many other people as possible. Remember that a Hispanic worker is probably learning to function in an unfamiliar culture. Try to make the newcomer feel comfortable. Demonstrate to the employee that the organization values all employees as members of an overall team, and that the opportunity to become a part of that team is real. The first impression is the most important. All the effort you invested in finding the right person will be wasted if the employee is not treated properly from the start. A personal welcome from a manager and director conveys a "we care" attitude.

Step 3: Acclimation

This step, accomplished with a caring attitude, can make a big difference to new employees.

- Provide a tour of the department.
- Introduce the individual to co-workers.
- Explain the duties of each person so the new employee can understand how each fits into the organization.
- Go over the day's planned activities and provide the employee with a schedule.
- Review any forms that the employee might have to complete or understand.

Step 4: Assignment of Experienced Co-worker as Counselor or Guide

Relationship building is always an important issue on the job. The quality of human relationships among the members of a workforce is closely related to retention and productivity. Tension, anger, and distrust tend to decrease productivity and can seriously reduce a business's ability to compete. Openness, friendliness, and trust in the workforce contribute to cooperation, productivity, and long-term employment. Human relationships are especially important with workers of Hispanic origin, because those workers are in many cases cut off from their native cultures. Understand that Hispanic workers may be struggling to overcome language and cultural barriers. Starting a new job and learning the procedures associated with it are further burdens, in addition to the communication and cultural problems. All these difficulties can add up to an extremely demanding situation for the new Hispanic worker.

An assigned buddy (preferably from a similar culture) can answer basic how-to questions, familiarize the employee with the habits and daily procedures of the staff, show the new employee the location of facilities (restrooms, cafeteria, equipment and supplies), take the new employee to lunch, and provide insight into informal department rules and procedures.

Here are a few ways to select a counselor or guide. You need someone who is:

- On a peer level with the new employee
- Well versed in the organization and department practices
- Experienced and with a good understanding of policies and procedures
- A positive role model with excellent work behaviors
- Friendly and enthusiastic

Step 5: Orientation

The purpose of new-employee orientation is to welcome and educate all new and transferring employees and provide them with critical information about the organization. HRM has an obligation to communicate with new workers in a way that each can understand. In many instances, this means having information normally provided in English also available in Spanish. This information is designed to maximize employees' safety, success, and commitment to the organization. Goals of an orientation program include:

- Reducing first-day jitters by helping new employees feel secure and welcome
- Instilling positive attitudes toward work
- Communicating what the organization offers, and also what it expects in the way of performance
- Providing basic information employees need to perform effectively and efficiently

Supervisors are crucial to the orientation and integration process. The supervisor is the first person the new employee will be dealing with and the person who will be most influential in the newcomer's first impressions. After general orientation, the supervisor introduces the employee to job duties and performance expectations. This department orientation might include where to get help in Spanish for understanding:

- Organizational structure
- Department policies and operating procedures
- Department goals and priorities
- General expectations and standards
- Safety rules
- Overtime requirements
- Breaks and meal periods
- Job description and responsibilities
- Opportunities for training and learning

Step 6: Job-Related Training

Structured training is a methodical approach to ensure competency. It is also used to determine the skills needed to perform the tasks and define minimum performance levels. The methods of instruction include demonstration, personal coaching, written instruction (procedure manuals, guides, and the like), and shadowing of more experienced employees.

Written standard operating procedures (SOPs) are an important part of business today. They are essential for businesses that employ more than one or two workers. They are not, however, a replacement for effective training. It is wrong to assume that all workers, whether they speak English or Spanish, can comprehend what they read. In both English and Spanish, basic communication entails clear postings in simple language, using block letters. Hispanic workers in particular seem to value visual learning very highly. Demonstration in a training setting and practice are critical to good retention and accurate work. Managers should supplement written SOPs with visual aids. Whenever possible, use diagrams, pictures, or photographs that help explain correct procedures. Consult extension and industry advisers for help with these materials. A wealth of support material is available.[5]

Step 7: Feedback and Communication

Because of key aspects of Hispanic culture, such as the cultural reluctance to question the status quo and engage in conflict on the job, managers must engage the new Hispanic worker in meaningful feedback. Hispanic workers are often afraid to ask questions when they don't understand some part of their training. They generally have a very strong desire to be successful in their work and to please their manager. This may lead them to feel very insecure about asking questions. They also don't want the manager to think they aren't as knowledgeable as everyone else. Hispanic workers often have no idea what the English-speaking manager thinks of their job performance. This can make them feel insecure—and insecure workers tend to let problems go rather than reach out to the manager for help. In many cases, minor problems or misunderstandings can lead to the loss of good workers, all due to poor communication. Sometimes, even managers who understand the importance of feedback for workers hesitate to provide it because of language and cultural barriers.[6] These measures will help you hardwire the feedback process:

- Schedule a periodic checkpoint meeting with buddies and supervisors to track performance.

- Provide an initial thirty-day review designed to ensure that individuals can do their jobs.

- When employees are doing well, ask if they need anything from their supervisor, or from you, to help do their job. It is important to reinforce good performance.

- When employees are faltering, provide coaching and feedback on areas needing improvement and recommend ways to improve.

An important part of feedback is checking in with a new employee at the end of the first month. Here are some sample questions that may be useful for the thirty-day discussion:

- Have the employee's co-workers been friendly and helpful?

- Does the employee know where to find supplies?

- Has the employee been properly introduced to other staff?

- Is the employee satisfied with the current schedule?
- Is the job what the employee expected?

Another important consideration of new employee orientation is safety. It may be helpful for HR to see what the Occupational Safety and Health Administration (OSHA) has to report specifically regarding Hispanic employees. While workplace fatalities for Anglos and African Americans have steadily declined in recent years, the opposite is true for Hispanics. Deaths among that demographic rose from 815 in 2000 to 891 in 2001, the most recent years for which the Bureau of Labor Statistics (BLS) has figures. Alarmed by that trend, OSHA recently began to investigate workplace fatalities more closely to see how often language was a factor. The resultant data shows that, for example, 61 percent of workplace deaths in Dallas in 2001 involved workers with a limited understanding of English. In response to the rise of fatalities among Hispanic workers, OSHA established the Hispanic Outreach Taskforce in late 2001 to address the issue and provide greater access to safety information for Spanish-speaking workers.

OSHA has also begun to translate all of its safety literature into Spanish, including "All About OSHA" and "OSHA to Serve You." It has even created a Spanish version of its Web site, but John Miles, a regional administrator of OSHA, admits that although these are important gestures on the part OSHA, they may not be as effective as intended. Literacy rates are notoriously low in Mexico, for example, meaning that safety manuals written in Spanish may not help the people who need them most. In addition, very few of the workers for whom the information on the Web site is intended have access to computers or the Internet. "You can't always just take an OSHA document and translate it from English to Spanish," Miles explains. "Some of these workers that come up from Mexico really don't understand Spanish very well, either. Many are only reading at a second-grade level."[7]

CONTINUING DEVELOPMENT OF HISPANIC EMPLOYEES

Hispanics tend to view training not as a bargaining chip but as a normal part of doing business. Hispanic cultures are inclined to view the employer-employee relationship as one in which both parties benefit, and people expect to build long-term bonds based on trust, respect, *simpatía,* and *confianza.* Table 12 identifies key areas where Hispanics express interest in having their employer facilitate training. For HR professionals, Hispanic employees represent a whole new world of neglected needs.

WHAT HISPANIC EMPLOYEES WANT

What do Hispanic employees respond to? In surveys and studies, most notably an exhaustive analysis conducted by Hispanic Economics, the three principal issues Hispanics identified as lacking in their employer were opportunities for continuing education, facilitation of English-language instruction, and programs on cross-cultural training.[8] These concerns reflect a marginalization of the Hispanic employee in the corporate workplace, as well as a conflict of expectations.

Training is a powerful tool for signaling management's commitment to the employee. "Training can be used to send messages to third parties (particularly other employees) about the organization's culture and strategy," Baron and Kreps note in *Strategic Human Resources.* "Although this point is obvious, we feel confident in asserting that it is overlooked with remarkable frequency,

TABLE 12

Training Strategies for Retaining Hispanic Employees

TRAINING STRATEGY	BENEFITS FOR EMPLOYER AND EMPLOYEE
Language skills	Providing language classes is more than offering English as a second language (ESL). Although for the vast majority of nonsalaried Hispanics, fluency in English remains a goal, additional aspects make a difference when it comes to retaining Hispanic employees: 1. For salaried Hispanic employees, managers, and executives, accent elimination classes can be seen as an enticing benefit that signals the organization's commitment to the Hispanic employee. 2. Spanish-language classes should be made available for English-speaking employees. Although many organizations involved in life safety—such as police departments, hospitals, and airlines—routinely offer Spanish classes for their employees, many other organizations do not. Such classes help English-speaking employees feel more comfortable with Spanish spoken in the workplace and also signal to Hispanics that their presence is a long-term one in which management has a vested interest.
Acculturation and assimilation	The life experience of many Hispanics is on the margin of the mainstream, or outside it. Acculturation into the norms of American life is highly coveted. At the same time, non-Hispanic employees may want a basic orientation to the dominant Hispanic group in their midst, and not only for Hispanic Heritage Month. Informal potlucks featuring traditional foods prove helpful in breaking barriers and fostering a convivial experience in the workplace. That Americans already eat more salsa than they do ketchup is an indicator of how what was once considered foreign has become a staple. Acculturation works both ways, and HRM must understand that while it is crucial for Hispanic success, it is also necessary for non-Hispanic employees who now find themselves in a changed workplace.

TABLE 12 cont'd	
TRAINING STRATEGY	**BENEFITS FOR EMPLOYER AND EMPLOYEE**
Geographic opportunities	Corporate management continues to confront the challenge that Hispanic managers are reluctant to relocate, compared to their non-Hispanic counterparts. Through the creation of internal opportunities, it can be possible to create incentives for Hispanic managers to move to distant geographic areas. This is a long-term proposition, one in which a series of extended assignments allow for Hispanics to become acclimated and comfortable in different parts of the country.

inasmuch as few organizations devote much effort to articulating for employees how the particular training programs that are sponsored reinforce specific aspects of corporate strategy and culture. In many organizations, it is not difficult to find dimensions of strategies or culture that are described by top leaders as absolutely pivotal (e.g., teamwork, ethics, diversity, learning) but that receive little or no emphasis in company education and training programs."[9]

For HR practitioners who are designing training programs for Hispanics, it is important to remember that Hispanics come from nations that have endeavored (though mostly failed) to establish social welfare states roughly along the lines of European nations, and Hispanics are likely to expect a higher level of paternalism from their employers than non-Hispanic employees do. The social commitment of the firm to the worker is often found lacking, and the three areas previously identified reflect a cultural misreading of roles and expectations in the workplace.

Continuing Education

In Hispanic culture, *superarse* literally means "to better oneself." Beyond Hispanics' deep-seated fear that their educational attainment level is lacking, they share a cultural recognition that no matter how well prepared one believes oneself to be, any field has more to know than any one person can possibly hope to master. This attitude stands in sharp contrast to the common U.S. view of the world, where American gung-ho and can-do enthusiasm generate both optimism and bravado. For Hispanics, whose societies have been humbled by limitations, hopes of career advancement take the form of a desire to *superar* (that is, to surpass) oneself. This means they look to their employer to facilitate continuing education programs, whether through assisting with tuition, accommodating requests for time off, or authorizing sabbaticals.

English-Language Instruction

The question of language is seen differently by Hispanics, generally depending on their role in the organization. For hourly employees, becoming fluent in English is of great importance. Millions of adult Hispanics spend countless hours attending continuing education classes to learn or improve their English language skills. They welcome and often expect recognition from their employers, through tuition subsidies or hours off from work to pursue these studies. HRM can enhance the commitment of its hourly Hispanic workers through a program that facilitates their efforts to become fluent in English.

For Hispanic salaried employees, the emphasis is not as much on learning English as it is on classes to eliminate their accents. This is not a new phenomenon—or a specifically Hispanic issue, for that matter. "There have been accent schools for a very long time, going all the way back to the 19th century, when accents first became a social issue," Tim Machan, an English professor at the University of Wisconsin-Madison, explains. "British public schools like Eton worked hard to erase regional dialects and to create in their students a standard variety which came to be known as 'Received Pronunciation.' That's what the British call their most prestigious form of English. You also call it the King's English or the Queen's English."[10] Hispanic professionals fear that accents affect how they are perceived within an organization and often impede their career progress. They would welcome HRM's recognition of the validity of this issue and employer development of, or support for, speech and accent-reduction classes. We discuss the question of language in further detail in this chapter under "Language in the Workplace."

Acculturation Versus Assimilation

A more immediate concern, and one that is more difficult to address, is the Hispanic employee's longing to be more informed about mainstream American life. Often described as the desire to become acculturated into American norms, this is a sensitive issue—if for no other reason than that many non-Hispanics mistakenly believe that Hispanic employees wish to assimilate American norms. Most do not.

Becoming familiar with American norms does not necessarily equate with a desire to adopt them. Most Hispanics report feelings of confusion over American norms: Why do Americans embrace Thanksgiving with such enthusiasm when they have worked so hard to destroy indigenous cultures? Why do Americans grant so much independence to their adolescent children when they have done such a poor job of teaching them respect and responsibility? Why do so many Americans place their older parents in nursing homes? (A move that looks to Hispanics like abandoning parents to horrific institutions where they are likely to be professionally neglected.) Hispanic misgivings about mainstream society inform the cynicism with which they see this society, including the corporate sector.

Cross-Cultural Training

Employer support for cross-cultural workshops or seminars constitutes an area where Hispanic employees consistently express an interest—not because they wish to assimilate into the American mainstream or adopt American norms, but because they feel a need to be knowledgeable about the greater society in which they live and work.

This makes workshops and seminars with titles like "Culture and Language Immersion" the fundamental tools for integrating Hispanics into the workplace. Fazioli's, an Italian food restaurant chain with nearly four hundred branches across the United States, has such a program in place. Ninety percent of its employees are Hispanics who speak little or no English. The company sponsors a Spanish Language Immersion program for its managerial-level staff. During the eight-day program, managers undergo an intensive study of Hispanic culture and customs. In addition, after the second day, participants must communicate in Spanish for the remainder of the course. The company hopes that the training enables managers to recruit and retain Hispanic workers more effectively. The program costs $1,500 per person and has led to sizable returns. Following the completion of four sessions, Fazioli's experienced an improvement of 24 percent in the retention of Hispanic employees.[11]

Hilton Hotels World Headquarters in Beverly Hills is ranked thirteenth in *Fortune* magazine's list of America's 50 Best Companies for Diversity in 2004. Benefit manager Anita Sarad says,

We translate much of our important communications to Spanish because Spanish-speakers comprise the largest language group outside of English. We realize that it benefits not only our employees with limited English, but also our native Spanish-speakers who have learned to speak English, as they can understand such information as their medical benefits so much better in their own language. They appreciate that we make the effort.

We had an instance where we had a document translated and the target employees didn't understand the translation. We learned that there is a difference in a document that is translated word-for-word and one that actually makes sense so it is understood. We then found translators able to analyze a document and thoroughly understand it so the intent would come across to our employees. When we hired new translators I really depended on references from experienced H.R. colleagues.[12]

Regulations vary from state to state. In California, for instance, companies with fifty or more employees and where 10 percent or more of the employees speak a language other than English as their primary language need to pay attention. These companies are legally required to translate certain policies and notices into the language or languages spoken by these groups of employees. Generally, businesses employing workers who have limited English reading skills should at a minimum translate the following: the equal employment opportunity policy, the policy against harassment, the at-will employment policy, pregnancy disability leave and family care leave policies, voting rights policies, rest and meal break policies, conflict resolution policies, disciplinary policies, and safety rules.

HRM policies that recognize the desire for continued education are sound business practice. "At one leading technology firm, over one-third of the salaried workforce participates in the tuition-reimbursement program, and nearly 10 percent of the employees have earned a degree through the program," Harriet Hankin writes in *The New Workforce*. "Those who received a degree have had higher performance ratings, earned greater merit pay increases, and advanced more rapidly than other employees."[13]

Where Hispanics are concerned, their anxiety and self-doubt about education levels lead them to place a premium on education as a benefit. "The success of Hispanics—and the importance of education as an ingredient for that success—has been documented for years, even if the mainstream culture tended to ignore it," Jesús Chavarría, editor and publisher, argues.[14] Aside from the obvious benefits of increased learning, Hispanic employees appreciate the extra effort that the company expends to further their development, generating increased goodwill and loyalty.

LANGUAGE IN THE WORKPLACE

The question of allowing another language, whether Spanish or any other, to be spoken in the workplace presents a daunting dilemma to HR professionals, managers, and employees alike. Research confirms that where language is concerned, HRM has three aspects to consider. Foremost is encouraging nonnative speakers to sign up for instruction in the English language by giving them time off to do so, along with providing such coursework in on-premises classes or subsidizing it through tuition reimbursement. Many organizations also recognize the importance of affording English-speaking employees introductory Spanish, in an effort to help them communicate more effectively with their co-workers *and* customers. With the switching back and forth between English and Spanish, it is not surprising that a third area is now emerging: the need for Spanish-language instruction to Spanish-speaking employees who lapse into "Spanglish."

English-Only Perspectives

Before examining each of these issues, let us first consider generally how the law is affecting the way HR practitioners approach the question of language. On September 1, 2000, the Equal Employment Opportunity Commission announced a $192,500 settlement in an "English-only" case involving eight Hispanic workers who were either disciplined or fired by a suburban Chicago manufacturer for speaking Spanish in the workplace.[15]

The settlement ended litigation filed by the EEOC eighteen months earlier against Watlow Batavia Inc. of Batavia, Illinois. The company manufactures various mechanical systems found in household appliances. The suit attracted local attention as the "'Buenos Dias' case" because one of the individuals was terminated after she greeted a co-worker by saying "good morning" in Spanish.

EEOC chair Ida Castro said the settlement demonstrates the commission's commitment to defending the civil rights of workers in disputes involving language and accent, which often camouflage illegal discrimination on the basis of national origin. She said that most employers still do not understand that most English-only work rules violate Title VII of the Civil Rights Act. EEOC guidelines contend that English-only rules established without a legitimate business justification are illegal. Between 1996 and 1999 the number of EEOC charges including English-only or accent allegations rose from 77 to 253.

According to case specifics, Watlow announced a blanket English-only rule on August 1, 1998. The policy affected only the assembly division. The policy barred communications in languages other than English during work hours, including breaks and lunch periods. At least three employees who voiced objection to the policy were fired under its provisions within four days of implementation. Of the five other employees disciplined under the policy, four were eventually laid off. Under the settlement, the workers were to receive various awards to compensate them for lost wages and other damages.[16]

English-only workplace rules have garnered considerable media attention. Many companies implement English-only policies because they may benefit employers in several ways:

- Reducing ethnic tension
- Improving employees' English proficiency
- Promoting safety and efficiency

Senior management and HR professionals, however, should proceed with caution when implementing English-only policies. The courts and the EEOC agree that employees may challenge English-only policies under two different legal theories: disparate treatment and disparate impact. Under the theory of disparate treatment, workers may allege that an employer intentionally discriminated on the basis of national origin by adopting such a policy. Under the disparate impact theory, employees can allege that employment practices that may appear to be neutral have the effect of discriminating against a protected minority group.

Under EEOC guidelines that presume English-only policies have a disparate impact on employees who do not use English as their primary language, the burden of proof is shifted to employers. If the rule applies at all times, such as during breaks and lunchtime, it is presumed to violate Title VII and will be scrutinized. If the rule applies only at certain times, the employer must prove a business necessity.

One of the most common reasons for employers to adopt English-only rules is to enhance workplace safety. Indeed, an employee's ability to communicate effectively with other employees in the workplace can be vital in industries such as construction or health care, where communication problems can lead to loss of property or even human life. Perhaps one of the most controversial justifications for adopting an English-only policy is to reduce ethnic tensions.

Many unions use workplace language rights to organize or to gain community or worker support. In one case, after a North Carolina State University housekeeper was reprimanded for speaking in Spanish to a co-worker, she filed a grievance with the help of UE local 150. Workers, students, and community supporters spoke at a press conference to bring attention to the discrimination at NCSU. Two newspapers and three television stations gave extensive coverage to the press conference, and there were significant "letters to the editor" on both sides of the issue. The press conference exposed the university's language discrimination to the community, creating pressure on the university for an appropriate response. The UE local has supported the employee in her case because, as a union, it stands against discrimination based on race, language, gender, and similar issues.

This is a workplace challenge that is here to stay. Some companies have taken actions like the following to alleviate the problems posed by language diversity in the workplace:

- Hire supervisors who speak the language of the non-English-speaking workers.

- Offer English classes either at the work site or through schools or community colleges.

- Offer incentives for workers to learn English.

- Ask employees who are considered to be part of the problem to become part of the solution.

- Allow workers as a group to decide what their language standards will be except on occasions when a common language is necessary.

Lee Gardenswartz and Anita Rowe, authors of *Managing Diversity: A Complete Desk Reference and Planning Guide,* offer the following steps to prevent language differences from hindering interactions:

- Understand the reasons why people speak another language on the job. Perhaps it allows for a more accurate exchange of information, or it relieves stress to speak in a native tongue.

- Recognize and question your assumptions. Could employees be talking about their family or the weather rather than about you?

- Create options and alternatives. Let people know how you feel. ("When you speak another language I feel left out.") Ask for a translation.

Against this background, how should language instruction be handled? There are several approaches to this subject. In fact, employer-sponsored language training programs vary widely in design and purpose, depending on the firm and the industry. Some organizations focus on conversational skills, while others focus on basic literacy or work-related vocabulary. The majority of language training courses focus on teaching English, but some companies are also making efforts to teach Spanish and other languages for business purposes.[17]

To address the language barrier, employers have implemented a wide variety of language training programs:

- Pace Foods provides English-language instruction for Hispanic employees on their own time, usually during lunch breaks or after shifts.

- Motorola offers English-language courses to company employees on company time.

- Westin Hotels and Resorts provides English courses to employees at multiple sites through coordination with local schools and agencies.

Before an organization begins offering foreign language training, it should establish some guidelines for consideration:

- Establish a task force to review workers' needs and identify proper methods for instruction.
- Adopt a common set of training methods and techniques.
- Consider self-instruction programs (such as audio- or videotapes or computer-based training).
- Offer incentives to attend language training.

Several restaurant chains with large non-English-speaking employee populations offer before- or after-hours English classes, or both. Chipotle, a Mexican food chain restaurant owned by McDonald's, started its ESL classes in 1996 and now offers basic to intermediate courses in both Spanish and English. The curriculum is based on textbooks and audiotapes developed in-house, lessons are free, and employees are paid for their in-class time.[18]

Individuals learn at different rates, or for various reasons, one consequence of which is that it is impossible to have all workers gain mastery of the English language in a uniform manner. For many line managers, particularly in trade, retail, and service industries that count on large numbers of Hispanic workers, effective communication is an everyday challenge. A common remedy is to rely on one employee who is fully bilingual to be the unofficial translator. This is a stop-gap measure, not sustainable over time. "Bilingual employees tend to get overworked because they are constantly translating," Jennifer Thomas, a Spanish-language consultant, argues. "It's better to have a few people that take the class and learn the skills rather than just one."[19]

Training in a Language Other Than English

With the emergence of a bilingual consumer economy in the United States, basic Spanish-language skills are of increasing importance. For governments, from municipalities to federal agencies, it can be a question of life safety and national security. Here are some of the kinds of professions and workplaces where basic Spanish is required in order to serve the public and customers:[20]

- Emergency 911
- Firefighters
- Bank tellers
- Financial institutions
- Child care facilities
- Airline staff
- Construction sites
- Correctional staff
- Hotel and motel staff
- Librarians
- Receptionists
- Law enforcement officers
- Paramedics and EMTs
- Probation officers

- Dental staff
- Respiratory therapists
- Restaurant staff
- Supermarket staff
- Secretaries
- Physician's office staff
- Postal employees
- Supervisors of Spanish-speaking employees
- Customer service staff
- Anyone doing business in Latin America
- Anyone requesting personal information and data

Spanish is also helpful in other industries. Consider the situation in the gaming industry. Hispanics make up a large part of the customer base, as well as significant numbers of employees, especially in California and Nevada. For casinos, the business case for offering training in Spanish is clear. Cache Creek provided guest-service training for more than nine hundred of its employees, in English and separately in Spanish, with the objective of enhancing competitive position.

Effective foreign-language training such as the program Cache Creek provided requires more than just translating the workbook or the lectures. It must be created from the ground up, taking cultural differences into account. Here are strategic guidelines to make your bilingual workplace training more effective:

- **Understand cultural differences that affect learning styles**—Most Spanish and Latin American classrooms are very traditional places where learners are not accustomed to participation, and it's difficult to start them on cooperative learning immediately.

- **Establish rapport**—Get to know trainees beforehand if at all possible, and call them by name. Personal connections are important in many cultures.

- **Provide hands-on practice, and test for comprehension**—Since many Hispanics are afraid to make waves and don't want to be noticed, they tend to be extremely reluctant to ask questions.

- **Think, pair, share**—Pair up each trainee with a neighbor. Pose a question, and ask everyone to think about the answer and jot a few notes. Then, ask learners to turn to their partners and discuss their answers, with the understanding that one member of each pair will share with the class—not the answer, but the nature of their discussion.

- **Put numbered heads together**—Group trainees into teams of four and assign each team member a number, one through four. Call out a question, and have the teams discuss the answer. Then call for the responses by number; the respondent whose number is called must speak for the whole team. This ensures that everyone on the team knows the answer and builds in individual accountability.

- **Provide variety in materials as well**—Adding visual aids and demonstrations to the training will enhance learning because many unskilled workers have little formal education and are unaccustomed to absorbing information from written sources or lectures.

- **Have company executives attend or participate**—Management needs to be involved even if they don't speak the language. Participants need to see the person at the top spending time with them. This is crucial to the success of multi-language programs.

- **Be careful with feedback**—In the United States, we like to think that criticism of work should be taken objectively as a way to improve performance. Hispanics often don't separate work and personal attitudes and may take criticism personally, especially if the correction takes place in front of others.[21]

Teaching Spanish or other languages to English-speaking employees is designed to make them more effective in dealing with their co-workers and with the public. Organizations where HRM encourages and provides Spanish-language instruction to native English speakers enjoy a competitive advantage, as measured in the profitability edge they maintain over other firms in their industries that do not have similar policies.[22] The factors cited for this range from increased goodwill from Hispanic customers who acknowledge (and reward) the effort made when a native English speaker knows some Spanish to the reduced employee turnover at firms where language is seen as way of uniting, rather than dividing, employees and creating a convivial work environment.

Bilingualism in the Workplace

This brings up the more peculiar situation with which to contend—Spanglish, as briefly mentioned earlier. "As socially acceptable as Spanglish is in Miami, it can cause problems for U.S. companies operating in Latin America and Spain, appearing sloppy or even snooty to Spanish-speaking customers. 'When you send an e-mail with 20,000 [grammatical] mistakes in it, the thought is, I'm dealing with an illiterate guy,' says Dario Gamboa, senior vice-president in charge of human resources at Visa International for Latin America and the Caribbean."[23]

It is not safe to assume that Spanish-speaking employees are fluent in proper Spanish. On one hand, corporate America's capacity to smooth linguistic transitions is time-tested. "In the thirty years between 1870 and 1900, nearly 12 million persons immigrated to the United States, more than had come to our shores in the previous two and a half centuries," Robert Putnam reports in *Bowling Alone: The Collapse and Revival of American Community*.

> In the following fourteen years nearly another 13 million would arrive. In 1870 one-third of all industrial workers in America were foreign born. By 1900 more than half were. In 1890 immigrant adults actually outnumbered native adults in eighteen of the twenty cities with a population over 100,000.... By 1890 the cacophony of strange tongues and strange customs of newcomers had triggered a national debate about "Americanization" and ethnic identity, similar in many respects to the debate about "multiculturalism" and "English only" today.[24]

HR practitioners must be mindful that Spanglish comes with business pros and social cons. On the pro side, "Spanglish can reflect impressive bilingual verbal skills as speakers choose from two languages. Switching back and forth between Spanish and English, or 'code switching' as linguists call it, people will often use Spanish to express emotions and English for analytical thoughts," Jennifer Bingham Hull argues.[25] On the con side, it can undermine harmony among colleagues in the workplace and, as a consequence, alienate other Hispanics who are offended by the cliquish nature of how Spanglish is used.[26] And those conversant in Spanglish face an overriding concern: remaining literate in both English and Spanish, which is the reason several Fortune 100 firms are adopting clear guidelines on the need to use proper Spanish in all business correspondence.

For the Hispanic employee, there can be ambivalence. "For me, Spanish and everything that went with it belonged at home and with family friends and relatives; and the language came to life most powerfully on our trips back to Puerto Rico and Ecuador," Roberto Suro writes in *Strangers Among Us: Latinos' Lives in a Changing America*.

> English belonged in all other places. . . . For me, Spanish could belong to one world and English to another, and the door between them was open. We were light skinned and middle class, and I could switch from one language to another, from one world to another. By becoming culturally ambidextrous, I fulfilled my parents' aspirations. When I passed through the door into America from my Spanish-speaking home, I did it quietly and no one much noticed.[27]

Among non-Hispanic managers and customers, there is a growing sense of tolerance and acceptance about the Spanish that surrounds them. "I feel, in order to really communicate, to explain products and new approaches, I need to know Spanish," Jack Lass, who owned a paint store in Wheaton, Maryland, explained over a decade ago. "My attitude is, these folks are going to be here, we should respect them. I absolutely agree they should learn English. But in the meantime, I'm in business, and it doesn't hurt you to know another language. I think we should all learn something, just to expand our tiny constricted little minds—Spanish, Japanese, something."[28]

The question of who needs to learn English, or Spanish, and of the limits (if any) on Spanglish is a matter of consequence as HR professionals analyze the impact on their employees, their customers, and the socioeconomic norms that are evolving as this century unfolds.

DIVERSITY TRAINING

For many companies, training for Hispanics will fall under the category of diversity training. Although diversity training is much broader than training that focuses purely on the Hispanic population, it is beneficial to examine those areas of diversity that have a crossover to Hispanic employees.

See Chapter 5 for a broader discussion of diversity as a factor in employee relations, with additional coverage of diversity programs.

Myths and Realities of Diversity

It may be advisable to confront the myths and realities of diversity in planning or presenting training programs. The idea of diversity as an objective to be fulfilled by HRM continues to evoke strong passions, particularly when it is associated with affirmative action programs. The subtext remains that diversity is an attempt to give opportunities to individuals who are not qualified for those positions, primarily at the expense of white men. Here are the leading misconceptions and myths about diversity:

Misconceptions About Diversity Programs

- Affirmative action results in the hiring of unqualified or less qualified people.
- Minorities and women take jobs away from more qualified white men.
- Women and some minorities have too many family responsibilities to make commitments to the firm.
- Minorities do not have an aptitude for math, accounting, or computers.

Myths About Diversity

- **Diversity is a problem.** No. It is an opportunity. The purpose is to allow individuals to contribute to organizations in ways previously unavailable to them. It is about enriching an organization's workforce to reflect the greater demographics that characterize the nation, and through this process, it promotes better customer service and establishes competitive advantage.

- **Diversity is the responsibility of HRM.** No. It is everyone's responsibility. HRM alone cannot create a welcoming and inclusive environment. Diversity is everyone's responsibility simply because this is a way of helping each person grow through learning about and from other people whose life experiences and heritages are different.

- **Diversity is about race and gender.** No. It once was, but now it has expanded to include cultural, social, and ethnic heritages that enrich the nation and constitute the consumer and client base for every organization's goods and services. Diversity encompasses both internal (colleagues and co-workers) and external (customers and prospective clients) aspects. It affords greater insights into the community and into facets that make multicultural issues important components of future growth. Without diversity, customer bases diminish simply because the organization is out of touch with clients' wants and needs.

- **Diversity is exclusive.** No. It is inclusive. It gives an opportunity for everyone to learn about others. The notion that diversity training is sensitivity training for white men is mistaken, simply because every individual stands to benefit by learning about others. The ultimate goal of diversity is to empower a culture where each individual can thrive and contribute to the organization.

Diversity is about empowering the workplace by taking advantage of talent, regardless of the person who brings that talent.

It is also about creating opportunities that enrich and benefit all employees, strengthening the firm and making it more responsive to the marketplace. "My customers are the 330,000 IBM employees," says Maria Villar, an IBM vice president who is the liaison for Hispanic employees at that organization. "If [IBM chairman] Sam Palmisano logs on to his computer and sees something wrong, he calls me."[29] As the executive sponsor of La Red Familiar, a Hispanic network for IBM's female executives, Villar promotes ethnic and racial diversity at Big Blue. (As noted earlier, *red* means "network" in Spanish. The group's title translates as "The Family Network.") "I want other Hispanics in the company to see what's possible," Villar argues, in keeping with the spirit of the mentoring program Lou Gerstner launched in the 1990s.

When it comes to making diversity work for Hispanic employees who are entering the organization, what HR practitioners must bear in mind is that promoting and maintaining diversity, like other aspects of becoming a strategic partner, involve a process of self-analysis to determine what actions are required to make management's mandate a reality. IBM's Maria Villar is an example of a proactive executive who has spearheaded an innovative effort to expand her organization's opportunities for all employees. What detractors misunderstand about diversity is that it isn't a question of dividing a pie in smaller slices; rather, it's about creating a program that results in a larger pie for everyone to share.

Of equal concern are the differences between the public goals of diversity and the private objectives sought. Table 13 outlines in broad terms how these goals diverge, and why the private sector, through the careful implementation of organizationwide diversity initiatives, has more to gain than simple compliance with the letter of the law.

Organizations throughout the United States face societal pressure to become more diverse and to work to resolve the

TABLE 13
Public Versus Private Objectives in Diversity Training

PUBLIC OBJECTIVES	PRIVATE OBJECTIVES
Government initiated	Voluntary (company driven)
Legally driven	Productivity driven
Problem focused	Opportunity focused
Quantitative	Qualitative
Assumes assimilation	Assumes integration
Internally focused	Internally and externally focused
Reactive	Proactive

Source: Adapted from Marilyn Loden and Judy B. Rosener, *Workforce America! Managing Employee Diversity as a Vital Resource* (Homewood, IL: Irwin Professional, 1991).

broad terms how these goals diverge, and why the private sector, through the careful implementation of organizationwide diversity initiatives, has more to gain than simple compliance with the letter of the law.

Organizations throughout the United States face societal pressure to become more diverse and to work to resolve the inequities that continue to characterize the American workforce. HRM has a responsibility to ensure that the organization's diversity program is consistent with efforts to meet societal expectations of how responsible corporate citizens meet their obligations.

Diversity Training as a Retention Tool

In light of the preceding discussion, HRM should understand the following key aspects of Hispanic culture before determining strategic direction regarding recruitment and retention. All are group support for Hispanics who have recently immigrated to the United States.

- **Team oriented**—Hispanics generally tend to work cooperatively and interdependently within authority structures.

- **Preference for direct treatment**—Despite a collectivistic culture and team-oriented working style, Hispanics usually prefer direct, individualized personal treatment when they are communicating.

- **Passivity as a form of respect**—From an early age, Hispanic children are expected to treat authority figures with strong deference, a trait often viewed as passivity.

- **Hesitancy to question the status quo**—Many Hispanics in the United States, particularly Hispanics who have immigrated, tend to be hesitant to question the status quo or complain for fear of recrimination.

- **Conflict aversion**—Most Hispanics tend to avoid conflict, particularly in contexts where they are the minority group, and correspondingly find accepting criticism and confrontation difficult.

Any attempt at creating a training strategy for retention of Hispanic workers has to be founded on an understanding of the key challenges they face in the workforce:

- **Cultural differences**—Employers should be aware of how cultural differences manifest themselves in the workplace—for example, how Hispanic and non-Hispanic workers communicate and interact.

- **Fear of discrimination**—Hispanic immigrants in particular fear discrimination, and this leads to lowered expectations and a perception of limited career advancement.

- **Inadequate affinity groups**—Diversity networks generally lead to engagement and retention of underrepresented groups. However, Hispanics have been slow to create such networks.

- **Poor English language skills**—Many employers interpret this as an indication of lower intelligence or lack of education.

Once an organization has defined diversity and determined what dimensions will have the greatest benefit for its employees, it must decide what strategy to pursue. The way organizations define diversity is usually reflected in mission and vision statements, of course, and each organization will develop its program according to its own criteria, but the following discussion raises points that are uniform across organizations and constitute a firm foundation.[31] Effective diversity statements should include the what and the why of diversity.

Common Guidelines for Developing a Hispanic-Sensitive Training Program

While the meaning and parameters of workplace diversity are still being defined, managing diversity depends greatly on training. The American Society for Training and Development (ASTD) has identified two basic models for this training. As a starting point, ASTD defines "managing diversity" as treating the diverse workplace as a resource to be managed to tap the potential of all employees.

Both "awareness-based" and "skill-based" training have the same long-range goals: to improve multicultural interaction, morale, creativity, productivity, and competitive position. Here's a brief look at each training type, followed by a discussion of the pitfalls to avoid and points to cover:

Awareness-Based Training

Designed to increase employee knowledge, awareness, and sensitivity, awareness-based training is the starting point for developing diversity. Its immediate objectives are to provide information, uncover hidden assumptions and biases, assess attitudes and values, correct myths and stereotypes, and foster individual and group sharing.

Skill-Based Training

Skill-based training is designed to provide the tools to promote effective interaction in a heterogeneous work setting. Immediate objectives are to increase knowledge, awareness, sensitivity, and appropriate attitudes; to build or reinforce interaction skills; and to inventory methods for skills building.

Ways to Avoid Common Pitfalls

- Avoid off-the-shelf programs. Every corporate culture is different. As a result, training must be tailored to each individual company's situation.

- Resist the urge to do mass training, and don't start prematurely in response to pressure for action. Most experts agree that diversity training isn't a one-shot fix-it for organizations. Instead, companies need to commit to diversity over the long term.

- Have a clear strategy in mind if you are committed to diversity training. It is essential to zero in on exactly what the company is trying to accomplish. This is proverbially easier said than done.

- Obtain support and commitment from top management.

- Avoid programs that bash or confront employees aggressively. Allowing an uncontrolled airing of differences can be dangerous. Programs that attack any gender or ethnic or racial group should be avoided, even if the attack is meant to teach people how others feel.

- Aim at behavior modification rather than changing anyone's personal opinions and moral beliefs. People are different, and making them the same is an impossible task. Focus instead on finding ways for people to work cooperatively despite their differing perspectives.

Topics to Include

In designing a Hispanic-sensitive training program, HR will want to consider common topics often covered in diversity seminars and workshops:

- The business case for diversity
- Components of the organization's diversity program
- The goals of the diversity program
- Skills training to support diversity goals and multicultural teamwork
- Stereotypes and conceptions of diverse groups
- The individual's role in diversity efforts

Getting Started

Training for the general employee population may occur in a variety of forums, including video presentations, instructor-led classroom training, storytelling sessions, lecture series or brown-bag lunches, or interactive CD-ROM courses. In addition, group discussions, role-plays among employees, and diversity board games are all excellent follow-up strategies or main training methods.

An organization may take a number of steps before embarking on a strategy for retention based on diversity training. Among them are creating external resources and measuring the effectiveness of various initiatives. For example, in 2001 Eastman Kodak Company created a diversity panel of external leaders to advise the organization on methods to integrate diversity and inclusion into all aspects of global strategy. The seven-member panel includes individuals from the private, public, and academic sectors and reports to Kodak's chairman and CEO. The panel meets two or three times a year and shares its recommendations with the public policy committee of Kodak's board of directors. Here are a few recommendations the panel has made:

- Establish a goal to maintain a workforce whose ethnic, racial, and gender makeup mirrors that of the available U.S. workforce.

- Establish an internal diversity advisory panel made up of senior leaders around the globe.

- Implement mechanisms to ensure all locations adhere to Kodak values.[32]

As another example, after benchmarking its practices against those of leading companies for diversity, in 2000 BellSouth implemented several new benefits to attract and retain diverse employees. To make sure such new programs are tied to improved business results, BellSouth instituted a diversity-balanced scorecard in March 2001. The scorecard measures success in the major areas of diversity: diversity in terms of actual numbers, the amount of success of diversity training, and the effectiveness of programs and policies intended to create and foster diversity.

Diversity initiatives can produce other positive effects for organizations and their communities. By expanding their community outreach, for instance, organizations can become recognized as desirable employers and can increase their recruitment base. They can do this through teaching ESL, establishing day care centers, holding open houses for spouses, sponsoring clothing drives, and more. Such actions can improve diversity and thus recruitment and retention and overall company goodwill.

IN REVIEW

- The orientation of the Hispanic employee from day one is critical since it will determine the employee's success within the organization.
  - HR practitioners have a strategic role in preparing line managers to incorporate Hispanic employees into their departments.
  - HR professionals can make themselves available as counselors or guides during the initial thirty- to ninety-day phase of an orientation program in order to achieve a successful introduction.

- Hispanic employees value continuing education as part of their development as employees of the organization and in their careers.
  - HRM policies should recognize that availability of training signals the company's commitment to employees.
  - HR practitioners need to recognize the three areas where Hispanics indicate the desire to develop: language skills, acculturation into mainstream American life, and willingness to consider geographic relocation.
  - Hispanics expect HRM to facilitate continuing education, English-language and accent elimination courses, and seminars on cross-cultural issues, all of which are necessary—if not for Hispanic integration into the mainstream, then at least for Hispanics to feel confident about their ability to navigate the greater American society around them.

- A consequence of the emergence of the United States as a bilingual consumer economy is that Spanish is an inevitable part of corporate life.
  - HRM policies must encourage Spanish-speaking employees to become fluent in English and should make accent reduction or elimination courses available.
  - HRM policies must recognize that many English-speaking employees should have a fundamental understanding of Spanish, not only to work with their Hispanic colleagues but to relate to increasingly bilingual external constituencies.
  - HR practitioners must be aware of, and perhaps wary of, the implications of English-only rules in the workplace and encourage Hispanic employees to avail themselves of company-provided language instruction.
  - HRM policies should discourage Spanglish since it is a form of slang that undermines efforts to communicate with external constituencies that demand to be addressed in standard written Spanish.

- Myths about diversity continually undermine efforts to integrate the American workplace.
  - The distinctions between affirmative action and diversity need to be understood by all employees throughout the organization.
  - The differences between the public and the private objectives of diversity training must be articulated clearly to all employees throughout the organization.

5

Employee Relations and Retention

HOW TO KEEP HISPANIC EMPLOYEES CHALLENGED AND SATISFIED

Once Hispanic employees are part of the organization, the day-to-day process of integration to some extent undoes efforts at diversity. This is a paradox, for while a specific department or division is composed of a variety of individuals, the department or division—as well as the entire firm—ideally should operate as a single unit, committed to fulfilling its purpose. For this to occur in a cohesive manner, a sense of defined mission and esprit de corps is required. How management believes this can be achieved, and how HRM policies are designed to fulfill this goal, is specific to the individual characteristics of an organization. It's impossible to obsess over "all diversity, all the time" without interfering with the ability of employees to perform their duties in the course of a normal business day.

A sound policy, therefore, is to incorporate certain aspects that speak directly to Hispanic employees in the organization's culture. This move is helpful on a broad front since many of the concerns Hispanics have also matter to other constituencies in the American workplace. Hispanic concerns about family, for instance, can be added to the voices of other employees who are lobbying for the option of either of a newborn's parents to take a leave of absence. Similarly, Hispanics' insistence that *family* be defined to include members outside the nuclear family resonates with other employees who want an expanded definition to afford benefits to their long-term partners, the parents of either partner, or whatever children they may adopt as a household.

In this chapter we will examine the enticing and exciting field emerging for HR practitioners as the nation's demographics encourage a rethinking, evolution, and introduction of pioneering HRM tools to allow organizations to achieve a sustainable competitive advantage in the fast-globalizing economy. Many new steps fall under the heading of *employee relations and retention,* since retention is a primary goal where employees are concerned. It is also useful to explore the proper role of diversity in a workplace with both Hispanic and non-Hispanic employees. This includes how to communicate effectively with Hispanic employees, how recognition and rewards can speak to Hispanic culture, what HRM needs to understand about how Hispanics see and understand work-life balance, how Hispanics approach conflict resolution, what HRM can do to support professional and trade organizations for Hispanic employees, and how to conduct exit interviews of Hispanic employees.

HISPANIC EMPLOYEES AND THE PROPER ROLE OF DIVERSITY

As noted in Chapter 4, mission and vision statements allow HR professionals to develop their organization's diversity training

---
EXAMPLE 4

Citigroup's Executive Summary on Diversity

For Our People . . . Employer of Choice	Citigroup values a work environment where diversity is embraced, where people are promoted on their merits, and where people treat each other with mutual respect and dignity. Around the world, we are committed to being a company where the best people want to work; where opportunities to develop are widely available; where innovation and an entrepreneurial spirit are valued; and where a healthy work/life balance is encouraged.
For Our Customers . . . Provider of Choice	Citigroup strives to deliver products and services to our customers that reflect both our global reach and our deep local roots in every market where we operate. The diversity of our employees enables us to better understand our customers, while the breadth of our product offerings allows us to serve them better.
For Our Suppliers . . . Business Partner of Choice	Citigroup works to create mutually beneficial business relationships with minority-, women-, and locally owned businesses. We recognize that working with a wide range of professionals, suppliers, and consultants strengthens the communities we serve and creates value for our shareholders.

---

program. We now turn to how companies position their diversity programs and communicate them to employees and the community. Examples 4 and 5 show how two major firms in the banking industry have articulated their positions. Once diversity has been defined by the organization, the company's stance must be communicated. According to a 2003 survey by the *New York Times* printed in its "Job Market" section, the two primary methods organizations use to support diversity programs are by communicating them as top priorities to employees (91 percent of respondents) and communicating them as top priorities to customers or

---
EXAMPLE 5
JPMorgan Chase's Diversity Vision

The JPMorgan Chase diversity vision identifies clear action steps to ensure that our firm continues its progress toward developing a workplace environment where diversity is encouraged to thrive. Our vision states:

"At JPMorgan Chase, we win by creating a culture that sparks creativity, leadership, and exceptional performance. Our success depends on enabling and challenging each other to contribute our best in an environment that is inclusive, open, flexible, fair, and courageous."

Our commitment to an inclusive workplace:

- We respect and harness individual strengths and differences to surface the best ideas and insights.
- We hold every colleague accountable for living our vision and for promoting our diversity efforts with colleagues, clients, suppliers, and communities.
- We excel by building diverse teams.
- We measure progress rigorously and often.
- We engage everyone in making this vision a reality.

---

the business community (73 percent). This emphasis demonstrates the critical need for clear and broad communication to make diversity part of the organization's culture and to illustrate to employees and managers their role in diversity-related processes.[1]

These articulations of intentions, while different in approach, share the same spirit, one of inclusiveness and desire to derive mutual benefit from the wealth of life experience, history, and insights different people bring to the organization. "One case for diversity is that it broadens the perspectives the firm can bring to bear in specific decisions," James Baron and David Kreps argue in *Strategic Human Resources,* affirming beliefs now almost universally shared in the American workplace.

Insofar as the firm is able to choose among alternatives with some discernment, then having more diverse viewpoints represented will widen the set of alternatives considered, leading on average to better decisions. Diversity can also help the firm to reach out to and then serve a broad clientele. An American firm, for example, that wishes to extend operations or sales to the Far East, South America, or virtually anywhere in the world, may find invaluable resources in the ethnically and racially diverse population of the United States, giving it a competitive advantage over firms that recruit from more homogeneous populations. Particularly in transactions involving trust, ambiguity, and intense communication, some similarity between an employee and the external constituencies with whom he or she interacts can be an asset.[2]

Communication regarding diversity programs should focus on ensuring that all employees understand the program's policies and goals. Figure 2 indicates how components of diversity-related communication may help employees understand the purpose and direction of a diversity program.[3] As an organization prepares to implement a diversity initiative, HR professionals, of course, need to define it and determine why it matters. Diversity is about intelligent management of employees—all employees. It is about encouraging and enabling everyone in the organization, regardless of background, ethnicity, or heritage, to draw fully on their talents and skills and contribute to their fullest potential.

Demographic research suggests the future workforce will continue to grow more diverse, including individuals of different genders, ages, races, ethnicities, and lifestyles. Effectively leveraging this human capital will play a large role in companies' future competitiveness and economic performance.[4] There is a strong business case for diversity. The *Academy of Management Journal* has conducted several studies over the years linking diversity to

FIGURE 2

Components of Diversity-Related Communication

Explain the Business Case	Explain the value of diversity to the organization; emphasize its impact on the bottom line, productivity, and achievement of company goals.
Build on Existing Values and Vision	Link existing organizational values related to ethics, responsibility, and empowerment to diversity efforts.
Show Employees What's in It for Them	Help employees understand how diversity benefits them individually. For example, emphasize more effective teams, less conflict, and greater undestanding of customers.
Utilize an Inclusive Definition of Diversity	Emphasize that diversity is more than race and gender and encompasses multiple dimensions of similiarity and difference. Without an inclusive element, many employees are likely to reject the process because they don't see themselves as part of a diverse mix.
Explain the Process	Explain the concrete steps in the diversity program, including individual responsibilities and available opportunities and events.
Demonstrate Commitment	Place a credible, powerful leader at the helm of the process or commit executive team members to such groups as diversity task forces to demonstrate the organization's strong commitment to diversity.

Source: Adapted from Corporate Leadership Council, "Developing, Communicating, and Measuring Diversity Initiatives," 2003.

corporate performance. Continuing research finds that having a diverse management team, including women, people of non-European descent, and people under the age of forty correlated with superior corporate performance. A Kotter and Heskett study, "Corporate Culture and Performance," documents the results of 207 large U.S. companies in twenty-two different industries over an eleven-year period. The study reveals that the organizations that managed their cultures well accomplished an increase in revenues of an average of 682 percent (as opposed to 166 percent increase for companies with weaker culture); an increase in net income of 756 percent (as opposed to 1 percent); and a rise in stock prices of 901 percent (as opposed to 74 percent).

Furthermore, diversity is also linked to reduced turnover, improved retention, and high employee morale. A survey conducted by the Society for Human Resources Management and *Fortune* found that the majority of the 121 U.S. HR professionals who responded said that diversity initiatives affect their organizations' bottom lines by improving culture, recruitment of new employees, and client relations.

During interviews, candidates—regardless of race or ethnicity—often ask questions about diversity in the organization. With greater frequency, if candidates do not see varied representation within management, they are discouraged from pursuing opportunities with an organization. This follows changes in society at large. "With the glaring exceptions of sex and skin color . . . the mold for a big-company CEO has been broken, and there isn't a new one to take its place," David Leonhardt reports. "The story is different in Washington, where political leaders are richer, older, more likely to have gone to an expensive college and more likely to have first held another elected office than they were in the past. So in some ways, corporate leaders now mirror the rest of society more closely than elected leaders do."[5]

Job applicants want to see greater diversity in management, which is a major selling point. Recruiting diverse employees makes this possible and improves retention. When employees feel valued and respected, when the promotional system is fair and open, and when resources are spent on developing staff, people stay with a company and often tell others about it.

Having championed diversity, it is important to advocate integration, mindful of the fact that while many Hispanics wish to acculturate to American society, most want to retain their distinct identity, whether they are Cuban, Puerto Rican, Mexican,

Dominican, or from some other country. In "Diluting Diversity: Implications for Intergroup Inequality in Organizations," published in *Journal of Management Inquiry*, Frank Linnehan and Alison Konrad make the strong case that, once diversity is a core value of an organization's culture, HRM should take the lead to reduce inequality—which should be understood as pointing out one group of employees, whether women, or gays and lesbians, or Hispanics, for special treatment or consideration—in the labor force. An analogy we all can relate to is the special attention showered on a newborn, which often leads to feelings of neglect in the older siblings. In the workplace, similarly, once the initial process of identifying how an organization's culture can best incorporate a specific constituency is complete, HRM must develop and implement policies that lay out an articulated effort to foster harmony by eliminating any perceived inequality that has been generated.

Linnehan and Konrad recommend a three-pronged approach to intergroup inequality:

> First, through human resource (HR) audits, organizations should assess the degree to which their HR practices serve to either create or perpetuate privilege based on group membership. . . . Removing preferential selection mechanisms that arbitrarily favor privileged groups is less likely to cause a negative backlash than introducing preferential selection mechanisms favoring historically excluded groups. . . . Sharing information with all employees on the specific nature of the HR interventions made as a result of the audit should help to generate positive attitudes.
>
> Second, diversity management initiatives should include training to address the interpersonal aspects of intergroup relations. Training should incorporate modules on stereotyping, prejudice, and discrimination. . . . Training modules on cultural differences are less likely to be emotionally charged than modules on prejudice and discrimination. . . .

The third prong of an effective diversity management initiative involves community action. Many companies already act to support the work of community groups to improve the life chances of historically excluded groups. Actions that help members of historically excluded groups attain the quality education and skills they need to compete on an equal basis will make the organization's job of reducing intergroup inequality easier over the years. Such actions also demonstrate the sincerity of the organization's commitment to equality, enhancing its reputation for social responsibility in the community at large.[6]

For organizations that have decades-old diversity programs, the growth of the Hispanic employee population represents a series of adjustments, and not necessarily the launching of entirely different programs.

EFFECTIVE COMMUNICATION WITH HISPANIC EMPLOYEES

To promote positive employee relations, HRM needs to be sensitive in providing communications and policies in both English and Spanish, not unlike major companies from airlines to banks that provide language options as a normal part of doing business. Chapter 2 provided a "code of ethics" and "workplace responsibilities" examples in both English and Spanish. These set the standard for improving the productivity and job satisfaction of rank-and-file Hispanic employees. The following steps give HR practitioners a checklist for improving communication with Hispanic employees:

- **Provide HR materials in English and Spanish**—This applies not only to company-written materials but also to literature from external constituencies and government agencies.[7]

- **Provide Spanish-language classes for supervisors and line managers**—A fundamental refresher course on the level of high school Spanish is the minimum standard for managers of nonsalaried Hispanic workers.

- **Communicate the importance of confidentiality**—When more than one language is spoken in the workplace, it is imperative that proprietary and confidential information not be inappropriately discussed in either language.

- **Take into account the Hispanic family model**—This is especially important for line manager awareness. Employers whose workforce consists of large numbers of Hispanics need to recognize that family leave, bereavement time, and other benefits considerations should include people outside the nuclear family.

- **Revitalize a diverse workforce**—Hispanics prefer to work where they are made comfortable and where they are understood. Careful listening to Hispanic employees who are not fluent or comfortable speaking English will benefit the individual employee while sending a powerful signal to all Hispanic employees.

Communication skills are vital, from the CEO on down, and being able to speak with anyone in the organization is a necessity. "Today's C.E.O. . . . has to be very comfortable talking about the business with folks on the factory floor or customers who are increasingly diverse," Robert A. Eckert, chief executive of Mattel and a University of Arizona graduate, argues. "While private schools have the advantage of smaller classes and the financial wherewithal to attract the world's greatest faculty, the public schools offer the diversity and variety that go along with the size they have there."[8]

When possible, use the passive voice in short memos or documents in English intended for nonsalaried Hispanic workers. This may seem counterintuitive, since in standard written English the passive voice is frowned on, but in Spanish it is used as way of being respectful and deferential. Instead of "Turn off the lights," use "The lights will be turned off"—that phrasing will reach the intended audience more effectively.

HRM must also understand that, through technology, globalization, and increased trade among Latin American nations, a "standard" Spanish is emerging in business and culture. "Accent-neutral Spanish is the sound of a coming media culture," Frank Ahrens informed the readers of the *Washington Post* in 2004. "Spanish-speakers make up the fastest-growing group of minority media consumers in the United States, according to Nielsen Media Research. [Television broadcaster] Univision encourages accent-free Spanish among its actors, even if it does not enforce it as [competing broadcaster] Telemundo does. And neutralized Spanish can be heard elsewhere, as well: both presidential campaigns [in 2004] employ[ed] it in their Spanish-language television ads targeting Hispanic voters."[9]

What is the net result? As Ahrens reports, "Mexican Spanish . . . hits a middle ground . . . [and as a result] Mexican Spanish is the broadest-appeal, easiest-to-understand Spanish. . . . In other words, [Mexican Spanish] becomes the Nebraskan of Spanish."[10] HR specialists, mindful of regional differences between, for instance, Puerto Rican and Cuban usages, must understand that in the United States and throughout corporate Latin America a "neutralized" Mexican Spanish is emerging as the Spanish of business and entertainment.

THE ROLE OF RECOGNITION AND REWARDS

HRM should develop a reward strategy that recognizes exceptional Hispanic employees. Diversity programs that have recognition and rewards built into them continue to prove successful in employee retention. HR practitioners must understand that, not unlike other minority groups, Hispanics respond favorably to structured programs that allow them to develop their own career and value greatly mentors who can guide them through the professional ropes of their industry. A "recognition and reward" program should be implemented within the context of an overall workforce planning strategy. Since initiatives must be supported by the organizational culture, retention strategies will vary by organization. Organizations can recognize and reward—and retain—exceptional Hispanic employees through employee networks, a variety of development and mentoring initiatives, and other measures related to HRM's awareness of cultural backgrounds.

Hispanic Preferences in Employer Recognition

Hispanics, like people of all backgrounds, want recognition for work well done. When compared with mainstream American society, however, Hispanics culturally respond more favorably to recognition that signals their employer is aware of the importance of family and the sentimentality attached to the giving and receiving of gifts.

Employer Recognition of Family Importance
Throughout, we have discussed the importance of family in Spanish cultures, but it bears mentioning in relation to recognition and

rewards. Hispanic employees, for instance, might consider it their right to attend a second cousin's wedding, or they might consider it appropriate to invite a dozen or so relatives to a company picnic. This is the reason it is imperative to have written policies in place to avoid misunderstandings in matters having to do with family, including how many guests are allowed for an event. For informal events, such as summertime picnics, separate events for children at the same location would be appropriate. For more formal events, such as corporate dinners, perhaps the firm might provide babysitters or babysitting, a perk that would be welcomed by all employees.

HR should be aware of other family-related characteristics of Hispanic culture that are quite different from those of other cultures in the United States. Hispanics tend to live at home when they go to college. They live at home until they are married. They live close to members of their extended family. Everyone takes responsibility for raising children; most babysitters are relatives and it is rare to entrust the care of a child to an adult who is not a relative. They tend to care for their elder parents at home and consider first cousins as close as siblings. Employer recognition that personal time is seen by Hispanics to be a right to attend funerals, weddings, and other life events generates goodwill and loyalty.

Gift Exchange

The second characteristic to consider centers on sentimentality, or the sign of caring that comes from the exchange of gifts. Hispanics, more than other groups, invest tremendous meaning into small gestures symbolized by gift exchange. The intrinsic value of what is given is secondary to the thought behind it. This may sound like a cliché, but HR practitioners are well advised to be cognizant of the strong signals that can be sent through gift exchange. This has long been recognized as a powerful motivator.

"Benefits and perks can also be particularly powerful symbols of gift exchange, moving the employment relationship from one with purely economic connotations to something more along the lines of kin or friendship relationship," Baron and Kreps explain in *Strategic Human Resources*. "Salary, wages, and even bonus payments all have the connotation of an economic exchange, in which (according to certain social norms, at least) each party should attempt to extract for itself the best possible (narrowly selfish) deal. Some forms of benefits and perks are of an entirely different flavor and can cause the worker to respond with reciprocal gifts or by internalizing the welfare of the organization. As examples of benefits that are strongly symbolic of gifts, consider gift packages distributed at Christmas and Easter or on other holidays, or bottles of wine given out on the employee's birthday, especially when employees observe that these gifts are personalized to the employee rather than generic."[11]

Of course, any gift-giving must be within the company's established guidelines and be across the board rather than extended to one group of employees only.

Tuition Reimbursement

The importance of tuition reimbursement cannot be overstated. "The tuition reimbursement program is . . . a significant retention tool," Harriet Hankin reports. "The turnover rate for those participating in the program was only 8 percent, compared to 13 percent for those not involved [at the organization studied]. Since a part-time graduate degree course typically takes at least four years to complete, this has been a significant benefit in retaining the high-potential workers who are most likely to pursue degrees."[12]

EMPLOYEE NETWORKS OR AFFINITY GROUPS

To signal organizational commitment to Hispanic employees' long-term career development, companies should provide training and development opportunities. The creation of affinity, or resource, groups constitutes official sanction for continued development of employees, just as diversity networks are critical to a diversity strategy. Affinity, or resource, groups offer management and employees alike seven benefits. They:

- Engage employees in company culture

- Establish informal networking opportunities

- Provide informal development opportunities

- Signal organizational commitment to diversity

- Serve as a forum for encouraging the discussion of issues of concern to the group in question

- Serve as a point of contact for recruiting efforts within targeted groups

- Generate feedback to HRM about the wants and needs of the members of that group

"When new hires discover that they share interests with others in the organization, they often collaborate more effectively on professional matters," Lauren Keller Johnson writes. For that reason, she recommends including personal information that people are comfortable sharing when introducing new managers to members of their network. She adds, "San Francisco–based biotechnology firm Genentech created cross-functional 'diversity groups'—each focused on a specific interest—to encourage socializing among staff at all levels. At quarterly networking gatherings for new employees, it encouraged participants to join one or more groups that were of interest to them. The social bonding in Genentech's diversity groups has inspired valuable work-related collaboration."[13]

Affinity groups can also be used to educate the workforce at large on diversity issues. Indeed, Ford Motor Company began formally sponsoring resource groups in 1996 and currently sponsors ten groups. One of those groups is called The Ford Hispanic Network, and its mission statement reads: "Drive the corporate effort in the employment, career development, and retention of Hispanics in the workforce. Continually enhance Ford Motor Company's image in the Hispanic Community as well as the Hispanic Image throughout the Company."[14]

Ford provides each group with an annual budget. Ford's leadership team also sponsored these groups individually, giving the groups insight and access to the company's leadership team. On a quarterly basis, Ford facilitates resource roundtables attended by at least one representative from each of the resource groups. These roundtables are used to help people understand one another's objectives and to offer mentoring advice. Although Ford allows the groups to determine their organizational structure, it requires that all resource groups maintain a governing structure, for example, having a board of directors with a chair and people in the roles of communications, membership, marketing, public affairs and media, and protocol. The board is overseen by a member of the executive team and the Office of Diversity & Worklife Planning. Each group may have subcommittees and local and international chapters.

Citigroup is another example of an organization that has taken the lead on affinity groups within its organization. With the full support of Chairman Sandy Weill, it established the Citigroup Hispanic Network in 2003 "to create a work environment where individual differences are embraced and celebrated." Currently the group has more than five hundred members at the company's New York headquarters and is cited as a beneficial resource for support, networking, and learning about opportunities company-wide.

Example 6 offers language that HR professionals can adopt to help their organization create an affinity group for Hispanic employees. Note that this is a structure for uniformly allowing any constituency to form a network and can be used for corporate consistency. How the group operates once it has been authorized to exist is up to HR—Chess Network employees can, for instance, agree to establish a chess league; Black Network employees can agree to commemorate Rosa Parks's birthday or other special times—but the structure for forming each network must be equal.

ENCOURAGEMENT FOR ADVANCEMENT OPPORTUNITIES

HRM can go a long way toward ensuring that Hispanic employees stay with the organization. Useful strategies include providing corporate role models and mentoring programs, which can contribute to greater Hispanic success and contributions to the organization.

Corporate Role Models

Corporate role models represent greater commitment on the part of leadership to Hispanic employees. "It's critically important that our employees have the capacity to work well with individuals whose backgrounds may be different from their own," Monica E.

EXAMPLE 6

[Name of Organization] Employee Networks

Thank you for your interest in creating a [Name of Organization] Employee Network Group. [Name of Organization] supports the development of networks that

1. Provide an opportunity for employees with common experiences and perspectives to network and enhance their professional growth

2. Promote education and awareness for all employees

3. Adopt a mission statement and goals and conduct activities that are consistent with [Name of Organization]'s values, objectives, diversity initiatives, and policies and practices.

4. Do not have religious, political, or other ideological objectives

5. Do not define their mission, goals, and activities or operate in opposition to another Employee Network Group or segment of the employee population

Employees interested in forming an Employee Network Group should complete and submit the attached proposal to the Office of Workforce Diversity for consideration by the company. Once the proposal is submitted, the Employee Network program manager in the Office of Workforce Diversity will contact you. The program manager will discuss the proposal and next steps with you. Upon acceptance of the proposal, a local HR diversity manager will be identified for you as the network's liaison to assist you in forming the network.

The proposal that you submit should be consistent with [Name of Organization]'s guidelines for employee networks, which you can obtain from your local HR manager or the Office of Workforce Diversity at [HR e-mail address]. If you do not know the name of your local HR manager, ask your business manager.

Proposals that are not consistent with the guidelines will not receive further consideration.

Here is the process for establishing an Employee Network Group:

- Interested employees submit a proposal for the formation of an employee network to the Office of Workforce Diversity.

- If the proposal is approved, the Office of Workforce Diversity will identify a local HR diversity liaison to help set up the Employee Network Group.

- The HR diversity liaison works with networks in formation to develop network bylaws and an organization structure.

EXAMPLE 6 cont'd

- Once a network has a leadership team identified and has developed proposed bylaws that include an organization structure and mission, the network leaders and the HR diversity liaison should present their proposed bylaws and organization structure to the Office of Workforce Diversity.
- Once the bylaws and organization structure are approved, the Office of Workforce Diversity will issue a statement of recognition to the network.
- If recognition is received, the network may begin operating.
- The Office of Workforce Diversity may delegate, at its discretion, the authority to establish a local network to a business or local diversity office.

Emerson, director of diversity and work/family at DaimlerChrysler, is quoted as saying. DaimlerChrysler sponsors The Project, an initiative founded by Carolyn M. Callahan to allow executives to become positive role models for minority students.[15] Studies confirm that the most successful executives recall mentors and role models that inspired and guided them. Korn/Ferry surveys, time and again, have indicated that more than half of successful executives credit role models for shaping their worldview and believing in their ability to succeed.[16]

A compelling role model for innumerable Hispanics during the past quarter century was Roberto Goizueta, the Cuban-born CEO of the Coca-Cola Company. Goizueta relished the "refugee-to-riches" story of his life and enjoyed telling people how he and his family arrived in the United States with nothing, only their determination to succeed. Before he fled Cuba, he had trained as an engineer and worked for the Cuban subsidiary of the Coca-Cola Company. In the United States, he resumed his career and rose through the ranks. When he took the helm at Coca-Cola in 1981, the company's stock was valued at $4 billion. At the time of his death in 1997, it had risen to a staggering $145 billion, and he had transformed Coca-Cola, in the words of the *Washington Post,* into "a global symbol of American style and affluence." In an interview in 1995, he reflected on the importance of being a role model. "In many ways I always wanted to show young people that hard work and dedication leads to success," Goizueta said. "It might have had something to do with trying to prove to people back in Cuba that working in a capitalist system is far superior, but if that was a motivation for wanting to be a positive role model to other Hispanic youth, then so much for the better."[17]

A measure of how far-reaching his achievements as a role model were can be found in the testimonials he received at the time of this death: "Perhaps no other corporate leader in modern times has so beautifully exemplified the American dream. He believed that in America, all things are possible. He lived that dream," former president Jimmy Carter told the Associated Press.[18] Successful Hispanics in an organization offer living proof that professional success is possible at that firm.

Mentoring Programs

Although organizations spend significant amounts on formal training, research suggests that informal relationship-based learning such as mentoring serves as the most consistently powerful source of enhanced performance. The Corporate Leadership Council's 2001 *Voice of the Leader* survey of more than eight thousand leaders asked what valuable contributions their internship and mentoring programs had on management. These inquiries revealed that "feedback and relationship programs" development outranked "experience-based" programs.[19] The benefits of mentoring had a multiplier effect on managers, where one would become enthusiastic after learning of another manager's

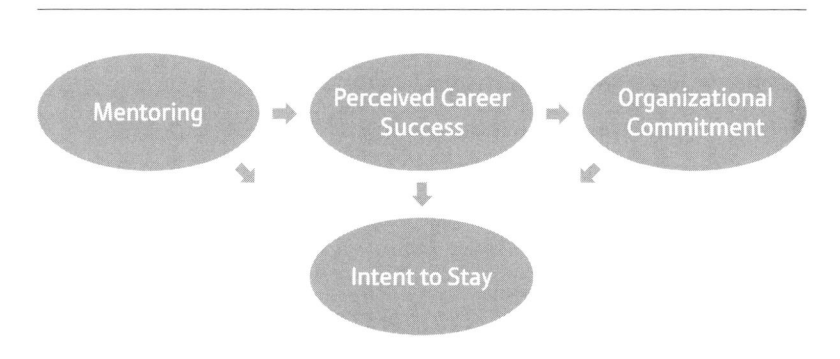

FIGURE 3

Effects of Mentoring in the Workplace

```
Mentoring → Perceived Career Success → Organizational Commitment
                    ↓
             Intent to Stay
```

Source: Adapted from Therese A. Joiner, Timothy Bartram, and Terese Garreffa, "The Effects of Mentoring on Perceived Career Success, Commitment and Turnover Intentions," *Journal of American Academy of Business*, 2004, 5 (1 & 2).

experience. Indeed, mentoring is a continuous process, one that allows for significant feedback not just to the participants but also to other employees and management. Figure 3 shows the feedback flows that occur when HRM takes a proactive role in the development of an organized mentoring program designed to integrate talented Hispanic employees into the organization.

Mentoring is traditionally defined as developmental assistance offered to a junior employee by someone more senior. The answers to the following questions define a mentoring program and how it applies to Hispanics.

What is the goal of the mentoring program?

Organizations may develop programs to provide relationship-based support and help every new employee feel welcome and at home in the workplace. A mentor is assigned to each new employee to help him or her learn about the culture and values of the organization. For Hispanic employees, the guidance of Hispanic mentors provides a greater comfort level and more learning opportunities.

What is a mentoring relationship?
Mentoring is a collegial relationship where old hands provide support, information, and guidance to new employees through the orientation process. It takes place at the department level, outside the supervisor-employee relationship.

What are the characteristics of a mentor?
A mentor is a positive role model who expresses a sincere desire to be a mentor and demonstrates a commitment to the values of the organization. A mentor should also be enthusiastic, caring, and flexible and a good communicator and sharer of information. A particular advantage to Hispanics occurs when a mentor can communicate effectively in the language of the protégé.

What is mentoring's impact on the organization?
Organizations use mentoring to impart key job skills. Increasingly, companies with a clear sense of vision, values, and strategy have a distinct competitive advantage. Corporate Leadership Council research suggests that employees' connection to organizational strategy is directly tied to their level of discretionary effort. Mentors foster the continuity of culture. Mentoring also serves to quickly connect employees to the organization from the start of their careers, a time when they are most likely to leave and seek their fortunes elsewhere. The end result is greater retention of Hispanic employees.

What is a mentor's role?
A mentor's role has four basic components:[20]

- **Adviser**—Recommends career direction, identifies and helps overcome obstacles
- **Ally**—Provides candid opinions
- **Broker**—Assists with establishing and increasing networking contacts
- **Communicator**—Facilitates discussion, interaction, and exchange of information

What are the benefits of mentoring?

A successful mentoring program can enhance new employees' perceptions of career success and commitment to the organization, which in turn should reduce their inclination to leave. Mentors can fill the role of initiating Hispanics into the subtleties and nuances of corporate life, including cultural differences between the American and Latin American workplace. Some distinctions are of legal consequence, and most center on familiarity. In Latin America, for instance, men shake hands firmly to greet and say good-bye upon first meeting, and women kiss each other and allow men to kiss them on the cheek. This is not acceptable in the American workplace. Men are less formal, and the failure to shake hands upon saying good-bye should not be seen as an affront. Of greater consequence, women should not kiss other women or allow men to kiss them. In many Latin American and European countries, men place their hands on another man's shoulders, and in some countries they lock arms while walking, practices almost unheard of in the American workplace. U.S. law governing sexual harassment is fraught with peril, and as a matter of policy, physical touching of any kind is discouraged. Hispanics should be made aware that this is not a sterile legacy of the American Protestant past but simply an effort to protect everyone from unwanted or inappropriate touching. Mentors can help Hispanics, particularly immigrants, adapt to the behavioral norms considered appropriate for the American workplace.

Here is a set of guidelines for instituting a mentoring program as part of recognition, rewards, and advancement for Hispanic employees.

The Mentoring Relationship

The first essential of a positive mentoring relationship is to create good rapport between the participants. The mentor can best do this by:

- **Demonstrating openness and sincerity:**
  - Meeting new employees with a pleasant, positive greeting, and trying to anticipate and meet their needs
  - Smiling; it's contagious! A warm smile can go far toward putting the new employee at ease.
  - Making good eye contact
  - Complimenting honestly
  - Speaking in Spanish to make the new employee feel welcome
- **Avoiding gestures and behaviors that convey power and authority.** New employees react with irritation and distrust if a superior makes them wait, ignores them, or dominates the conversation, interrupting them and otherwise making them feel put down.
- **Discussing language as an issue.** Mentors need to know whether Hispanic employees are fully bilingual. Does the new employee expect to be able to speak Spanish in the office? Believe that managers should learn some Spanish? Fully understand the firm's policy on Spanish in the workplace?

Whatever the circumstances, the new employee will integrate more smoothly into the workplace with a clear idea of what the real situation is on each point.

- **Describing culturally acceptable norms and helping protégés find ways of living with them.** Culturally, Hispanics need to develop trust in all relationships before any meaningful exchange can take place. Mentors should spend time getting to know their protégés' families and personal concerns. It is especially important to foster the Hispanic employee's sense of acceptance and safety.

- **Being receptive, showing empathy, and validating feelings.** Mentors should listen attentively and communicate effectively, demonstrating genuine concern; honor any confidentiality agreements; and provide consistent support. They should provide feedback, but avoid being judgmental—people almost universally intend to do well, and they react better to help in doing so than to criticism that implies they deliberately did wrong. Consistently conveying a sense of respect and equal dignity in the relationship, and consequently the privilege of serving as an adviser, will do much to win the trust of the new employee.

- **Being a role model and providing peer support.** Time spent with the new employee can be best used to provide support, initiate networking opportunities, model and discuss company norms and culture, and discuss job expectations and work protocols. At the same time, mentors must always respect the new employee's right to make personal choices. By promoting his or her independence and self-direction from day one, mentors can launch the person on a trajectory toward a successful career with the firm.

- **Managing the farewell at the end of a formal mentoring relationship.** Mentors should celebrate the end of the commitment with an event where both mentor and protégé can laugh and have fun. Mentors should lavish the new employee with sincere praise, offering words of confidence, compassion, and consideration while avoiding the urge to dispense warnings or to lecture. They should try to remember that setting the relationship free requires time, and avoid following up too soon.

Communication Skills for Mentors

Active listening is key to a successful relationship.[21] Listening is more than just hearing what someone has to say; it involves careful attention to the words and the feelings expressed and reflecting the content—that is, paraphrasing the statement so speakers know they have been understood. "Reflecting the content" means expressing the meaning of the information you are hearing. For example:

New employee: My supervisor had to retrieve the storage room key from my desk again.
Mentor: Sounds like you are having difficulty returning the key to the designated spot.

This kind of attentive reflection supports and encourages the speaker. It shows that the listener understands the speaker—and gives the speaker the chance to eliminate any misunderstanding that may be revealed. This helps the person clarify thoughts and keeps the conversation focused.

"Reflecting feelings" means expressing the feelings you are hearing from the person, not just the facts:

New employee: I really don't want to tackle that project today.
Mentor: Sounds like you are not motivated to begin work on the project.

This attention to feelings further supports and encourages the speaker. It lets the speaker know that the listener is sensitive to what is happening on an emotional level, and it helps the speaker recognize and accept the feelings—which is a necessary precursor to adjusting their impact.

"Paraphrasing" means repeating in your own words what the person says.

New employee: Sometimes I feel what I say to my supervisor falls on deaf ears.
Mentor: Sounds like you feel your supervisor sometimes does not listen to you.

As with summarizing the content, restating the message lets the speaker know that you are listening and are interested in what is being said. It shows that you understand—and gives the speaker the chance to eliminate any misunderstanding that may be revealed. And the simple effort to restate the point can be very helpful in developing understanding in the first place.

Beyond active listening, several strategies can help you communicate effectively as a speaker. They will allow you to obtain the information you need to understand the new employee, to show that you have been listening, and to verify you understand the information relayed:

- Use "I" statements
- Seek clarification
- Ask questions
- Summarize information

It is also useful to avoid communication roadblocks—comments or behaviors that hinder rather than facilitate communication because they tend to discount the validity of feelings, opinions, and rights of the other person. Roadblocks include any behaviors and responses that

- Order or command ("You must . . ." or "You have to . . .")
- Moralize or preach ("You should . . ." or "You ought to . . .")
- Provide answers or solutions ("You should . . ." or "It would be best for you to . . .")
- Criticize or judge ("You are not thinking straight" or "You are really messed up")
- Use sarcasm ("You think you know it all?" or "Yeah, I'm sure you're better qualified")

Positive Effect of Minority Mentors

Continuing research reaffirms the importance of the race and ethnicity of the mentors in developing an organization's leaders internally. "Minority executives attributed much of their later success to their immediate bosses, other superiors, and peers who helped them develop professionally," David A. Brown reports in the *Harvard Business Review*. He continues,

> Of course, such developmental relationships are important for everybody climbing the corporate ladder, regardless of race, but what distinguished minority executives from white executives and plateaued managers was that they had many more such relationships and with a broader range of people, especially in the early years of their careers. . . . These mentors provided critical support in five ways:
>
> - The relationships opened the door to challenging assignments that allowed the minority executives to gain professional competence.
> - By putting the future executives in high-trust positions, the mentors sent a message to the rest of the organization that

these people were high-performers, thus helping them gain confidence and establish their credibility.
- Mentors provided crucial career advice and counsel that prevented their protégés from getting sidetracked from the path leading to the executive level.
- Mentors often became powerful sponsors later in the minority executives' careers, recruiting them repeatedly to new positions.
- Mentors often protected their protégés by confronting subordinates or peers who leveled unfair criticism, especially if it had racial undertones.[22]

Selecting Hispanics for Mentoring Roles

It may be highly beneficial for HRM to grant Hispanic managers ownership in the development of Hispanic talent throughout the organization. For such a mentoring approach to be successful— that is, for Hispanic managers to become owners of the process of nurturing Hispanic employees through a mentoring program, however, they require training. Such an approach can help HR professionals identify which Hispanic managers or executives are both willing and suited to participate actively in the internal development of Hispanic talent already working for the organization. The purpose, of course, is not to diminish the leadership role HRM plays in nurturing the Hispanic employee but to determine how managers already in the organization can contribute in a supporting and complementary role, facilitating both support and guidance.

Of equal importance, HRM must be able to elicit sufficient information on which to base decisions about who is suited to the program. Example 7 offers a list of questions that will help Hispanic candidates respond openly, since they exclude areas of inquiry that may either be distractions for Hispanics or provoke anxiety and thus result in poor interviews. This is still the case

---
EXAMPLE 7

Preparing to Interview Hispanic Managers for Mentoring Roles
---

1. **Develop a game plan.**

    a. Review the position description.

    b. Review official employee files.

    c. Prepare questions.

    d. Determine whether or not you will use a panel to conduct the interviews.

    e. Arrange a suitable place and time as free as possible from interruptions.

    f. Schedule interviews.

2. **Develop interview questions.** Since your prime concern is to gather information, take time to listen to what the candidate has to say—get the interviewee to talk. Avoid selling the job; it's better to state the facts exactly as they are. Avoid promises of promotion or privileges that may not materialize. Establish a friendly but businesslike atmosphere. Questions must meet these criteria:

    a. Be job related

    b. Not appear to constitute a test

    c. Be open ended (Allow the candidate to expand on the question)

    d. Move from general to specific probes for information.

    e. Pick up on earlier answers (Building on what the candidate says shows interest by the interviewer)

3. **Conduct the interview.**

    a. Go meet the candidate. Use the candidate's name; shake hands. Make sure the candidate knows who you are. (If you are using a panel, introduce all panel members.)

    b. Establish a friendly but businesslike atmosphere.

    c. Make the candidate comfortable.

    d. Inform the candidate that you will take notes during the interview.

    e. You may allow the candidate to review the job description prior to asking your interview questions. If you choose to do this, you must do it for all candidates for the specific position.

    f. Establish rapport.

EXAMPLE 7 cont'd

   g. Go through questions. Document responses. (Note that any additional questions added to the original list of intended questions must also be documented, along with the responses.)

   h. Treat men and women in the same way.

   i. You can talk about the job, its duties and responsibilities, and about the organization, its mission, programs, and achievements. Discuss career possibilities and opportunities for growth, development, advancement, where the job is located, travel, mobility, equipment, and facilities available—but keep to specifics and avoid overselling or taking up too much time.

   j. Ask if the candidate has any questions, and then close the interview by thanking the candidate for coming.

4. **Build good listening habits.** Every communication has at least one sender and one receiver. When interviewing a candidate, you have a responsibility to be first a receiver, and second a sender. You must use good listening habits to be an effective receiver. Here are some of the most recognized good listening habits:

   a. Stop talking. You can't listen if you are talking.

   b. Put the candidate at ease. Help people feel free to talk.

   c. Show the candidate you want to listen by looking and acting interested.

   d. Remove distractions. Don't doodle, tap, or shuffle papers. Close the door to outside noise, and turn off any unnecessary noisy equipment (or appliances such as radios or computer speakers).

   e. Empathize. Try to put yourself in the candidate's place and see things from the candidate's point of view.

   f. Be patient. Don't rush the candidate. Don't interrupt a candidate in the middle of a response because you think you know what is going to be said.

   g. Avoid argument and criticism—this will put the candidate on the defensive.

5. **Monitor your body language.** Throughout the interview, ask yourself the following questions, questions that will help you acquire and maintain positive body language.

   a. Are you smiling enough? Wait for an opening in the conversation. Listen to what the person is saying, and smile when appropriate.

   b. Are your eyes directed toward the speaker? You don't like to feel ignored, and neither does the other person. As you become more skilled in conversation, you will become so absorbed that eye contact will just happen naturally.

EXAMPLE 7 cont'd

c. Are you standing, sitting, and walking straight? Keep reminding yourself not to slump or slouch. When you are alone, practice good posture. Even your voice projects better when your posture is good. Stand up straight. Sit up straight. Walk tall. Your posture says a lot about you as a positive person.

d. What do you sound like? Only other people can really hear you. But you can listen to the sound of your voice. Does it sound too monotonous? Is it too low? Is it too high? It is practically inaudible? Does it sound too abrupt? Your voice should be pleasant and well modulated. You can practice on a tape recorder.

e. How is your handshake? When you greet someone with a handshake, be sure your hand acts as your private diplomat. Put a lot of energy into your handshake. Shake hands firmly and positively. A good handshake projects a self-assured image.

Source: Adapted from Martin Army Community Hospital minority development policies, Fort Benning, GA.

despite the enormous strides Hispanics are making in the technical fields of engineering, mathematics, operations research, and related disciplines.[23] The line of inquiry of these questions also offers insight into the qualifications for most white-collar positions and gives line managers enough information to form more accurate opinions about individual candidates and make more informed decisions about how they might perform in the job and fit into the organization.

The results from these internal inquiries can facilitate the creation of committees designed to address the specific needs of Hispanic employees, help in the development of workshops and seminars that educate line managers across the organization, and assist in the formation of HRM policies that are consistent with management objectives.

Proof That It Works

Time and again, this approach has proved invaluable, particularly where management makes it a stated and supported objective.

"The commitment of senior management was cited as an important corporate attribute in retaining minority employees by 85 percent of executives and 82 percent of professionals; the next most frequently mentioned attribute was 'making diversity an integral part of the business strategy,' cited by 66 percent of executives and 62 percent of professionals," the Korn/Ferry Best Practices for Diversity study finds. It continues,

> There is significant disagreement on the effectiveness of programs and organizations. Corporate executives say that "relationships with minority-oriented organizations" are the most effective programs for attracting minority employees (cited by 91 percent), but just 61 percent of professionals view such programs as effective. Professionals believe that internships (cited by 65 percent) are most effective in attracting minority employees. Skills training is considered by corporate managers to be the most effective program to retain minority employees (cited by 98 percent), but just 70 percent of professionals view such programs as effective. Some 80 percent of managers believe that mentoring programs are effective programs for retention, but just 57 percent of professionals agree. Managers and professionals also disagree on how effective larger corporations are, in general, in achieving diversity goals.[24]

Armed with commitment from management and results from interviewing Hispanic managers, HR professionals are better able to assess their capabilities for identifying and recruiting internal mentors and role models who can participate in Hispanic employee development. With this feedback, HR professionals can also fine-tune the orientation process for new Hispanic employees.

HRM must understand the importance of incorporating new Hispanic employees into the organization. Intentional efforts to improve current and future performance by increasing capabilities include employee socialization—teaching employees about corporate culture and philosophies—as well as training designed to improve skills needed today or in the near future, along with development programs designed to improve skills over the long term.

HISPANICS AND THE CHALLENGES OF WORK-LIFE BALANCE

Hispanics stand to transform how organizations view the challenge of work-life issues. To be sure, Hispanics join their voices to other constituencies—those based on gender or age, for example—that wish to expand the options for American workers.

The frustration of competing interests between employees' personal lives and their career ambitions is not new. "Workplace surveys still register high levels of employee stress stemming from work/life conflicts. Large groups of women and minority workers remain unemployed or underemployed because of family responsibilities and bias in the workplace. And in too many cases, the programs have reached only the workers who need them least," Fay Hansen reports. "Many [HR professionals] acknowledge difficulty, however, in creating a culture that supports these programs, extending flexibility to nonprofessional employees, and building solid tools to measure results."[25]

The results over the past decade have been mixed, at best. "We have a senior vice president who works a four-day week, so we work with that and try to promote it, but it has limitations," Dennis Stern, a human resources manager, told Hansen. "The vice president has a small department where there is flexibility in scheduling, but it doesn't automatically translate to other parts of our business."

Yet the concept that personal life is important to an employee's total job satisfaction holds great currency among management. "The idea [is] that the longer a worker is happily employed by a particular employer, the greater will be the worker's commitment and loyalty to the firm," Baron and Kreps explain in *Strategic Human Resources*.[26]

As mentioned previously, holidays are an important part of work-life balance to Hispanic employees. A bold affirmation of identity stems from management recognition that other days of the year may be more important than some mainstream holidays for the Hispanic workforce. In the same way that Yom Kippur is an important part of Jewish life—and employers accommodate this fact—other holidays merit similar consideration for Hispanics.

Appendix 2 shows a list of important holidays for Hispanics, with notes regarding demographic differences. Some holidays that are important for Cubans may have little resonance for Puerto Ricans or Mexicans. This appendix will allow each organization to identify what may be important to employees in any specific location. HR practitioners would be prudent to use surveys for this purpose, and to recommend HRM policies that reflect these priorities. Culturally important holidays tend to draw in members of the extended family and form a significant part of the core value system that contributes to each employee's happiness. For many Hispanics, for instance, the option of having December 12 as a paid holiday instead of Thanksgiving Day, a holiday to which they have little emotional attachment or affinity, would signal goodwill from management—if such an arrangement is at all possible in a specific work environment—and would allow them to affirm their identities in a traditional way.

In addition, many Hispanics wish to include grandparents, cousins, aunts and uncles, and nieces and nephews among the family members whose weddings, funerals, and other life events warrant taking time off. This broadened definition of *family* stands to shift the conversation between HR practitioners and management about the kinds of initiatives that are necessary to resolve the work-life issues Hispanics face.

Another area that is of critical concern to Hispanics, who generally have larger families and are apt to be primary caregivers for elderly parents, is access to health care. A good health care program is important to them, but at the same time, they feel their health matters are personal and private. Some companies that are critically observant of the levels of wellness among their employees may advocate consumer-driven health plans that are more attractive to healthier employees as a tactic to help control health care costs.

In light of such perceptions, Hispanic employees feel a sense of urgency about how their needs and their respect and dignity are regarded—and for one simple reason: Hispanics are *four times* as likely to resign and leave the labor market as they are to sacrifice their families and stay on the job.[27] This "take it or leave it" attitude is a challenge for HR practitioners across all industries throughout the entire nation.

NEW AND OLD CONFLICTS FOR HISPANICS AND HR

What happens when there is a dramatic change in the demographics of a workforce, for either an individual firm or an entire community? In late 2005 and beyond, major employers with operations in New Orleans—from national hotel chains to home improvement companies and from restaurant chains to supermarkets—confronted an employee relations issue that few had ever anticipated: the wholesale displacement of black workers by Hispanics. Many of the jobs held by African Americans before Hurricane Katrina were subsequently performed by Hispanics. The dramatic demographic upheaval occasioned by Katrina in

New Orleans is not unlike the impressive growth of the Hispanic population, on a slower scale, in other parts of the country.

The resulting question has become: How does HRM address the workplace conflicts that are emerging between African Americans and Hispanics?

While no HR practitioner in America can do anything to stop this generations-old conflict, every HR practitioner in America needs to understand its origins, for the simple reason that the United States is undergoing a demographic process in which Hispanics are displacing African Americans in the labor market. This is a serious issue, one that evokes strong passions and generates anger throughout the American workplace. This is not to say, however, that HR professionals are ill equipped to address the challenge and develop strategies for overcoming it.

In the 1960s, HRM acknowledged that decades of segregation had denied African Americans equal opportunities to prosper in the workplace. Remedies were designed. In the 1970s, HRM confronted how sexism had deprived women of the chance for career advancement. Remedies were developed. In the 1980s, HRM accepted that homophobia had excluded many talented individuals from the opportunity to contribute to their organizations. Remedies were implemented. In the 1990s, HRM addressed the challenges that handicapped Americans encounter in fulfilling their career ambitions. Remedies were approved. In all these areas, social concerns have spilled into the workplace, and whether it is with the rallying cry "equal pay for equal work" or the enactment of the Americans with Disabilities Act, HRM has been able to work, on a continuing basis, to become more inclusive and welcoming of the rich diversity that constitutes the American workforce.

It is from this legacy of achievement that HRM is now confronting the workplace conflict emerging between African Americans and Hispanics. In the development of seminars, classroom instruction, and workshops, HRM must take the lead in spearheading a dialogue between African Americans and Hispanics within their organizations. Two components must be included in these discussions aimed at recognizing the conflict, defusing the tensions, and addressing the concerns that are raised by the displacement of African Americans by Hispanics. The two aspects, African American resentment of Hispanics and the Hispanic tendency to view African Americans negatively, are integral to how HRM develops these programs.

Recognition of the Problem

HRM must recognize that African American resentment toward Hispanics is a relatively new phenomenon; American blacks have historically admired Hispanics. In the nineteenth century Mexico provided sanctuary to American slaves escaping the South, and abolitionists used Mexican territory to operate segments of the Underground Railroad. In the twentieth century Mexican artists, as part of the New Deal, welcomed their African American counterparts and worked with them on joint projects. Unfortunately, through a peculiar set of quintessentially American traits, Hispanics tend to adopt antiblack attitudes as they acculturate into mainstream society, and this is an impediment to maintaining harmony within the labor force.

Workshops developed to address the "brown versus black" conflict must involve give-and-take, acknowledging that both African Americans and Hispanics have legitimate issues and concerns. For African Americans, a prevailing sentiment is that Hispanics are interlopers, benefiting from the civil rights movement that American blacks fought to achieve, and that Hispanics are aliens who did not earn these benefits and privileges. Many African Americans (not unlike most Americans of all backgrounds), however, tend to have a collective historical amnesia, forgetting that vast stretches of the United States were Hispanic in origin and that there is a strong legacy of enriching collaboration between American blacks and Hispanics.

A value-neutral way of broaching this subject is to focus on how, as part of the New Deal, Mexican and African American artists participated in workshops and worked side by side in studios in Mexico City, Guadalajara, and Los Angeles. The result of this collaboration was an infusion of influence from the Mexican muralist movement that helped redefine the development of black art in the United States. Art critic David Bonetti explains:

> Alain Locke, the primary theorist of the New Negro movement, wrote that racial progress would more likely occur through the exercise of culture than overt political activity. He proposed that study of the culturally pure and undiluted customs, beliefs and mores of the uneducated Southern black, who he suggested formed America's true peasantry, would result in cultural riches. When African American artists who were open to Locke's suggestions surveyed the contemporary arts, they saw that the Mexican muralists, whose work was rooted in indigenism—the exaltation of the Indian who survived the Spanish Conquest carrying aspects of his ancient civilizations into the modern world—was a perfect example for them. Not only were the Mexicans sensitive to historically oppressed peoples, they were politically militant. By embracing their work, African American artists could assert their own cultural pride and lodge powerful protests against racist conditions endemic to mid-century America.[28]

This discussion forms the basis of constructive engagement, one in which the concerns of black employees can be raised and discussed without conflict or confrontation. The increasing presence of Hispanics in the workforce is a legitimate issue for African Americans, simply because positions traditionally held by blacks are now being filled by Hispanics; unemployment among urban blacks is twice that of Hispanics in key metropolitan markets.[29]

Attitudes Regarding Others

The second component must include Hispanic acknowledgment that the longer Hispanics live in the United States, the greater their tendency to view blacks in a negative light. This phenomenon, at times referred to as "creeping racism," is a paradox, but it is an undeniable part of Hispanic life in the United States. Hispanics are reluctant to acknowledge how they begin to adopt anti-black attitudes as part of living in the United States. Mirta Ojito reported for the *New York Times* on how conditions change attitudes:

> Havana, sometime before 1994: As dusk descends on the quaint seaside village of Guanabo, two young men kick a soccer ball back and forth and back and forth across the sand. The tall one, Joel Ruiz, is black. The short, wiry one, Achmed Valdés, is white. They are the best of friends.
>
> Miami, January 2000: Valdés is playing soccer, as he does every Saturday, with a group of light-skinned [Hispanics] in a park near his apartment. Ruiz surprises him with a visit, and Valdés, flushed and sweating, runs to greet him. They shake hands warmly. . . . [But] in ways that are obvious to the black man but far less to the white one, they have grown apart in the United States because of race. For the first time, they inhabit a place where the color of their skin defines the outlines of their lives—where they live, the friends they make, how they speak, what they wear, even what they eat.[30]

A prominent Hispanic who has pondered this point is Juan Gonzalez, a columnist for the New York *Daily News*. "While the de facto segregation has been a pernicious part of this society since the end of slavery, in our case, it became an unbearable assault on our family bonds," he writes in his book *Harvest of Empire,* describing how Puerto Ricans in New York were forced to step inside "the racial box" of American life. "'*Y tu abuela, donde esta*' ('And your grandmother, where is she?') is a familiar Puerto Rican refrain and the title of a popular poem by Fortunato Vizcarrondo. The phrase reminds us that black blood runs through all Puerto Rican families. Puerto Ricans resisted the sharp racial demarcations so prevalent in this country, and their implicit diminishment of our human worth."[31]

Gonzalez then continues, describing how generations of Puerto Ricans, and other Hispanics, have been forced to make a Faustian bargain: become accepted by American society by becoming racist. He describes the haunting realization of what America demands this way:

> But gradually, almost imperceptibly, I watched my aunts and uncles begin to adopt antiblack attitudes, as if this were some rite of passage to becoming authentic Americans. "A hostile posture toward resident blacks must be struck at the Americanizing door before it will open," is how writer Toni Morrison so aptly describes it.
>
> The social imperative to choose a racial identity, and then only in purely black-and-white terms, impelled those of us in the second generation at first to jettison our native language and culture, to assimilate into either the white or black world.[32]

Every HR professional in the United States needs to understand the dynamics at work here in order to manage the single most important source of conflicts Hispanics have in the workplace.

The Problem of Misconstrued Language

Another minefield for HR specialists resides in the nature of language. In English, for instance, terms of endearment often center on food. One calls another *cupcake, pumpkin, sweetie pie,* or *honey* as a way to show affection. In Spanish, on the other hand, such terms often focus on physical attributes. Hispanics call one another *gordito* (fatty), *flaquito* (skinny), *guerito* (blondie), or *negrito* (darkie) to show intimacy and friendship. In the United States, because of the unfortunate legacy of racism, it can be seen as shocking or offensive for anyone to call another person *darkie,* especially since *negrito* sounds so similar to an English-language racial slur.

African Americans (and Caucasians as well) who are unaware of the linguistic and cultural nature of terms of endearment in the Spanish language are often offended by what is innocuous and innocent in Spanish. The conflicts that arise from this cultural misunderstanding, however, are real; they affect perceived hostility in the workplace and give rise to conflicts between African American and Hispanic employees. HR specialists need to address this concern and the origins of this conflict.

For someone to accuse a Hispanic of racism for using the term of endearment *negrito,* for example, in the workplace demonstrates a cultural misunderstanding. HRM must endeavor to educate non-Hispanic employees while also informing Hispanic employees, many of whom are unaware of the legacy of racism in the American mainstream culture, about the cultural and social implications of using a word like *negrito* in the United States.

With this in mind, it is important for HR specialists to understand the two interrelated issues here. Foremost is the question of acceptable language in the U.S. workplace. Many employees find any terms of endearment condescending, *sweetie pie* no less than *flaquito.* What is culturally acceptable language in society at large is not necessarily acceptable in a workplace environment. HR specialists seldom have difficulty making management staff understand this, but it may become more difficult where factory, warehouse, service, and retail workers are concerned. It's one thing to have professionals refrain from using such language, and it's quite another to get the rank-and-file hourly staff working a late night shift to refrain as well. The second point is the need to mitigate cultural misunderstanding, which entails educating all employees about the cultural differences.

Use of Discipline in Conflicts

Yet another aspect of Hispanic concerns about conflict focuses on how discipline is used to settle conflicts. To assuage these concerns, HRM policies need to be articulated clearly.

What is a conflict? It is a struggle between parties who perceive their goals as incompatible. Where Hispanics in the workplace are concerned, counterintuitive conflicts emerge in some areas: In matters of language, is it speaking Spanish or the inability of a manager to speak Spanish that is the source of a conflict? Is a Hispanic employee putting a religious icon on the wall creating a conflict for other employees? What about race—is there resentment among African Americans that a Hispanic who is also black identifies not with them but with Hispanics instead, opting for language and culture over biological race? Managers need to understand what kind of conflict they are dealing with to select the best tool to resolve it. Conflicts that arise from performance issues, behaviors that contradict established workplace rules and standards, or legal or ethical infractions might be best managed using a formal progressive discipline process; those that arise from workplace misunderstandings, personality conflicts, or miscommunication, in contrast, might be better off with conflict resolution.

Progressive Discipline

This method is founded on the basic principle that employees deserve the opportunity to understand what is expected of them in terms of performance and behavior. It relies on the use of a warning notice as a tool to explain to employees what is unacceptable and to give them the opportunity to change their behavior or performance through corrective action to avoid termination. If the employee is unable to meet performance standards and expectations, then termination may be in order.

Conflict Resolution

Conflicts can occur in the workplace over facts or data, over process or methods, over purpose, or over values, which are the most serious and oftentimes most emotional and difficult conflicts to resolve. Managers typically have choices when presented with a conflict. They can ignore it and hope it goes away, encourage people to get along, separate employees, restructure job duties, *mediate*, or *terminate*. The purpose of mediation is to reach and record a balanced, mutually acceptable agreement that defines everyone's future behavior with regard to the business problem caused by the conflict. Mediation helps employees step back out of the conflict and think about what they really want.

HR staff should encourage managers to consult them and discuss the organization's policies before making a decision about using any kind of resolution or discipline process.

PROFESSIONAL AND TRADE ORGANIZATIONS SUPPORTING HISPANICS

Employers can send powerful signals of encouragement by endorsing efforts to nurture and develop the career aspirations of Hispanic employees through professional and trade organizations. Appendix 3 offers a list of major organizations that provide support, primarily to salaried Hispanics. For HR practitioners and management alike, this is a very straightforward proposition since it does not differ from the way other constituencies organize support for their trades or professions. Having HRM and line managers voice encouragement or facilitate these efforts by actions such as providing conference rooms after hours to employees who wish to hold regional meetings of the organization of which they are members is a concrete step that a company can offer. Hispanic managers expect the same consideration for their trade and professional affiliations as their employers provide to other employees with similar affiliations.

Another aspect to supporting the efforts of Hispanic workers: helping them send remittances to their families and communities in their home countries. This is an area where HRM can position itself at the forefront of ensuring an organization is a socially responsible corporate citizen where the firm's Hispanic workers are concerned. Most Hispanics, whether they are immigrants or not, support development programs in their hometowns. In the past decade these endeavors have grown and become more structured. Hometown associations, known as HTAs, have sprung up throughout the United States, though they flourish primarily in the Midwest and west of the Mississippi. Xóchitl Bada, of the Sociology Department at the University of Notre Dame, has studied the emergence of HTAs and the role they play in the social and economic life of Hispanics. She explains:

> Contemporary Mexican HTAs represent values of commitment, solidarity, altruism, and patriotism. HTAs in the United States are heirs to the historical mutual aid societies and welfare organizations created in the late nineteenth and early twentieth century in order to provide sickness care and death benefits at a time when such services were unavailable for many immigrant groups.... In the last decade, these HTAs have received financial and technical support from the Mexican government through its consular offices.... There are currently more than 600 Mexican hometown clubs and associations registered in 30 cities in the United States. In Los Angeles alone, there are 218 Mexican HTAs.[33]

Employers that recognize Hispanic involvement in HTAs as an area in which the firm can validate its recognition of, and commitment to, the integrity of the Hispanic experience in the United States enjoy a sustainable, competitive advantage in attracting Hispanics to the ranks of their workforce. Xóchitl Bada also gave us listings for a number of resources HR professionals can use to identify HTA organizations that address the specific needs of various Hispanic constituencies:

Selected Hispanic Hometown Association (HTA) Resources

Asociación Tepeyac
Web site provides critical support and resources for the undocumented Mexican and Hispanic population living and working in the New York City area.
www.tepeyac.org.ns50.alentus.com/intro.asp

Enlaces América
Supports the development of Latin American immigrant–led organizations as national and regional leaders in the Americas.
www.enlacesamerica.org

League of United Latin American Citizens (LULAC)
Largest and oldest Hispanic organization in the United States, empowering the Hispanic community at the local, state, and national levels through education programs, citizenship and voter registration drives, housing advocacy, and youth leadership training programs.
www.lulac.org

Mexican American Legal Defense and Education Fund (MALDEF)
Ensures and protects the civil rights of Hispanics throughout the country through litigation, education, and outreach.
www.maldef.org

Mexico Solidarity Network
Posts news, reports, and analysis of issues affecting U.S.–Mexico relations.
www.mexicosolidarity.org/site

National Council of La Raza
Web site offers extensive resources and links to support and strengthen Hispanic community–based organizations, as well as research, policy analysis, and advocacy on issues such as education, immigration, housing, health, employment and training, and civil rights enforcement.
www.nclr.org

Other HTA organizations:
Federación de Clubes Zacatecanos
http://federacionzacatecana.org/index.php

Asociación Nacional de Empresa Comercializadoras de Productores del Campo (ANEC)
www.laneta.apc.org/anec/

Illinois Coalition for Immigrant and Refugee Rights (ICIIR)
www.icirr.org

Embassy of Mexico in the United States (Washington, DC)
Has contact information on Mexican consulates throughout the U.S.—contact to learn about local HTA resources in each consulate's specific region.
www.embassyofmexico.org

    For all Hispanic workers, one overriding factor in deciding whether an employer is attractive or unattractive is how they perceive an organization's sensitivity to their identity. Hispanic sensibilities, for instance, are offended by the failure of HRM to acknowledge their identity. Over the past decade a significant body of research concludes that proper HRM incorporates the development of "social capital" through programs that address issues of importance to the workforce. "Recent work on communities and various aspects of knowledge management promote a kind of managerial intervention that encourages natural development, that orients rather than orders, that provides nourishment rather than blueprints," Dan Cohen and Lawrence Prusak write in the *Harvard Business Review*. "Some describe the difference in terms of a distinction between management and leadership. Some use the analogy of gardening or husbandry, the stewardship of an ecology as opposed to the construction or maintenance of a machine. Successful investment in social capital—which of course includes investment in communities—demands this kind of organic approach. Networks of social connection, trust, and commitment cannot be manufactured or engineered, only encouraged. Social capital thrives on authenticity and withers in the presence of phoniness or manipulation."[34]

EXIT INTERVIEWS FOR HISPANIC EMPLOYEES

In an ideal world, long-term employment would be the norm, particularly when finding suitable employees is a difficult task. That Hispanic employees leave the firm undermines efforts at sustained diversity.

This is a decades-old challenge, and one that is noticeable to an organization's external constituencies. "Many early diversity officers started with the obvious—recruitment and hiring. Efforts to fill positions with qualified candidates from underrepresented communities were stepped up, and diversity officers strategically partnered with staffing agencies and leadership groups that serve women, minorities and persons with disabilities," Bill Picture notes in his report, "Are Diversity Officers Changing the Face of Corporate America?" published in *Asian Week*. "But these efforts did little more than colorize a sector of the workforce. Creating a truly diverse workplace, they soon realized, was going to require applying diversity management principles across the board."[35]

Employees do leave, after all. When they go, they have valuable information and insight that they can offer to improve the work environment, opportunities, and productivity of the employees who remain. Exit interviews allow HR professionals to improve their understanding of their own firms and the mind-set of their Hispanic employees. Indeed, one purpose of the exit interview is to help management nurture and reward Hispanic talent within the organization, as well as to attract Hispanic talent from outside.

Exit interviews represent a prime opportunity to gain candid information on employment conditions within the organization. Such debriefings can provide objective feedback on the conditions or patterns of management behavior that may have contributed to an employee's decision to leave.[36] HR specialists must be aware, however, that Hispanic employees who are leaving nonmanagement positions may still have considerable reticence in speaking their minds, or in being critical of the company, colleagues, or managers. Culturally, Hispanics usually are taught that being respectful of others entails being slow to criticize. One strategy for addressing this concern is simply to ask questions in a positive tone: How can we improve your department? What can your manager do to become a better manager? Is there a practice that your colleagues follow that could be made better?

Normally an exit interview is conducted at the time an employee is terminating employment with a company, but it may also be done at the time of an internal transfer. With the usual departing-employee interview, some companies have chosen to wait a while, conducting the interview well after the termination to gain additional information without the employee being concerned about some form of retribution by the employer.

To gain the employee's confidence and get the most candid answers, it is best to have a neutral party conduct the interview. This usually means someone not involved with the day-to-day supervision of the employee or someone not in a direct line of authority to the supervisor. In many organizations, this is someone from HR. A word of caution here: Make sure the person conducting the interview is perceived by the terminating employee as someone who will take the resulting information seriously. Of course, this individual must also have good listening and interviewing skills and use good judgment in evaluating and following up on the answers provided. For as much valuable insight as possible, it is imperative to steer conversations away from too much negativity. Before exit interviews, gently remind the departing employees that *how* things are said is more important than *what* is said; this will help keep things positive while protecting departing employees from burning their bridges or saying things they will subsequently regret.

Many companies use both internal and external (third-party) exit interview sources. At times outside parties can provide data to the organization aggregated in a variety of ways, such as by job classification, department, division, or race and ethnicity. Also, if a company has an employee opinion survey, it would beneficial to ask the same or similar questions at an exit interview, so that trends in responses can be more easily detected. If terminated employees' responses mirror active employee responses, it allows the HR professional to refine the area of need. Furthermore, there is the general understanding that information or opinions volunteered can, or will be, quoted and distributed within the organization. The only expectation for confidentiality during an exit interview is in the case where there is a claim of discrimination, sexual harassment, or unlawful activity. In such instances, information from the exit interview is to remain confidential until the matter is investigated thoroughly and a written report of findings has been completed and filed.

Example 8 presents a representative set of questions for an acceptable exit interview. The purpose is to engage the employee in one final, official conversation that elicits information about the workplace environment for the Hispanic employee, which can be used constructively to improve the organization's diversity program.

CONCLUSION

Over the past quarter century HRM has evolved into a powerful tool that has served the nation well. Through innovative, forward-thinking, and developing efforts, the nation's workplace has grown tremendously in diversity, affording entire categories of Americans opportunities that a mere generation ago seemed implausible. Each new "first" has validated the ability of HR practitioners to expand opportunities for all. With Hispanics speedily emerging as a major part of the workforce, management now depends on HRM to develop, define, and refine policies that can help organizations throughout the entire nation incorporate Hispanic employees. The hot-button issues, from bilingualism in the workplace, to resentment from African Americans at being displaced as the nation's largest minority, to Hispanics' demand that the family be redefined, have sent shock waves reverberating throughout the nation, and HRM is at the forefront of confronting the socioeconomic consequences of these changes. The challenges facing HR professionals are tremendous, but the rewards are well worth the efforts they require.

EXAMPLE 8

Exit Interview

Employee Name ....

Dept. .... Title ....

Manager ....

Length of Service .... Last Day of Work ....

1. Overall, what did you enjoy the most at [Company]?
2. Did you know what was expected of you at work? If so, how did you know?
3. How did your manager regularly communicate with you and tell you what was going on?
4. Did you have the materials and equipment you needed?
5. Was your department adequately staffed for the workload?
6. Were your skills, abilities, and experiences fully utilized in your position?
7. When was the last time you received recognition or praise for doing good work?
8. How did your supervisor or manager encourage your development?
9. Were you treated with fairness and respect as an employee of [Company]?
10. Do you feel that your supervisor was trusting and concerned for your welfare and supported you? If not, be specific.
11. What was the main reason that you decided to leave?
12. Before you decided to leave, what changes would have kept you from leaving [Company]?
13. Please let us know which organization you are joining and what it offers that [Company] does not?
14. What suggestions for change or improvement do you have that would make your department or [Company] a better place to work?
15. Was either language or your comfort as a Hispanic an issue for you, your colleagues, or the manager in your department or in [Company] as a whole?
16. Would you recommend either your department or [Company] to a family member?

Source: Adapted from materials used by Human Resources, Baptist Health South Florida.

IN REVIEW

- Hispanics, who are the fastest-growing segment of the U.S. workforce, require diversity programs that integrate them into the workplace.

  - HRM must develop diversity programs that speak to the specific linguistic, cultural, and family needs of Hispanic employees.

  - HRM policies must allow for a seamless integration of Hispanic workers through diversity programs that make them feel welcome and comfortable—and then incorporate them into the organization.

- Effective communication skills are crucial to Hispanics' success.

  - Language remains a crucial concern as the nation evolves into a bilingual consumer economy.

  - English as a second language (ESL), accent reduction and elimination courses, and introductory Spanish need to be provided or facilitated as part of a sound diversity program.

- Recognition of work well done and nonpecuniary rewards are important aspects of Hispanic culture.

  - HRM policies must reflect the value that Hispanics place on continuing education as a reward for a job well done.

  - Affinity programs that are endorsed or facilitated by the organization can strengthen the bonds between the organization and its Hispanic workforce.

- Mentoring programs, a time-honored mechanism for rewarding Hispanic employees, should include tools for assessing the needs for, and the identification of, mentors.

- Hispanic employees challenge HRM's concept of work-life balance.
  - Hispanic employees add their voices to other constituencies in seeking to expand how organizations define *family*.
  - Hispanic employees are more likely to choose to remain the primary caregivers for elderly parents, so they seek to have health benefits extended to include these responsibilities.
  - Hispanic employees are extremely likely to leave the workforce if necessary to fulfill what they understand to be their obligations to family.

- Workplace conflicts and dispute resolution center on the growing "black versus brown" tensions in American society.
  - The increasing population of Hispanics is fast displacing African Americans, a fact that is creating tension between the nation's two largest minorities.
  - HR professionals need to understand the tension that is invading the workplace, and to develop seminars, workshops, and classroom instruction that fosters a dialogue between African American and Hispanic employees.
  - HR professionals must also be aware of the peculiar phenomenon that, as Hispanics become acculturated, they tend to adopt antiblack attitudes.
  - HRM policies need to embrace conflict resolution and progressive discipline processes that are crucial to the seamless integration of Hispanics in the workplace.

- Supporting professional and trade organizations is an indispensable way for management to support their Hispanic employees.

  – Management must encourage Hispanic employees to participate in professional and trade organizations that are appropriate to their professions or interests.

  – HRM policies must, for firms that have a significant number of nonsalaried Hispanic employees, endorse hometown associations (HTAs) in order to send a powerful signal to employees about the organization's commitment to their concerns.

- When Hispanics leave the organization, HR practitioners can elicit information that will strengthen their diversity program.

  – Proper exit interviews are valuable tools to improve the working environment for the Hispanic employees who remain.

  – Exit interviews can provide HR professionals with insights that are indispensable to strengthening the organization's diversity program, for the good of all employees.

APPENDIX 1

Hispanic Versus *Latino* in the Workplace

Hispanic and *Latino* are not synonyms; they cannot be used interchangeably.

While every Latino is a Hispanic, not every Hispanic is a Latino. The increasing presence of Hispanics in the workforce requires a clear understanding of terminology.

It is not an obvious matter, but it is one fraught with perils. Five centuries after Columbus's voyage to America, the word *Hispanic* has come to describe the process of acculturation through which indigenous peoples (Native Americans throughout Latin America) adopt Western norms: language, religion, technology, and political economies. Throughout Latin American colonial history, *Hispanic* has referred to the process of becoming Christian and learning Spanish; a person can be a full-blooded Zapotec and, by virtue of being Christian and speaking Spanish, not be indigenous or Native American but simply *Hispanic* in a cultural sense, an identity that is second only to their ethnic or national identity.

Hispanic first came into widespread use throughout Europe in the tenth century. Saxon writer Hrotsvit of Gandersheim, a nun familiar with the court of Holy Roman Emperor Otto I, is credited with first documenting use of the word outside the Iberian peninsula. "The brilliant ornament of the world shown in the west, a noble city newly known for the military prowess that its Hispanic colonizers had brought, Cordoba was its name and it was wealthy and famous for its pleasures and resplendent in all things," she reported to the Teutonic court.[1]

Latinoamericano as a cultural moniker came into widespread use throughout the second half of the eighteenth century, culminating in the independence movement beginning in 1810. Throughout Spanish America, *Latino* came to denote pride, a brotherhood that encompassed an affinity for the other nations emerging from the ruins of New Spain (Mexico and Central America) and New Granada (most of South America, save Brazil). This is how *Latino* came to be used and understood throughout Latin America from colonial times to the present. During colonialism, individuals born in the New World of Spanish (or European) parents were called *criollos*. After independence, while concepts of nationalism were formative, some landowning elites called themselves *ladino* (with a "d") or *americano* (with a lower case "a," as for all adjectives in Spanish).

Latino first appeared in American English in the mid-1940s, as slang, a shortening of *latinoamericano*. (This came into use through the military, primarily because many Latin American immigrants joined the armed forces to improve their lives in the United States.) Latin Americans living in the United States who were not fluent in English were the first to use it. Throughout the 1970s and 1980s, it supplanted *Chicano* among civil rights activists, primarily in California, who wanted to reach out to Hispanics who were not of Mexican ancestry. This is instructive, for it underscores the political nature of how *Latino* was embraced by activists promoting a specific social, political, and economic agenda. The term *Chicano*, for instance, was used by Mexican immigrants in the United States as a bold affirmation of identity. Today, *Chicano* has been supplanted by *Hispanic* generally, and by *Latino* or *Latina* in colloquial use. Cultural anthropologists studying American society, following in the pioneering work of Renato Rosaldo, identify *Latino* or *Latina* as a linguistic marker that denotes the concept of "cultural citizenship."

APPENDIX 2
Important Hispanic Dates and Events

JANUARY

1

Año Nuevo, New Year's Day.

6

Día de los Reyes Magos or Día de los Santos Reyes, Epiphany. In many Catholic countries, this is the time for Christmas fun. Traditionally, the children receive gifts on this day rather than on Christmas. Since the Three Kings brought gifts, people exchange presents and children put out their shoes for the magi to leave presents inside.

10

Birthday of Eugenio Maria de Hostos (Puerto Rico). An educator and writer who fought Spanish colonial rule and helped abolish slavery in Cuba and Puerto Rico.

21

Feast of Nuestra Sra. de Altagracia, or Our Lady of Highest Grace, the patron virgin of the Dominican Republic.

26

Juan Pablo Duarte Day (Dominican Republic). Commemorates the hero of Dominican independence from Haiti.

28

Birth of José Martí (Cuba). A political activist, independence hero, and poet who led the fight for Cuba's independence from Spain.

FEBRUARY

2

Treaty of Guadalupe Hidalgo (Mexico). This treaty, which marked the end of the Mexican War, established U.S. sovereignty over 1,193,061 square miles of formerly disputed or Mexican territory, including the present states of Texas, Arizona, California, and Utah, and parts of New Mexico, Colorado, and Wyoming.

5

Día de la Constitucion, Constitution Day (Mexico).

24

Flag Day (Mexico).

27

Dominican Republic Independence Day and beginning of Dominican Carnival. The pre-Lenten celebration coincides with the anniversary of the Dominican Republic's independence from Haiti.

MARCH

5

Carnaval, an official Mexican holiday that kicks off a five-day celebration of the libido before the Catholic Lent. Beginning the weekend before Lent, Carnaval, is celebrated exuberantly with parades, floats, and dancing in the streets.

21

Birth of Benito Juarez (Mexico). One of the national heroes of Mexico, Juarez served his country as president during the turbulent period from 1855 until his death in 1872 and instituted a number of civil reforms. He led the military resistance to the French emperor's attempt to impose Maximilian of Austria as emperor of Mexico.

22

Emancipation Day (Puerto Rico). Slaves in Puerto Rico were freed on this date in 1873.

31

Cesar Chavez holiday (U.S. Southwest). This holiday honors the Mexican-American labor and civil rights activist who gained attention in the 1960s as the leader of the United Farm Workers. His nonviolent advocacy approach earned him worldwide respect. California, Arizona, and Texas have made the day a state holiday; other states are considering doing so.

APRIL

Varies

La Semana Santa, or Easter and the Holy Week. Observed in Spain, Mexico, and all of Latin America. Easter is one of the highest holy days of the year. The week leading up to Easter involves solemn processions, prayer, masses, and other preparation for Jesus's rebirth. Customs in the United States include *cascarones*, the Mexican version of an Easter egg: eggshells filled with confetti.

11

Battle of Rivas Day (Costa Rica). Anniversary of victory over Confederate invaders in 1856. An army consisting mainly of farmers armed with machetes forced William Walker, an American who planned to enslave Central American countries, back into Nicaragua.

19

Landing of the 33 Patriots Day (Uruguay). Anniversary of the landing of thirty-three exiles in 1825, who began a campaign leading to Uruguay's independence.

MAY

1

Primero de Mayo or Día del Trabajo or Día del Trabajador. A national holiday celebrated in most Spanish-speaking countries, equivalent to the U.S. Labor Day.

5

Cinco de Mayo (Mexico). Commemorates the victory of Mexican forces over the French army at the Battle of Puebla on May 5, 1862. It is primarily a regional holiday celebrated in the Mexican state and capital city of Puebla and in other parts of Mexico. It is also celebrated in U.S. cities with a significant Mexican population. It is not, as many people think, Mexico's Independence Day, which is actually September 16.

10

Día de las Madres, or Day of the Mothers, observed on this date in Mexico and other Latin American countries.

15

Día de Independencia. Independence Day for Paraguay.

18

Battle of Las Piedras (Paraguay). Anniversary of the end of the conflict between Uruguay and Brazil in 1828.

20

Cuba's birth as an independent republic in 1902.

25

May Revolution Day for Argentina. It commemorates the establishment of an autonomous government resulting from the revolution on this day in 1810. This date is known in Argentina as Revolución de Mayo.

JUNE

19

Artigas Day (Uruguay). Celebrates the birthday of General José Gervasio Artigas, an early hero of Uruguay.

24

Feast of San Juan Bautista, or St. John the Baptist, patron saint of Puerto Rico's capital, San Juan. Other Latin Americans celebrate the day as El Día de San Pedro.

29

San Pedro y San Pablo, St. Peter and St. Paul. Celebrated in Spain and many Latin American countries.

JULY

5

Independence Day for Venezuela.

6–14

Los Sanfermines, or the San Fermin Festival or the Running of the Bulls in Pamplona, Spain.

9

Independence Day for Argentina.

19

Revolution Day (Nicaragua). Anniversary of the day the National Liberation Army declared victory over the Somoza dictatorship.

20

Independence Day for Colombia.

24

Birth of Simón Bolívar (Colombia, Venezuela, Panama). Known as El Libertador, the Liberator, he led the rebellion against Spanish rule that established the independence of Venezuela, Colombia, Ecuador, Peru, and Bolivia.

25

Constitution Day in Puerto Rico.

25

Santiago Apostol, St. James (Spain). Celebrates the patron saint of Spain.

26

Communist Revolution Day, Cuba.

28

Independence Day for Peru.

AUGUST

1–6
Feast of El Salvador del Mundo, Savior of the World, the patron saint of El Salvador. Salvadoreans celebrate with street fairs and a *bajada,* a procession honoring the saint.

6
Independence Day for Bolivia.

7
Battle of Boyacá (Colombia): A public holiday celebrating the anniversary of the defeat of the Spanish in 1819 in the province of Boyacá.

10
Independence Day for Ecuador.

15
Feast of the Assumption, celebrated by Catholics in Spanish-speaking countries. It celebrates the belief in Mary's ascent to heaven.

17
San Martín Day. Anniversary of the death of General José Francisco de San Martín, liberator of Argentina.

25
Independence Day for Uruguay.

SEPTEMBER

8
Feast of Nuestra Señora de la Caridad del Cobre, patron saint of Cuba.

15
Independence Day for Central American nations (El Salvador, Costa Rica, Guatemala, Honduras, and Nicaragua). Commemorates the declaration of independence from Spain in 1821.

16

Mexican Independence Day or 16 de Septiembre. Celebrates the day that Miguel Hidalgo delivered El Grito de Dolores and announced the Mexican revolt against Spanish rule.

18

Independence Day for Chile. Also known as Fiestas Patrias and El Dieciocho.

23

Grito de Lares. Anniversary of the uprising that initiated the movement for Puerto Rican independence from Spain.

OCTOBER

10

Grito de Yara (Cuba). The revolt of Yara began Cuba's struggle for independence from Spain on this day.

12

Día de la Hispanidad, Spanish National Day (Spain). In most Spanish-speaking countries this is celebrated as *Día de la Raza,* Columbus Day, or Panamerican Day. This holiday commemorates the arrival of Christopher Columbus in America. A holiday with complex and changing meanings. Hispanics in the United States are split on their political feelings about the holiday.

18

Señor de los Milagros, or Our Lord of Miracles (Peru). Also called the holiday of the Purple Christ. The holiday stems from the 1700s, when a huge earthquake destroyed Lima, but a painting of the Purple Christ was not affected.

NOVEMBER

1

Día de Todos los Santos, All Saints' Day. This Christian holiday celebrates the memory of all early martyrs and saints.

2

Día de los Muertos, or Day of the Dead (Mexico, Central America). (This is All Souls' Day in English-speaking countries.) Traditionally, it is a day to celebrate and honor one's ancestors. It's based on the belief that there is interaction between the living world and the world of spirits. On the Día de los Muertos, the *almas,* or the spirits of the dead, are said to come back for family reunions. Many Hispanics celebrate by setting up *ofrendas* (altars) in their homes to honor the memory of deceased loved ones and to welcome their visiting souls. Others visit their loved one's cemetery plot and decorate it with flowers, candles, and food. The holiday is celebrated with family and community gatherings, music, and feasting, and the festivity of its observance acknowledges death as an integral part of life.

3

Independence Day for Panama.

5

First Call for Independence (El Salvador). Commemorates the first battle for independence in 1811, led by Padre José Matías Delgado.

11

Cartagena Independence Day (Colombia). Commemorates the city of Cartagena's declaration of independence in 1811.

19

Feast of Nuestra Señora de la Divina Providencia, or Our Lady of Divine Providence, Puerto Rico's patron virgin.

20

Mexican Revolution Day. Anniversary of the Mexican Revolution of 1910 against dictator Porfirio Díaz.

DECEMBER

6

Day of the Constitution, Spain.

8

Immaculate Conception, celebrated in many Spanish-speaking countries.

12

Día de la Virgen de Guadalupe, or the Feast Day of Our Lady of Guadalupe, patron saint of Mexico. The Virgin Mary is said to have appeared to an Indian named Juan Diego on this date in 1531.

16–24

Las Posadas (Mexico, Guatemala, and other Central American countries). *Las Posadas* commemorates the journey of Mary and Joseph to Bethlehem and their search for a place to stay. Family and friends visit one another in their homes and enjoy conversations and traditional foods, and visitors sing carols. Colombians celebrate a similar holiday called La Novena, where, for nine days, families pray and sing traditional carols.

24 & 25

La Nochebuena y Navidad, Christmas Eve and Christmas. In many Catholic countries, people attend midnight mass on Christmas Eve. Preparing traditional foods is also an integral part of the holiday. Mexicans get together for a *tamalada,* or a tamal-making session. (A *tamal* is usually made of shredded pork and corn meal called *masa,* tucked into a corn shuck or leaf.) Puerto Ricans prepare *pasteles puertorriqueños,* which are plantain leaves stuffed with pinto beans, pork, raisins, and other ingredients. Cubans and Puerto Ricans often have a *lechón asado,* a roasted pork dish.

APPENDIX 3

Organizations for Hispanic Employees

PROFESSIONAL AND TRADE ASSOCIATIONS

Association of Hispanic Advertising Agencies (AHAA)
Founded: 1996. *Members:* 170 (2002).
From mission statement: "The mission of AHAA is to grow, strengthen and protect the Hispanic marketing and advertising industry by providing leadership in raising awareness of the value of the Hispanic market opportunities and enhancing the professionalism of the industry."

Association of Hispanic Healthcare Executives (AHHE)
Founded: 1988. *Members:* 166 (2002).
From mission statement: "AHHE was founded in 1988 as a national voluntary organization seeking to foster programs and policies to increase the presence of Hispanics in health administration professions. AHHE is the first organization devoted exclusively to Hispanic healthcare executives and to the education of the healthcare industry about the Hispanic healthcare marketplace."

Association of Latino Professionals in Finance and Accounting (ALPFA)
Founded: 1982. *Members:* 2000 (2002).
From mission statement: "ALPFA is the leading professional association dedicated to enhancing opportunities for Latinos in the accounting, finance and related professions. ALPFA is a not-for-profit entity registered with the Internal Revenue Service."

Hispanic Association on Corporate Responsibility (HACR)
Founded: 1986.
From mission statement: "HACR's mission is to ensure the inclusion of Hispanics in Corporate America at a level commensurate with our economic contributions. HACR focuses on four areas of corporate

economic activity and refers to them as indicators of corporate responsibility and 'Market Reciprocity.' They are: Employment, Procurement, Philanthropy and Governance. In pursuit of its mission, HACR offers Corporate America access to the Hispanic community—its talents, its entrepreneurs and its leadership—creating a forum to ensure corporate responsibility and market reciprocity for the nation's Hispanic population."

Hispanic Dental Association
Founded: 1990. *Members:* 1,950.
From mission statement: "To provide leadership and represent professionals who share a common commitment to improve the oral health of the Hispanic community."

Hispanic Designers (HDI)
Founded: 1985.
From mission statement: "Dedicated to highlighting Hispanic talent and cultural contributions in the design industry; provides a national focus on positive contributions by Hispanics in the U.S. by showcasing Hispanic excellence; works to create educational opportunities and build public awareness about major issues affecting education, health and overall well-being of Hispanic-Americans."

Hispanic National Bar Association (HNBA)
Founded: 1972. *Members:* 22,000 (2002).
From mission statement: "HNBA is a professional association representing the interest of over 25,000 Hispanic American attorneys, judges, law professors, and law students in the United States and Puerto Rico."

Hispanic Organization of Latin Actors (HOLA)
Founded: 1975. *Members:* 530 (2002).
From mission statement: "HOLA is an arts service organization committed to exploring and expanding available avenues for projecting Hispanic artists and their culture into the mainstream of Anglo-American industry and culture. HOLA exposes the entertainment and communications industries to the availability, diversity and quality preparation of Hispanic artists. HOLA is recognized and recommended as a reliable source of information on Hispanic talent."

Hispanic-Serving Health Professions Schools, Inc. (HSHPS)
Founded: 1996.

From mission statement: "HSHPS is a non-profit organization established in 1996 in response to the President's Executive Order 12900, 'Educational Excellence for Hispanic Americans.' The Association was established with support from the U.S. Department of Health and Human Services as a part of their 'Hispanic Agenda for Action Initiative.' HSHPS currently represents 23 medical schools and 3 public health schools."

National Association of Hispanic Journalists (NAHJ)
Founded: 1984. *Members:* 1,500 (2002).

From mission statement: "Organization dedicated to the recognition and professional advancement of Hispanics in the news industry. Scholarships and internships for Latino students of journalism are offered annually."

National Association of Latino Elected and Appointed Officials (NALEO)
Founded: 1976.

From mission statement: "Hispanic elected and appointed officials and people who support them, including both individuals and corporate members; associate members are others interested in furthering association goals. A comprehensive advocacy and leadership network dedicated to the advancement of the Hispanic people. Serves as a vehicle through which Hispanic needs and concerns may be articulated, particularly in Washington, DC and the southwestern U.S., on issues such as economic development, U.S. citizenship, legalization, and Latino child poverty. Serves as a clearinghouse on citizenship information; compiles Hispanic voting statistics."

National Hispanic Corporate Council (NHCC)
Founded: 1985. *Members:* 90.

From mission statement: "Membership organization of Fortune 1000 companies, serving as their principal resource for information, expertise, and counsel on selected Hispanic issues affecting corporate objective, and advocating for increased employment, leadership, and business opportunities for Hispanics in corporate America."

United States Hispanic Chamber of Commerce (USHCC)
Founded: 1979. *Members:* 100,000 (2002).
From mission statement: "Hispanic and other business firms interested in the development of Hispanic business and promotion of business leadership and economic interests in the Hispanic community."

United States–Mexico Chamber of Commerce (USMCOC)
Founded: 1973. *Members:* 2,000.
From mission statement: "A non-profit business association chartered in Washington D.C. The coalition of businessmen created a bilateral organization to promote trade, investment and joint ventures on both sides of the border."

EDUCATIONAL AND CULTURAL ASSOCIATIONS

American Association of Teachers of Spanish and Portuguese (AATSP)
Founded: 1917.
From mission statement: "Since its inception in 1917, AATSP has promoted the study and teaching of Hispanic, Luso-Brazilian, and other related languages, literatures, and cultures at all levels. Through an exchange of pedagogical and scholarly information, the AATSP encourages heritage and second language study and supports projects to that end."

ASPIRA Association
Founded: 1969.
From mission statement: "The ASPIRA Association promotes the empowerment of the Puerto Rican and Latino community by developing and nurturing the leadership, intellectual, and cultural potential of its youth so that they may contribute their skills and dedication to the fullest development of the Puerto Rican and Latino community everywhere."

Association of Hispanic Arts (AHA)
Founded: 1975.
From mission statement: "AHA is a not-for-profit organization dedicated to the advancement of Latino arts, artists and art organizations as an in-

tegral part of the cultural life of the nation. We facilitate projects and programs designed to foster the appreciation, growth and well being of the Latino cultural community."

Hispanic Association of Colleges and Universities (HACU)
Founded: 1986.
From mission statement: "The HACU is a national association representing the accredited colleges and universities in the United States where Hispanic students constitute at least 25 percent of the total student enrollment. HACU's goal is to bring together colleges and universities, schools, corporations, governmental agencies and individuals to establish partnerships for: promoting the development of Hispanic-serving colleges and universities; improving access to and the quality of postsecondary educational opportunities for Hispanic students; and meeting the needs of business, industry and government through the development and sharing of resources, information and expertise."

Hispanic Educational Telecommunications System (HETS)
Founded: 1993.
From mission statement: "HETS is a telecommunications consortium of colleges and universities in the United States and Puerto Rico. Its mission is to widen the access of Hispanics to higher education and training opportunities through educational telecommunications and distance learning. HETS members connect to each other through a diversity of telecommunications and information technologies. These technologies may include the HETS C-band satellite network system or compressed video through telephone lines or ISDN. All member institutions connect to each other through the Internet."

Hispanic Genealogical Society
Founded: 1993.
From mission statement: "People interested in Hispanic genealogy. Aims to increase awareness in the field of Hispanic genealogical research. Produces newsletters, annual journal and holds meetings."

Latin American Studies Association (LASA)
Founded: 1966.
From mission statement: "LASA is the largest professional Association in the world for individuals and institutions engaged in the study of Latin America. With over 5,500 members, thirty percent of whom reside outside the United States, LASA is the one Association that brings together experts on Latin America from all disciplines and diverse occupational endeavors, across the globe."

The Mexican American Legal Defense and Educational Fund (MALDEF)
Founded: 1968.
From mission statement: "MALDEF is the leading nonprofit Latino litigation, advocacy and educational outreach institution in the United States. MALDEF's mission is to foster sound public policies, laws and programs to safeguard the civil rights of the 40 million Latinos living in the United States and to empower the Latino community to fully participate in our society. MALDEF achieves its mission by concentrating its efforts on the following areas: employment, education, immigration, political access, language and public resource equity issues. Headquartered in Los Angeles, MALDEF has regional offices in Atlanta, Los Angeles, San Antonio, Chicago, and Washington, D.C., with a satellite office in Sacramento and program offices in Phoenix, Albuquerque, and Houston. The thirty-five member board of directors is comprised of leaders from the public and private sector, government, and law firms. MALDEF's staff of 75 employees includes 22 attorneys."

National Association of Latino Arts and Culture (NALAC)
Founded: 1989.
From mission statement: "Today NALAC serves more than 300 Latino arts organizations in the United States, including organizations found in Mexican American, Puerto Rican, Cuban, Dominican, Central American, and South American communities within the United States. Through its regional meetings, publications, and programs NALAC provides direct services to its constituency and collects information about current needs and challenges for Latino artists and organizations."

National Hispanic Scholarship Fund (NHSF)
Founded: 1975.
From mission statement: "The Hispanic Scholarship Fund (HSF) is the largest Hispanic scholarship-granting organization in the nation. HSF recognizes and rewards outstanding Hispanic students in higher education throughout the United States, Puerto Rico and the U.S. Virgin Islands. These students represent every region of the country, hundreds of institutions of higher learning and every segment of the Hispanic community. Founded in 1975, HSF has awarded more than 53,000 scholarships in excess of $89 million."

CIVIC AND SOCIAL ASSOCIATIONS

American GI Forum of the United States
Founded: 1948. *Members:* 20,000 (2002).
From mission statement: "Veterans of the Armed Forces of the U.S., primarily of Mexican origin, and their families."

Black, Indian, Hispanic, and Asian Women in Action (BIHA)
Founded: 1983. *Members:* 200 (2002).
From mission statement: "BIHA was established in recognition of a lack of communication and information sharing within and between Communities of Color regarding family violence. The unveiling of the size and growth of the tragedy of family violence in our society had resulted in the coming together of battered women from all corners of Minnesota. During the process of working on law changes and building a financial base to provide services to the victims of family violence, Communities of Color remained untapped and unassisted. BIHA was created to provide education, information and advocacy for and by Communities of Color and to serve as a forum for translating current concerns (family violence, racism, ageism, AIDS, chemical abuse) within communities of color for presentation to society as a whole."

Cesar E. Chavez Foundation
Founded: 1997.
From mission statement: "The Cesar E. Chavez Foundation was created to inspire today's and future generations by promoting the ideals of

César's life, work and vision. Through programs, events, and the development of educational materials, the Foundation works to ensure that César's vision of non-violence and hope will reach out to children, youth and to the general public. The Foundation will establish the César E. Chávez Library Complex at La Paz, in Keene, California—the site of the historic offices of the United Farm Workers, and César's own office until his passing. Here the Foundation will build a mission-style plaza encompassing César's graveside, establish an education center and create a library which will be open to the public."

Cuban American National Council (CNC)
Founded: 1972.
From mission statement: "Aims to identify the socioeconomic needs of the Cuban population in the U.S. and to promote needed human services. Services the needy through research and human services while advocating on behalf of Hispanics and other minority groups."

Dominican American National Roundtable (DANR)
Founded: 1972.
From mission statement: "The Dominican-American National Roundtable (DANR) is a non-partisan, non-profit corporation seeking to bring together the different voices of all people of Dominican origin in the United States. DANR is a national forum for analysis, planning, and action to advance the educational, economic, legal, social, cultural, and political interests of Dominican Americans. DANR aims to ensure for U.S. Dominicans the full exercise of the rights and freedoms guaranteed in the Constitution of the United States of America. With those objectives in mind, DANR is committed to enriching the quality of life in the United States by highlighting the contributions of Dominicans to the larger American society. The Dominican American National Roundtable has as its central mission to serve as 'a national forum for analysis, planning, and action to advance the educational, economic, legal, social, cultural, and political interests of Dominican Americans.'"

League of United Latin American Citizens (LULAC)
Founded: 1929.
From mission statement: "LULAC is the oldest and largest Latino civil rights organization in the United States. Advances the economic condi-

tion, educational attainment, political influence, health and civil rights of Hispanic Americans through community-based programs operating at more than 700 LULAC councils nationwide."

MANA: A National Latina Organization

Founded: 1974.

From mission statement: "Association dedicated to advancing the status of American women of Hispanic descent. It hopes to reach this goal by promoting leadership among Hispanic women, advocating for public policies that benefit Latinas and their families, improving communication and furthering parity with Hispanics. Before 1994 this organization was known as: Mexican American Women's National Association."

National Alliance for Hispanic Health

Founded: 1973. *Members:* 1,000.

From mission statement: "National coalition of health, mental health, and human service agencies and organizations and professional individuals serving Hispanics. Primary mission is to improve health and human services to Hispanic communities throughout the United States, including Puerto Rico."

National Council of La Raza (NCLR)

Founded: 1968. *Members:* 7,000 (2002).

From mission statement: "NCLR is a private, nonprofit, nonpartisan, tax-exempt organization established in 1968 to reduce poverty and discrimination, and improve life opportunities for Hispanic Americans. NCLR is the largest constituency-based national Hispanic organization, serving all Hispanic nationality groups in all regions of the country."

National Puerto Rican Forum (NPRF)

Founded: 1957.

From mission statement: "NPRF is a leadership organization working to enhance the socio-economic conditions of the Latino population and other underserved communities through information, advocacy and direct services.... Designs and implements programs in areas of job counseling, training and placement, and English language skills, to deal effectively with the problems of Puerto Ricans and other Hispanics. Sponsors Career Services and Job Placement Program at the national level. Also provides specialized programs in New York, such as: Employment Placement Initiative, Access and Family Services in the schools, and job counseling."

Puerto Rican Legal Defense and Education Fund (PRLDEF)
Founded: 1972.
From mission statement: "Established to protect the civil rights of Puerto Ricans and other Latinos and to ensure their equal protection under the law. Involved in litigation, advocacy, and legal work."

POLITICAL AND LABOR ASSOCIATIONS

Congressional Hispanic Caucus (CHC)
Founded: 1976. *Members:* 18.
From mission statement: "The Congressional Hispanic Caucus (CHC) is an informal group of 18 members of Congress of Hispanic descent. The Caucus is dedicated to voicing and advancing, through the legislative process, issues affecting Hispanic Americans in the United States and the insular areas. The CHC was founded in December 1976 as a legislative service organization of the U.S. House of Representatives. Today, the CHC is organized as a congressional member organization, governed under the Rules of Congress and comprised solely of Members of the United States Congress."

Cuban American National Foundation (CANF)
Founded: 1981. *Members:* 3000 (2002).
From mission statement: "CANF is a non-profit organization dedicated to advancing freedom and democracy in Cuba. Established in Florida in 1981, CANF is the largest Cuban organization in exile, with thousands of members across the United States and other countries, representing a cross section of the Cuban exile community as well as friends of Cuban freedom from around the world."

Hispanas Organized for Political Equality (HOPE)
Founded: 1989.
From mission statement: "HOPE is a nonprofit, non-partisan organization committed to ensuring political and economic parity for Latinas through leadership, advocacy, and education to benefit all communities and the status of women."

Hispanic Elected Local Officials (HELO)
Founded: 1976. *Members:* 150 (2002).

From mission statement: "The Hispanic Elected Local Officials (HELO) constituency group was established by the National League of Cities (NLC) in 1976 to serve as a forum for communication and information exchange among Hispanic local government elected officials and NLC colleagues. In addition to providing training and information services to its members, HELO also provides guidance to the NLC Board and to its policy committees on major public policy issues affecting the Hispanic and Latino communities."

Labor Council for Latin American Advancement (LCLAA)
Founded: 1973.

From mission statement: "A National Hispanic trade union association representing 1.4 million Hispanic working men and women in 43 international unions in 45 chapters in 17 states and Puerto Rico, LCLAA strives to achieve social dignity, economic and political justice, and higher living standards for every Hispanic worker."

United Farm Workers of America AFL-CIO (UFW)
Founded: 1970.

From mission statement: "A trade union representing American farm workers."

Notes

A Note on Terminology

1. See "Hispanic Economic Report on Nomenclature," February 2003, www.HispanicEconomics.com. HispanicEconomics.com is one of the nation's leading sources of information about Hispanic Americans.
2. See http://pewhispanic.org/files/reports/40.pdf. See also Juan Delgado-Moreira, "Cultural Citizenship and the Creation of European Identity," *Electronic Journal of Sociology,* 1997, 2(3).
3. For more information on the evolution of cultural identity among Hispanic Americans, see the work of Renato Rosaldo. His pioneering work on explaining the origins of the political nature of *Latino* identity in the United States has proved useful to European officials contemplating what it means to create a common European identity for the whole of Europe. For a greater understanding of these ideas, see R. Rosaldo, *Culture and Truth* (Boston: Beacon Press, 1989); R. Rosaldo, "Cultural Citizenship in San Jose, California," *PoLAR,* 1994, 17(2): 57–63; R. Rosaldo, "Cultural Citizenship and Educational Democracy," *Cultural Anthropology,* 1994, 9(3): 402–411; and R. Rosaldo, "Social Justice and the Crisis of National Communities," in *Colonial Discourse/Postcolonial Theory,* edited by F. Barker, P. Hulme, and M. Iversen (Manchester, England: Manchester University Press), pp. 239–252.

Introduction

1. Lynette Clemetson, "Hispanics Now Largest Minority, Census Shows," *New York Times,* January 22, 2003.
2. Roberto Suro is quoted in Clemetson, 2003.
3. See Samuel Huntington, "The Hispanic Challenge," *Foreign Affairs,* March/April 2004.
4. Figures taken from the Census Bureau; Department of Labor Statistics, *Hispanic Business;* and International Credit Monitor.
5. For reviews of this analysis, please see Morris M. Kleiner and others (eds.), *Human Resources and the Performance of the Firm* (Madison, WI: Industrial Relations Research Association, 1987); Brian E. Becker, Mark A. Huselid, Peter S. Pickus, and Michael F. Spratt, "HR as a Source of Shareholder Value: Research and Recommendations," *Human Resource Management,* Spring 1997, 36: 39–47; George Milkovich and Alexandra Wigdor (eds.), *Pay for Performance: Evaluating Performance Appraisal and Merit Pay* (Washington, DC: National Research Council, 1991); and James M. Rebitzer, "Efficiency Wages and Implicit Contracts: An Institutional Evaluation," in

Microeconomic Issues in Labor Economics: New Approaches, edited by Robert Drago and Richard Perlman (New York: Harvester Wheatsheaf, 1989).
6. See James N. Baron, Michael T. Hannan, and M. Diane Burton, "Determinants of Managerial Intensity in the Early Years of Organizations," Research Paper 1550, Graduate School of Business, Stanford University, n.d.
7. The studies controlled for various factors, including industry, public versus private status, and occupational mix.
8. James N. Baron and David M. Kreps, *Strategic Human Resources: Frameworks for General Managers* (New York: Wiley, 1999), p. 11.
9. For an intriguing discussion of HRM as a management strategy, see Jeffrey Pfeffer, *Competitive Advantage Through People* (Boston: Harvard Business School Press, 1994).
10. See Edward Lawler III, "HR on Top," *Strategy + Business,* Summer 2004; available online: www.strategy-business.com/press/article/04202?pg=all; access date: June 8, 2006.
11. See "Research Shows Young Urban Hispanics Making Impressive Gains in Income and Education" (press release), Media Audit, July 31, 2001; available online: http://themediaaudit.com/hispanics.htm; access date: June 8, 2006.
12. These are the markets surveyed: Akron, OH; Albany–Schenectady–Troy, NY; Albuquerque, NM; Allentown–Bethlehem, PA; Ann Arbor, MI; Atlanta, GA; Austin, TX; Baltimore, MD; Boise, ID; Boston, MA; Buffalo, NY; Charleston, SC; Charlotte, NC; Chicago, IL; Cincinnati, OH; Cleveland, OH; Colorado Springs, CO; Columbia, SC; Columbia–Jefferson City, MO; Columbus, OH; Dayton, OH; Daytona Beach, FL; Denver, CO; Des Moines, IA; Detroit, MI; Dallas–Ft. Worth, TX; San Diego, CA; Eugene–Springfield, OR; Ft. Myers–Naples, FL; Hartford–New Haven, CT; Houston, TX; Indianapolis, IN; Jacksonville, FL; Jackson, MS; Kansas City, MO; Knoxville, TN; Lexington, KY; Little Rock, AR; Louisville, KY; Los Angeles, CA; St. Louis, MO; Las Vegas, NV; Madison, WS; Melbourne–Titusville–Cocoa, FL; Memphis, TN; Miami–Ft. Lauderdale, FL; Milwaukee, WI; Minneapolis–St. Paul, MN; Myrtle Beach, SC; Nashville, TN; New Orleans, LA; Norfolk, VA; New York, NY; Ocala, FL; Oklahoma City, OK; Omaha–Council Bluffs, NE; Orlando, FL; Peoria, IL; Philadelphia, PA; Phoenix, AZ; Pittsburgh, PA; Portland, OR; Raleigh–Durham, NC; Reno, NV; Rochester, NY; Sacramento, CA; San Antonio, TX; Sarasota–Bradenton, FL; Seattle–Tacoma, WA; San Francisco, CA; San Jose, CA; Spokane, WA; Tampa–St. Petersburg, FL; Toledo, OH; Tucson, AZ; Tulsa, OK; Washington, DC; West Palm Beach, FL; Wilmington, DE.
13. "Research Shows Young Urban Hispanics . . ."
14. Personal communication with Douglas Massey of the University of Pennsylvania's Mexican Migration Project, May 2001.

15. Dave Ulrich and Wayne Brockbank, "HR's New Mandate: Be a Strategic Player," *Harvard Business Review*, June 20, 2005.

Chapter 1

1. For more information on the cost of employee turnover, see Human Resources Management of the Industrial Labor Relations School at Cornell University, www.ilr.cornell.edu/library/research/eCornellGuides/humanResourcesManagement/selectionAndStaffing.html
2. James N. Baron and David M. Kreps, *Strategic Human Resources: Frameworks for General Managers* (New York: Wiley, 1999), pp. 95–96.
3. See Todd Raphael, "Creating a 'Third Culture' for Growing Hispanic Workforce," *Workforce Management*, June 20, 2005.
4. Personal communication with officials at FedEx and American Airlines in spring 2003.
5. Although *diversity* is almost always thought of as multiculturalism, it can be the reverse: customers may *resist* dealing with certain groups of people, even though individuals from those groups may constitute a significant part of a local market's demographics.
6. Harriet Hankin, *The New Workforce* (New York: American Management Association, 2005), p. 115.
7. See "Hispanics Spreading Out Across U.S.; 28 Cities Now Have More than 100,000" (press release), Media Audit, August 8, 2004; available online: http://themediaaudit.com/44HispanicPopulationCenters.pdf; access date: June 8, 2006.
8. See "Hispanics Spreading Out Across U.S."
9. In the Fortune 500 companies in 2005, Hispanics occupied only 5 percent of management positions, a percentage far lower than the national Hispanic population proportion of 14 percent would suggest.
10. The Media Audit and International Demographics, Inc., 3355 West Alabama, Suite 500, Houston, TX 77098.
11. See "Research Shows Young Urban Hispanics Making Impressive Gains in Income and Education" (press release), The Media Audit, July 31, 2001; available online: http://themediaaudit.com/hispanics.htm; access date: June 8, 2006.
12. "Mexican Hispanics in the U.S. and Language as a Barrier," unpublished white paper, International Credit Monitor, 2004.
13. For an analysis of these challenges, see Sonia Perez, *Moving Up the Economic Ladder: Latino Workers and the Nation's Future Prosperity* (Washington, DC: National Council of La Raza, 2000).
14. Hispanic Economics, P. O. Box 3479, Grand Central Station, New York, NY 10163. See www.HispanicEconomics.com.

15. "The top companies' reports on the Hispanic percentage of their total work force ranged from 3.2 percent to 31.0 percent," Andrea Lehman reported. "The firms with the highest percentages were in the service industry, and the firms with the lowest percentages were in technical fields." Andrea Lehman, "Hispanic Labor Market Gap Continues," *Hispanic Business,* October 2005.
16. Lehman, 2005.
17. Figures provided by HispanTelligence, published by *Hispanic Business,* October 2005.
18. Personal communication, July 2005. To understand the differences between Knight-Ridder's operations in Florida and California, consider the fates of the company's Spanish-language newspapers. While *El Nuevo Herald* rivals the *Miami Herald,* it was impossible to duplicate this success in the San Francisco Bay Area. "The *San Jose Mercury News,* which has won accolades for the diversity of its newsroom and coverage, announced Friday it plans to drop its Spanish and Vietnamese-language newspapers because the free publications aren't profitable," the *News & Observer* reported October 24, 2005. "The company plans to stop printing *Nuevo Mundo* and is selling *Viet Mercury* to a group of businessmen. Their last editions as Mercury News publications will be Nov. 11, Mercury News Publisher George Riggs said.... 'We're very saddened by the news, but we respect the business decision,' said *Nuevo Mundo*'s editor and publisher Marina Hinestrosa."
19. Personal communication, July 2005.
20. Robert Putnam, *Bowling Alone: The Collapse and Revival of American Community* (New York: Simon & Schuster, 2000), p. 371.
21. See "Parity Project Newspapers Continue to Outpace Industry Trends," National Association of Hispanic Journalists *Summer Roundup* 2005 Newsletter.
22. Graham Gori, "Fears About Microsoft Return, in Mexico," *New York Times,* April 24, 2002.
23. Robert Haskett, *Indigenous Rulers: An Ethnohistory of Town Government in Colonial Cuernavaca* (Albuquerque: University of New Mexico Press, 1991), pp. 144–145.
24. Abby Ellin, "High-Tech Philanthropy in a Low-Tech Guatemalan Village," *New York Times,* June 4, 2000.
25. "Cramming Them In," *The Economist,* May 9, 2002.
26. Diana Jean Schemo, "Finances Hold Back Hispanic College Students, Study Finds," *New York Times,* September 6, 2002.
27. Dale Maharidge, *Denison, Iowa* (New York: Free Press, 2005), pp. 32–33.
28. Baron and Kreps, 1999, p. 340.
29. Ted Mouw, "The Use of Social Network Among Hispanic Workers: An Indirect Test of the Effect of Social Capital" (Chapel Hill: University of North Carolina, 2003); available online: www.unc.edu/~tedmouw/papers/contacts/hispcontacts.pdf; access date: June 8, 2006.

30. Mary Cheddie, "Do Employee Referral Programs Really Work?" SHRM white paper, June 2002.
31. Even for factory work, co-worker referrals are falling short, one reason some Fortune 100 companies have resorted to placing radio commercials in Mexico. Indeed, the siren calls of American business are heard each day throughout the towns and villages of central Mexico. The commercials, beckoning Mexicans to emigrate to the United States, are staples on Mexican radio, intermingled with ranchero songs and ballads. The ads, often disguised as public service announcements, promise "secure work" at factories where "wages are in dollars" and that "housing is affordable." The work itself "assures the economic well-being of your family" and an "opportunity to improve your life." Listeners, who are told they can earn more in one day in the United States than they can in almost a month in their hometowns, are directed to an agency or office, sometimes in a nearby town, where they will learn the details. Scores of thousands of unemployed Mexican men are seduced by these promises, follow instructions, and make their way to these "offices," which are often small travel agencies, check-cashing places, or rooms in the back of billiard joints. They are then given the details: the jobs are at a prestigious meat-packing plant in a town called Tar Heel in a state called North Carolina. "Ask for Mr. So-and-so and your job is guaranteed." With a contact name and phone number, they then embark on a journey north to the border with the United States: Mexican bus companies sell more one-way tickets than any other type. The trek from the towns and villages of central Mexico to North Carolina is a journey each must make on his own, and there are no guarantees that anyone will make it: hundreds of thousands are caught at the border and deported; scores of others die of exposure in the desert. But enough make it through, and American demand for illegal immigrants is insatiable enough, that it makes sense for corporate America to flood Mexican radio with these appeals for laborers. Corporate America's tactics sometimes backfire. "The indictment of Tyson Foods Inc., the nation's largest meat processor, on charges that it conspired to smuggle illegal immigrants to work at its plants, is a sign of how dependent the American food and agriculture system has become on foreign-born workers, many of them here illegally," reported the *New York Times*. (See David Barboza, "Meatpackers' Profits Hinge on Pool of Immigrant Labor," *New York Times*, December 21, 2001.)
32. Ayesha Khan is quoted in Julie Bennett, "Recruiters Develop Strategies to Uncover Diverse Candidates," CareerJournal.com, 2004; available online: www.careerjournal.com/myc/diversity/20040408-bennett.html; access date: June 8, 2006.
33. Andrea Poe, "Reeling Them In: The Art of Employee Referral Programs," SHRM Online, June 2002.
34. Bernie Eisenberg, Cydney Kilduff, Susan Burleigh, and Kevin Wilson, "The

Role of the Value Promotion and Employment Branding in Retaining Top Talent," SHRM white paper, June 2002.
35. Robert Rodriguez, "Tapping the Hispanic Labor Pool," *SHRM Magazine*, April 2004, 49(4).
36. Carla Joinson, "Strength in Numbers?" *HR Magazine*, November 2000, 45(11).
37. Rodriguez, 2004.
38. Ana Guzman is quoted in Joinson, 2000.
39. "Discrimination Against Racial/Ethnic Minorities in Access to Employment in the United States: Empirical Findings from Situation Testing," 1998; available online: www.ilo.org/public/english/protection/migrant/papers/usempir/index.htm; access date: May 29, 2006.
40. "Discrimination Against Racial/Ethnic Minorities . . . ," 1998, section 4.5.1. For another compelling study, see F. Bovenkerk, *A Manual for International Comparative Research on Discrimination on the Grounds of "Race" and Ethnic Origin* (Geneva, Switzerland: International Labour Office, 1992).
41. Joinson, 2000.
42. Here is the exact statement on accents: "A. Accent Discrimination: Because linguistic characteristics are a component of national origin, employers should carefully scrutinize employment decisions that are based on accent to ensure that they do not violate Title VII. An employment decision based on foreign accent does not violate Title VII if an individual's accent materially interferes with the ability to perform job duties. This assessment depends upon the specific duties of the position in question and the extent to which the individual's accent affects his or her ability to perform job duties. Employers should distinguish between a merely discernible foreign accent and one that interferes with communication skills necessary to perform job duties. Generally, an employer may only base an employment decision on accent if effective oral communication in English is required to perform job duties and the individual's foreign accent materially interferes with his or her ability to communicate orally in English. Positions for which effective oral communication in English may be required include teaching, customer service, and telemarketing. Even for these positions, an employer must still determine whether the particular individual's accent interferes with the ability to perform job duties."
43. One exception is native French speakers who learn English: many Americans are drawn to that accent and are enamored of the way it sounds.
44. Whether it was art imitating life or vice versa, in real life, Desi Arnaz (who portrayed Ricky Ricardo) was often seen as being the lesser of the business team with his wife, Lucille Ball. That it was Arnaz who was the mastermind behind Desilu Productions' ascent in Hollywood remains discounted, in part because reruns reinforce the idea that his accent is something worthy of ridicule.

45. Dianne Markley is quoted in Joinson, 2000.
46. Andrew Lam, *Perfume Dreams: Reflections on the Vietnamese Diaspora* (Berkeley, CA: Heyday Books, 2005), pp. 113–114.
47. In the late nineteenth and early twentieth centuries the same concerns were expressed about waves of European immigrants from other predominantly Catholic countries: Ireland, Italy, and Poland.
48. Samuel Huntington, "The Hispanic Challenge," *Foreign Policy,* March/April 2004.
49. See Eric Schmitt, "For First Time, Nuclear Families Drop Below 25 Percent of Households," *New York Times,* May 15, 2001.
50. John Kenneth Galbraith, *The Good Society: The Humane Agenda* (Boston: Mariner Books, 1997), p. 11.
51. Kenneth T. Jackson, "Once Again, the City Beckons," *New York Times,* March 30, 2001.
52. Joseph Straubhaar, Consuelo Campbell, and Kristina Cahoon, "From National to Regional Cultures: The Five Cultures and Television Markets of NAFTA," n.d.; available online: www.orbicom.uqam.ca/in_focus/publications/archives/straubhaar.html; access date: June 8, 2006.
53. Straubhaar, Campbell, and Cahoon, n.d.
54. Huntington, 2004.
55. Law enforcement officials often recognize that day laborers, for instance, are not interested in breaking any law but merely want to find work. "You cannot criticize the day laborers," Chief Gerard Larsen Jr. of the East Hampton Village police told a reporter for the *New York Times.* "They're trying to make a living. By going after the employers it seems right." See Peter Beller, "Crackdown Deters Day Labor Employers," *New York Times,* November 22, 2005.
56. Victor Cardoso and Andrea Becerril, "Remittance Income Surpasses Oil Revenue in Mexico," *La Jornada,* November 11, 2004.
57. For more information, see "Back to Ethnic America: Italian Immigration," *Digital History,* 2006; available online: www.digitalhistory.uh.edu/historyonline/italian_immigration.cfm; access date: June 8, 2006.
58. Donatella Lorch, "Is America Any Place for a Nice Hispanic Girl?" *New York Times,* April 11, 1996.
59. Personal interviews with Antonio Ek, February 2001.
60. This list was adapted from one used at Martin Army Community Hospital, 7950 Martin Loop, Fort Benning, GA 31905.
61. David A. Thomas, "Diversity as Strategy," *Harvard Business Review,* 2004, 82(9).
62. David Thomas is quoted in Judith Ross, "What It Takes: Minorities in the Executive Suite," *Working Knowledge: A Report on Research at Harvard Business School,* Winter 1999.

63. To the question, "How important is being satisfied with how you perform your job to your overall happiness?" the figures for those who replied "Very Important" are Hispanics, 93 percent; non-Hispanic whites, 89 percent; African Americans, 81 percent; and Asian Americans, 91 percent. Hispanic Economics, P. O. Box 3479, Grand Central Station, New York, NY 10163. See www.HispanicEconomics.com.
64. Corporate Leadership Council, "Becoming an Employer of Choice for Hispanic Workers," Washington, DC, Corporate Executive Board, September 2001.
65. Hispanic Economics compiled an exhaustive analysis of Hispanics in 2005. "Attitudes and Opinions of the Hispanic Employee in the United States, 2005" is available from Hispanic Economics, P. O. Box 3479, Grand Central Station, New York, NY 10163. See www.HispanicEconomics.com.

Chapter 2

1. Brian E. Becker, Mark A. Huselid, and David Ulrich, "The HR Scorecard: Linking People, Strategy, and Performance," *Harvard Business Review*, April 2, 2001.
2. Bill Picture, "Are Diversity Officers Changing the Face of Corporate America?" Pacific News Service, November 26, 2005; available online: http://news.pacificnews.org/news/view_article.html?article_id=cbfb7d2fa1378927c9744978a8142d96; access date: October 31, 2006.
3. Representative Peter Deutsch is quoted in Richard Brand, "Spanish Language Radio Gets Tainted," Knight-Ridder News Service, February 15, 2004.
4. Joseph Contreras, "Under-the-Radar Radio," *Newsweek*, May 3, 2005.
5. Picture, 2005.
6. Charles Gibson, "Employee Relations 101," SHRM white paper, May 1999.
7. R. Stup and T. Maloney, *Managing Hispanic Workers: Perceptions of Agricultural Managers* (University Park, PA: College of Agricultural Sciences, Cooperative Extension, Penn State University, 2003).
8. W. Imberman, "From Furnace to Finishing: Managing the Hispanic Worker," *Foundry Management & Technology*, February 2004; available online: www.foundrymag.com/full_story.php?WID=11403; access date: March 18, 2006.
9. Stup and Maloney, 2003.
10. Stup and Maloney, 2003.
11. Christopher Conte and Albert R. Karr, "Continuity and Change," in *Outline of the U.S. Economy*, U.S. Department of State, Washington, DC, February 2001; available online: http://usinfo.state.gov/products/pubs/oecon/chap1.htm; access date: June 8, 2006.
12. Jim Heskett, "What's the Future of Globally Organized Labor?" *Harvard Business Review*, October 3, 2005.

13. See James N. Baron and David M. Kreps, *Strategic Human Resources: Frameworks for General Managers* (New York: Wiley, 1999), p. 121.
14. Conte and Karr, 2001.
15. See "An American Hero," Cesar E. Chavez Foundation, n.d.; available online: www.cesarechavezfoundation.org/cesarechavez.html; access date: June 8, 2006.
16. Becker, Huselid, and Ulrich, 2001.
17. "Treating Employees Well Is Good for Business," Costco Wholesale Corporation in partnership with the International Brotherhood of Teamsters," n.d.; available online: www.americanrightsatwork.org/docUploads/LDL%202005%5FCostco%2Epdf; access date: June 8, 2006.
18. Baron and Kreps, 1999, p. 129.
19. Baron and Kreps, 1999, p. 524.
20. "The Labor Day List: Partnerships That Work," American Rights at Work, n.d.; available online: www.americanrightsatwork.org/srb/ldl.cfm; access date: June 8, 2006.
21. A former Smithfield worker, Carlos Martinez, described the dangerous pressure he labored under while on the assembly line: "I was working with this electric saw and they were pushing us to work so fast and I cut my finger. I never saw a doctor. They gave me first aid right there and said get back to work ... and told me to work with one hand." See "Why Smithfield Workers Want a Union Fighting for a Safer Workplace," www.americanrightsatwork.org; access date: October 14, 2004. In this instance, management attempted to pit black and Hispanic employees against one another, creating tension between the minorities, as a strategy for undermining efforts to unionize their workers.
22. Hispanic Economics, P. O. Box 3479, Grand Central Station, New York, NY 10163. See www.HispanicEconomics.com.

Chapter 3

1. James N. Baron and David M. Kreps, *Strategic Human Resources: Frameworks for General Managers* (New York: Wiley, 1999), p. 216.
2. Baron and Kreps, 1999, p. 224.
3. Mike Deblieux, *Performance Appraisal Source Book* (Alexandria, VA: SHRM, 2003).
4. Kathryn Tyler, "Performance Art," *HR Magazine,* August 2005.
5. Personal communication from William Lambert, April 1983.
6. Based on J. L. Farh, G. H. Dobbins, and B. S. Cheng, "Cultural Relativity in Action: A Comparison of Self-Ratings Made by Chinese and U.S. Workers," *Personnel Psychology,* 1991, 44: 129–147.
7. Hispanic Economics, P. O. Box 3479, Grand Central Station, New York, NY 10163. See www.HispanicEconomics.com.

8. Robert J. Greene, "Effective Performance Appraisal: A Global Perspective," SHRM white paper, April 2005.
9. F. Trompenaars and C. Hampden-Turner, *Managing People Across Cultures* (London: Wiley, 2004).
10. G. Hofstede, *Cultures and Organizations* (New York: McGraw-Hill, 1990).
11. Greene, 2005.
12. See Ann Murphy, "Hiring Across Borders," *Grounds Maintenance,* January 1, 2001; by Ann Murphy, available online: http://grounds-mag.com/mag/grounds_maintenance_hiring_across_borders/index.html; access date: June 8, 2006.
13. Baron and Kreps, 1999, p. 266.
14. Elizabeth A. Mannix, "Negotiating as a Team," *Harvard Business Review Online,* August 8, 2005, available online: http://hbswk.hbs.edu/item.jhtml?id=4940&t=strategy; access date: June 8, 2006.
15. Personal interview with Alex Penelas, May 2004.

Chapter 4

1. For information on the Parity Project, see www.nahj.org/parityproject/parityproject.shtml; access date: June 8, 2006.
2. Judith A. Ross, "What It Takes: Minorities in the Executive Suite," *Harvard Business Review,* October 19, 1999.
3. Corporate Leadership Council, "Recruiting and Retaining Hispanic Employees in the Financial Services Industry," Washington, DC: Corporate Executive Board, 2004.
4. See Joseph Baccarro, "The Hidden Cost of Employee Turnover," *Grant Thornton Benefits and HR Advisor,* Grant Thornton, 1992. Grant Thornton, 175 West Jackson Boulevard, Chicago, IL 60604.
5. Doug Speicher and Richard Stup, "Successfully Training Hispanic Workers," *Managing a Hispanic Workforce,* January 2001.
6. Speicher and Stup, 2001.
7. Matthew Halverson, "Lost in Translation," *Electrical, Construction & Maintenance Magazine,* June 2003.
8. Hispanic Economics compiled an exhaustive analysis of Hispanics in 2005. "Attitudes and Opinions of the Hispanic Employee in the United States, 2005" is available from Hispanic Economics, P. O. Box 3479, Grand Central Station, New York, NY 10163. See www.HispanicEconomics.com; access date: June 17, 2006.
9. James N. Baron and David M. Kreps, *Strategic Human Resources: Frameworks for General Managers* (New York: Wiley, 1999), p. 379.
10. Tim Machan is quoted in Nahal Toosi, "Free Speech: Experts Help Foreign-Born Professionals Shed Unclear Accents," *Milwaukee Journal Sentinel,* August 10, 2003.

11. Corporate Leadership Council, "Fostering an Inclusive Organizational Culture," Washington, DC: Corporate Executive Board, 2004.
12. Carol Hastings, "How to Avoid Getting Lost in Translation," available online: www.shrm.org/diversity/library_published/nonIC/CMS_012405.asp; access date: March 2005.
13. Harriet Hankin, *The New Workforce* (New York: American Management Association, 2005), p. 191.
14. See "Influentials Coverage: A School-Job Disconnect," *Hispanic Business*, October 2005.
15. See *EEOC v. Watlow Batavia Inc.*, N.D. Ill., No. 99 C 1435, consent decree 9/1/2000.
16. *BNA Daily Labor Report,* March 14, 2001.
17. Bureau of National Affairs, "Language Training," *BNA Policy and Practice Series,* August 2001.
18. Dina Berta, "Language Smarts: Shared Ideas from ESL Programs," *Nation's Restaurant News,* September 16, 2002. (Obtained though Corporate Leadership Council.)
19. See Ann Murphy, "Hiring Across Borders," *Grounds Maintenance,* January 1, 2001; available online: http://grounds-mag.com/mag/grounds_maintenance_hiring_across_borders/index.html; access date: June 8, 2006.
20. In *"Fun Lessons for Law Enforcement* and *Fun Lessons for Emergency Responders,"* www.spanishforpoliceandfire.com/products.htm#pfinstruction, the Dees Multilingual Services states, "Don't reinvent the wheel! Develop and teach professional classes at police/sheriff/fire departments, colleges or academies using our police or fire/paramedic instructor manuals. Even if you lack classroom techniques and language teaching experience, you can be successful using our classroom methods and experience, basing your course on our hands-on presentation of a 36-hour beginning Spanish classes for Law Enforcement for police officers/deputies or Spanish for Emergency Responders for firefighters and paramedics."
21. Jennifer Salopek, "Lost in Translation," *T & D,* 2003.
22. In a comparative analysis of firms that provided Spanish-language instruction to their English-speaking employees with those that did not, those firms that encouraged learning Spanish had, on average, 17 percent higher profits than those that did not. Hispanic Economics, P. O. Box 3479, Grand Central Station, New York, NY 10163. See www.HispanicEconomics.com.
23. Jennifer Bingham Hull, "Habla Spanglish?" *American Way*, August 1, 1999. "If you're in South America and you suddenly say something in English, it's a snobby thing to do. It's bad for business. You are going to upset the other person. It sounds like you are trying to show that the person doesn't speak English," Rosa Sugranes, chairman of Miami-based Iberia Tiles Corporation, is quoted as saying, underscoring the challenges of being fluently bilingual.

24. Robert Putnam, *Bowling Alone: The Collapse and Revival of American Community* (New York: Simon & Schuster, 2000), p. 371.
25. Hull, 1999.
26. See Janny Scott, "In Simple Pronouns, Clues to Shifting Latino Identity," *New York Times*, December 5, 2002. The nuances of language make Spanish in the United States an interesting field of research. "Now a team of linguists is studying the consequences of the collision of Spanish dialects in New York, looking not only at how that contact is affecting Spanish spoken but also at what the outcome might suggest about the evolution of Latino identity in the city and beyond," Janny Scott reports. One outcome, of course, is that it is imperative to be proficient in both standard English and Spanish, simply because the inability to converse properly in either is seen as a lack of education. Throughout Latin America few things are as annoying as speaking with a Hispanic who, living in the United States, is unfamiliar with Spanish and makes errors such as using the word for *network (red)* when they really mean the color. And in the United States, few things impede one's career advancement as thoroughly as the inability to speak and write in standard English; memoranda with "ain't" don't impress readers in the boardroom favorably.
27. Roberto Suro, *Strangers Among Us: Latinos' Lives in a Changing America* (New York: Vintage Books, 1999), pp. 11–12.
28. Sue Anne Pressley, "Multicultural D.C. Area Becoming Multilingual," *Washington Post*, February 11, 1992.
29. See Stephen Pounds, "Top IBM Exec Also Latino Liaison," *Palm Beach Post*, November 20, 2005.
30. Patricia Amason and others, "Social Support and Acculturative Stress in the Multicultural Workplace," *Journal of Applied Communication Research*, November 1999.
31. This discussion is based on material provided by the Diversity Network, a project of Cornell/IRL and the National Conference.
32. Corporate Leadership Council, "Fostering an Inclusive Organizational Culture," Washington, DC: Corporate Executive Board, 2004.

Chapter 5

1. For more information, see Stanley Rothman, "Affirmative Action—and Reaction: Is Diversity Overrated?" *New York Times*, March 29, 2003.
2. James N. Baron and David M. Kreps, *Strategic Human Resources: Frameworks for General Managers* (New York: Wiley, 1999), p. 339.
3. Society for Human Resource Management, *Launching an Initiative*, www.shrm.org; access date: August 30, 2002.
4. Corporate Leadership Council, "Developing, Communicating, and Measuring Diversity Initiatives," 2003.
5. David Leonhardt, "Who's in the Corner Office?" *New York Times*, November 27, 2005.

6. See Frank Linnehan and Alison M. Konrad, "Diluting Diversity: Implications for Intergroup Inequality in Organizations," *Journal of Management Inquiry*, 1999, 8(4): 399–415.
7. Partial listing of legal documents readily available in Spanish for HRM to offer Hispanic employees:
   - Discrimination (Title VII, Civil Rights Act of 1964)
   - Hiring (Title VII) and termination
   - Wages and hours (Fair Labor Standards Act, minimum wage, child labor)
   - Employee benefits (health care, 401(k), IRS, ERISA requirements)
   - Family and medical leave (FMLA, return to work protection)
   - Health and safety (OSHA regulations, workers compensation)
   - Workers with disabilities (Americans with Disabilities Act)
   - Types of workers: permanent and contractors
   - Unions (National Labor Relations Act)
   - Internal human resources practices (for example, taxes, personnel practices, and documentation)
8. Robert Eckert is quoted in Leonhardt, 2005.
9. Frank Ahrens, "Accent on Higher TV Ratings," *Washington Post*, August 2, 2004.
10. Ahrens, 2004.
11. Baron and Kreps, 1999, p. 303.
12. Harriet Hankin, *The New Workforce* (New York: American Management Association, 2005), p. 191.
13. See Lauren Keller Johnson, "Getting New Managers Up to Speed," *Harvard Business Review Online*, July 4, 2005; available online: http://hbswk.hbs.edu/item.jhtml?id=4884&t=leadership; access date: June 9, 2006.
14. Corporate Leadership Council, "Ford Motor Company: Supporting Employee Resource Groups," Washington, DC: Corporate Executive Board, 2004.
15. See "B-Schools That Look Like America," *BusinessWeek*, June 21, 1999.
16. For more information, see KornFerry.com.
17. Personal interview with Roberto Goizueta, May 1995.
18. Jimmy Carter is quoted in Paul Farhi, "Coca-Cola Chief Roberto Goizueta Dies," *Washington Post*, October 19, 1997.
19. See Corporate Leadership Council, "Voice of the Leader," Washington, DC: Corporate Executive Board, 2001.
20. Corporate Leadership Council, "Mentoring: From Theory to Action," Washington, DC: Corporate Executive Board, 2005.
21. The sections of Chapter 5 titled "The Mentoring Relationship" and "Communications Skills for Mentors" are based on material developed by the Baptist Health South Florida Employee Mentoring Program.
22. David A. Brown, "Race Does Matter in Mentoring," *Harvard Business Review*, 2001, 79(4).

23. For a discussion on the state of Hispanics in the hard sciences, see Paul Barton, "Hispanics in Science and Engineering: A Matter of Assistance and Persistence"; report available from the ETS Policy Information Center, MS-04R, Rosedale Road, Princeton, NJ 08651.
24. See Korn/Ferry, "Korn/Ferry's Best Practices for Diversity: Corporate and Candidate Perspectives," 2001; summary available online: www.korn ferry.com/Library/Process.asp?P=Pubs_Detail&CID=297&LID=1; access date: June 9, 2006.
25. Fay Hansen, "Truth and Myths of Work/Life Balance," *Workforce*, December 2002, pp. 34–39; available online: www.workforce.com/section/02/feature/23/36/99/; access date: June 9, 2006.
26. Baron and Kreps, 1999, p. 171.
27. Hispanic Economics, P. O. Box 3479, Grand Central Station, New York, NY 10163. See www.HispanicEconomics.com.
28. See David Bonetti, "Mexican Muralists Who Inspired Black Artists," *San Francisco Examiner*, March 20, 1998.
29. Hispanic Economics and the Bureau of Labor Statistics, Washington, DC.
30. Mirta Ojito, "Best of Friends, Worlds Apart," in *How Race Is Lived in America*, by correspondents of the *New York Times*; introduction by Joseph Lelyveld (New York: Henry Holt, 2001), p. 23.
31. Juan Gonzalez, *Harvest of Empire: A History of Latinos in America* (New York: Penguin, 2000), p. 92.
32. Gonzalez, 2000, p. 92.
33. Xóchitl Bada, "Mexican Hometown Associations," International Relations Center, March 1, 2003; available online: www.irc-online.org/content/1696; access date: June 9, 2006. The article also discusses HTAs for towns in other Latin American countries.
34. Dan Cohen and Lawrence Prusak, "Making Social Capital Work," *Harvard Business Review*, June 11, 2001.
35. Bill Picture, "Are Diversity Officers Changing the Face of Corporate America?" *Asian Week*, November 26, 2005.
36. Nina Drake and Ian Robb, "Exit Interviews," SHRM white paper, 1995.

Appendix 1

1. Katharina Wilson, *Hrotsvit of Gandersheim: A Florilegium of Her Works* (Cambridge: Brewer, 1998).

Index

accent: discrimination based on, 38–40; insecurities about, 54
accent-neutral Spanish, 191
acclimation, 144
acculturation, 151, 154–155
achievement-oriented cultures, 123
administrative authority, 69
advocacy, 74–75
affinity groups, 195–197
affirmative action, 169
African American workplace conflicts with Hispanics: description of, 92, 96–98, 100, 223; history of, 217–218; overview of, 216–217; recognition of, 218–219
American Society for Training and Development, 174
applicant self-selection, 27–28
ascription-oriented cultures, 123
assimilation: acculturation vs., 154–155; description of, 151; by immigrants, 51–52
awareness-based training, 175

Baccaro, Joseph, 141
backlash, 92, 96–98, 100
Bada, Xóchitl, 225
Baron, James, 3, 13–14, 27, 80, 103, 125, 150, 184, 194
Battz, Emilio, 24
Becker, Brian, 67, 84
Bendick, M., Jr., 37
benefit plans, 48, 53, 61
bias: based on what the candidate lacks, 36–37; performance appraisal affected by, 132; substantiation of, 54. *See also* discrimination

bilingual consumer economy, 14, 21, 44, 68, 180
bilingual employees, 162–163
bilingualism, 166–168
"black on brown" hostility, 98, 218
Bonetti, David, 219
brand: employment, 33–34; product, 33–35
Brockbank, Wayne, 8
Brown, David A., 208–209
Burton, M. Diane, 3

Callahan, Carolyn M., 199
candidates: attracting of, 16–21; employment branding for, 33–34; general profile of, 43; interviewing of. *See* interviewing; job offer, 59–63, 65; overview of, 13–14; preemployment screening and testing, 57–59, 65; recruiting of, 26–35; referral of, 28–31; summary of, 64. *See also* employee selection
career counseling and development, 78
Castro, Ida, 158
change agent, 69, 111
Chavarría, Jesús, 157
Chavez, Cesar, 83
civic associations, 255–258
Civil Rights Act, 158
clannishness, 42
Clemetson, Lynette, 1
code of ethics, 93, 189
Cohen, Dan, 228
collectivistic cultures, 123, 172–173
college graduates: family influences on, 46–47;

275

college graduates, *cont'd*
geographic distribution of, 17–18; statistics regarding, 5, 19–20
communication: description of, 75–76; diversity-related, 185–186; effectiveness of, 189–191; importance of, 190–191; listening as form of, 205, 207; management-labor relations considerations, 88–91; by mentor, 206–208; with new employees, 145; paraphrasing, 206–207; performance management effects on, 106; roadblocks in, 207–208; summary of, 233
community trust, 35
company tour, 143
complementarities, 4
confianza, 61–62, 83, 111
confidentiality, 190
conflict aversion, 173
conflict resolution: description of, 78, 224; discipline used for, 223–224; summary of, 234
constructive engagement, 219
consultants, 125
continuing development, 150
continuing education, 153, 156–157, 179
Contreras, Joseph, 72
corporate benefits, 48, 53, 61
corporate role models, 197, 199–200
counselor, 144–145
co-worker referrals, 28–31
creeping racism, 220
cross-cultural psychology, 119
cross-cultural training, 155–157
Cubans, 18–19, 85, 191, 215
cultural associations, 252–255
cultural awareness, 115
cultural differences: human resource management affected by, 120–123; learning styles affected by, 164–165; mentoring in, 203; performance appraisal affected by, 134; training about, 173; in workforce, 120
culturally equitable performance appraisal, 118–119
culture: achievement-oriented, 123; ascription-oriented, 123; collectivistic, 123, 172–173; Eastern, 121; individualistic, 123; Northern, 121; performance appraisal affected by, 117, 119–120, 122–123; performance ratings affected by, 117, 119–120; Southern, 121; "third," 124–127; Western, 121

dates and events, 239–248
defense mechanisms, 47–48
demographics: description of, 6, 15; employment recruitment affected by, 32
demonstration effects, 53
Deutsch, Peter, 72
discipline, 223–224
discrimination: accent-based, 38–40; based on what the candidate lacks, 36–37; employee manual documentation regarding, 94–95; fear of, 173; race-based, 37–38, 92, 96–98, 100; stereotype-based, 40
diversity: benefits of, 184, 187; corporate performance and, 185–187; defining of, 185; description of, 15–16, 94; integration of, 187–188; language-related, 160; in management, 187; management's commitment to, 141; myths and misconceptions about, 169–170, 180; opportunities created through, 170–171; promoting and

maintaining of, 171; responsibility for, 170; role of, 182–189
diversity training: affinity groups for, 196; awareness-based, 175; benefits of, 172–174, 177–178; communication about, 185–186; description of, 168–169; employee retention and, 172–174, 177, 187; guidelines for, 174–176; public vs. public goals, 171–172; skill-based, 175; summary of, 233; support for, 183–184
Dominicans, 85
drug-free workplace, 95

Eastern cultures, 121
Eckert, Robert A., 190
education: attainment levels, 17–20, 26, 153; continuing, 153, 156–157, 179; English-speaking skills and, 38; factors that affect, 19; financial barriers, 25; geographic locale and, 18–19; graduate degrees, 5–6; lack of, 22–26; in Mexico, 22–25; of working-class Hispanics, 49
educational associations, 252–255
Eleta de Cacho, Graciela, 27–28
Emerson, Monica E., 199
e-Mexico program, 22, 24
employee(s): acclimation of, 144; advocacy for, 74; benefit plans explained to, 61; bilingual, 162–163; concerns of, 150–157; exit interviews for, 228–232, 235; expectations for employers, 59, 61–62; feelings of, 77; education on workplace hostility, 97–98; orientation of. See orientation; performance management systems, 112–114; referral programs, 28–31; training and development of. See training and development; values of, 62; welcoming of, 143–144
employee advocate, 69
employee champion, 69
employee feedback, 109
employee manuals: code of ethics, 93; drug-free workplace provisions, 95; holidays, 91; language in the workplace, 91–92; language issues, 70–73; racial discrimination addressed in, 92, 96–98, 100; safety provisions, 96; summary of, 101; workplace responsibilities explained in, 94–96
employee networks, 195–199
employee relations: beliefs, 77; career counseling and development, 78; communication, 75, 88–91; conflict resolution, 78; criteria for success, 86–87; definition of, 73–74; ethics, 76; expectations, 77–78; fairness, 77; feelings, 77; perceptions, 77; trust, 75–76
employee retention: corporate role models and, 197, 199–200; diversity training and, 172–174, 177, 187; management commitment and, 212; training strategies for, 151–152; tuition reimbursement and, 194
employee selection: challenges for, 22–35; interview. See interviewing; job offer, 59–63, 65; market demands and, 14–16; overview of, 13–14; preemployment screening and testing, 57–59, 65. See also candidates
employee turnover: costs of, 141; description of, 13
employers: employee expectations for, 59, 61–62; paternalism from, 152
employment branding, 33–34

employment recruiting: applicant self-selection, 27–28; co-worker referrals, 28–31; resistance to, 26–35; search firms, 31–32; staffing agencies, 31–32
employment relationship: description of, 13–14; evolving nature of, 74
English as a second language, 151, 162
English-language instruction, 153–154
English-language television programming, 45
English-only workplaces, 158–163
Equal Employment Opportunity Commission, 38, 85, 158–159
ethics, 76
exit interviews, 228–232, 235
expectations: by employees, 59, 61–62; of managers, 77–78
extended family, 42–43
eye contact, 52

fair employment practices, 94
fair management practices, 60
fairness, 77
family: clannish nature of, 42; college selection and, 46; Corporate America's definition of, 43; employer recognition of importance of, 192–193; extended, 42–43; focus on, 46, 193; importance of, 190, 192–193; members of, 215; opinions of, 59
farm workers, 83
Federal Communications Commission, 72
feedback: description of, 109–110, 116, 123; training uses of, 147–149, 166
feelings, 77, 206
focus groups, 109–110
401(k), 61

Gamboa, Dario, 166
gaps of experience, 47
Gardenswartz, Lee, 161
Gerstner, Lou, 57–58
gift exchange, 193–194
global competition, 105
globalization, 53
Goizueta, Roberto, 199–200
Gonzalez, Juan, 220–221
Gori, Graham, 24
graduate degrees, 5–6
Guzman, Ana, 36, 47

halo effect, 132
Hampden-Turner, Charles, 121
Hankin, Harriet, 15
Hannan, Michael, 3
harassment, 94–95
health care, 215–216
hiring, 60
Hispanic Hometown Association resources, 226–227
Hispanics: ancestry of, 18; anti-black attitudes by, 219–221; backlash against, 92, 96–98, 100; demographics of, 6, 15; diversity of, 43; facts regarding, 1–2; geographic distribution of, 15, 17–18; identity of, 227; indigenous, 49–50, 119; nurturing of, 140–141
Hofstede, Geert, 121–122
holidays, 62–63, 91, 194, 214–215, 239–248
hostility, in workplace: awareness of, 96; "black on brown," 98, 218; education about, 97–98
hourly positions: English-language instruction for, 153; interviewing for, 48–56
Hughes, Abe Tomas, 33
Hull, Jennifer Bingham, 167
human capital, 3
human capital developer, 69
human resource management: case study of, 85–86; company examples of, 89–91; competitive

advantage through, 4; components of, 3; cultural differences, 120–123; integrated approach to, 15; management benefits of, 107; management's view of, 4; organization's performance affected by, 3; proactive use of, 3; purpose of, 62; role of, 69; as structural system, 4; studies of, 3; summary of, 231; technology effects on, 4
human resources: advocacy role of, 74; hiring obstacles for, 20–21; union participation role of, 84
human resources materials, 189
human resources policies: employee manuals. *See* employee manuals; employee relations. *See* employee relations; evolving of, 68; strategic partnership, 67–70, 84
Huntington, Samuel, 2, 40, 49
Huselid, Mark, 67, 84

illegal immigration, 7
immigrants: assimilation by, 51–52; increase in, 2; remittances sent by, 51, 225
immigration: economic benefits of, 43–44; by Native American population, 24; statistics regarding, 7, 167; urban revitalization due to, 44
indigenous Hispanics: cultural assimilation resistance by, 49–50; self-image of, 119
individualism, 79
individualistic cultures, 123
insecurities, 52–54
intelligence levels: accent and, 39; English-speaking skills and, 38
intergroup inequality, 188–189
Internet, 24
internship programs, 32
interviewing: difficulties in, 47–48; exit interviews, 228–232, 235; of Hispanic managers for mentoring roles, 210–212; for hourly positions, 48–56; for management positions, 47–48; overview of, 43–47; performance appraisal, 130–131; sample questions for, 55–56; scripts used in, 48; summary of, 64–65

Jackson, Kenneth, 44
job offer, 59–63, 65
job-related training, 147
Johnson, Lauren Keller, 195
Joinson, Carla, 38
Jordan, Robert, 5, 17–18
journalism, 20–21, 140

Konrad, Alison, 188
Kreps, David, 3, 13–14, 27, 80, 103, 125, 150, 184, 194

labor associations, 258–259
Lam, Andrew, 39
Lambert, William, 119–120
language: culturally acceptable, 221–222; misconstrued, 221–222; obscenities in, 72–73; safety materials, 149–150; in workplace, 70–73, 91–92, 157–168
language training: company examples of, 161–162; description of, 151, 153–154, 161; economic benefits of, 166, 168; guidelines for, 162, 164–166; jobs that require, 163–164; summary of, 180
Latino, 49, 237–238
latinoamericano, 238
Lawler, Edward, 4
learning: cultural differences in, 164–165; opportunities for, 26; relationship-based, 200
legal issues, 115
Lehman, Andrea, 19

Leonhardt, David, 187
Linnehan, Frank, 188
listening, 205, 207
Lorch, Donatella, 51

Machan, Tim, 154
management: commitment by, 141, 150, 152, 212–213; communication concerns, 88–91; diversity in, 187; fair practices by, 60; human resource management effects on, 107; interviewing for positions in, 47–48; labor relations with, 79–82, 89
manager: accountability of, 106; appraisals performed daily by, 104; bottom-line focus of, 74; ethics of, 76; fairness by, 77; education on workplace hostility, 97–98; as mentor, 209–212; performance management systems concerns, 112–114; sensitivity to employee feelings, 77; training of, 114–116
Markley, Dianne, 39
mediation, 224
mentor(s): communication skills for, 206–208; description of, 202–203; managers as, 209–212; minority, 208–209; positive effect of, 208–209; selection of, 209–212
mentoring: benefits of, 203–204; definition of, 201; description of, 32, 57–58; success of, 212–213
mentoring programs: goal of, 201–202; overview of, 200–201; summary of, 234
mentoring relationship: definition of, 202; development of, 204–205; rapport building in, 204
Mexico: middle class of, 23; money sent back to, 51; Native American population in, 24; private schools in, 23; public education in, 22–25;
public universities in, 23; remittances to, 51, 225; television programming in, 45
minority mentors, 208–209
misconstrued language, 221–222
mission statement, 15, 182
motivation, 52

new employees: acclimation of, 144; feedback given to, 147–149; orientation of. *See* orientation; welcoming of, 143–144
noncompetition, 60
North American Free Trade Agreement, 14, 45–46
Northern cultures, 121
nuclear family, 42

obscenities on Spanish-language radio, 72–73
Occupational Safety and Health Administration, 149
Ojito, Mirta, 220
onboarding, 142
organized labor: communication issues, 88–91; in Europe, 80; growth of, 78–79; Hispanic views on, 82–84; human resources professional's role, 84; management relationship with, 79–82, 89; political influences, 81; right to, 80–81; summary of, 101
orientation: communication during, 145–146; department-related, 146; description of, 142; goals of, 146; purpose of, 145–146; safety during, 149; summary of, 179
Ortiz, Leonardo, 24

paraphrasing, 206–207
passive voice, 191
paternalism, 152
peer support, 205
perceptions, 77

performance: conflicts caused by, 223; employee beliefs and, 77; human resource management effects on, 3
performance appraisal: advance notice of, 109; assessment of, 133–134; auditing of, 133; conducting of, 127–135, 137; cultural difference effects on, 134; cultural influences on, 117, 119–120, 122–123, 133–134; culturally equitable, 118–119; errors in, 132; human resource management assessment of, 133; interview, 130–131; postinterview, 131; preinterview, 129–130, 135; rater error effect on, 132; summary of, 136–137; task force for, 109; three-part approach to, 128–131
performance management system: bias concerns, 106; continual process of, 104–108; cultural considerations, 108; elements of, 105; employee concerns, 112–114; focus groups, 109–110; implementation of, 108–117; managers and, 104, 112–114; overview of, 103–104; pilot project, 110–111, 113; purpose of, 105–106; summary of, 136
"personalismo," 126
Picture, Bill, 68, 228–229
pilot project, 110–111, 113
political associations, 258–259
population: assimilation of, 1; college degrees as percentage of, 20; demographics of, 6, 15; geographic distribution of, 15, 17–18; growth of, 1, 5, 44; workforce changes, 1
population growth, 1
preemployment screening and testing, 57–59, 65
private schools, 23

probationary periods, 57, 59
problem solving, 125
product brand, 33–35
professional organizations, 224–228, 235, 249–259
progressive discipline, 223
Protestant work ethic, 40
Prusak, Lawrence, 228
public universities, 23
Puerto Ricans, 19, 85, 191
Putnam, Robert, 167

questions: cultural considerations, 147–148; interview, 55–56

racial discrimination, 37–38
Raphael, Todd, 14
rapport, 130, 165, 204
referrals, 28–31
reflecting feelings, 206
reflecting the content, 206
relationship: employment, 13–14, 74; management-labor relations, 79–82, 89
relationship building, 144
relationship-based learning, 200
remittances, 51, 225
retention of employees. *See* employee retention
rewards and recognition: description of, 192; family importance of, 192–193; gift exchange, 193–194; Hispanic preferences, 192–194; summary of, 233–234; tuition reimbursement, 194
risk aversion, 126
role models: corporate, 197, 199–200; mentors as, 205
Ross, Judith, 140
Rowe, Anita, 161

safety: during employee orientation, 149; English-only workplace and, 159–160

safety equipment, 53
Schemo, Diana Jean, 25
search firms, 31–32
self-appraisal, 130
self-image, 117
service brand, 33
silence, 52–53
simpatía, 61–62, 83
skill-based training, 175
social associations, 255–258
social capital, 228
socialism, 80
Southern cultures, 121
Spanglish, 167
Spanish: accent-neutral, 191; "standard," 191
Spanish language: classes in, 151, 157, 166, 190; endearment terms used in, 221–222
Spanish-language radio, 72–73
staffing agencies, 31–32
standard operating procedures, 147
stereotype-based discrimination, 40
strategic partnership, 67–70, 84
structured training, 147
supervisors, 146
surnames, 52
Suro, Roberto, 2, 168

teamwork, 127
technology, 4
television programming: English-language, 45; Mexican, 45
Temple, John, 21
"third" culture, 124–127
"Third World" mentality, 49
Thomas, David A., 58
Thomas, Jennifer, 124, 162–163
time management: discrimination based on, 40; social class and, 42
trade organizations, 224–228, 235, 249–259
training and development: acclimation, 144; continuing, 150; co-worker assigned as counselor or guide, 144–145; cross-cultural, 155–157; description of, 116–117; environment for, 141; feedback, 147–149; getting started, 176–178; human resource management's role in, 141–142; job-related, 147; management's commitment expressed in, 150, 152; of manager, 114–116; methods of, 176–177; onboarding, 142; orientation, 142, 145–146; prearrival, 143; steps involved in, 142–150; strategies for, 151–152; structured, 147; welcoming new employees, 143–144. *See also* diversity training
Trompenaars, Fons, 121
trust: building of, 35, 78, 205; communication affected by, 75–76; employee relations and, 75–76
tuition reimbursement, 194

Ulrich, David, 8, 68, 84
unemployment rates, 19
unions: communication issues, 88–91; employer partnerships with, 87; Hispanic views on, 82–84; human resources professional's role, 84; right to, 80–81; summary of, 101. *See also* organized labor

Villar, Maria, 171
vision statement, 182

Wagner Act, 81
Western cultures, 121
women: earning power of, 5–6; with graduate degrees, 5–6
workforce: challenges in, 173–174; cultural differences in, 120; diversity of, 15–16, 133; economic considerations, 14–15; globalization

effects on, 53; growth of, 127, 139–140; Hispanic population effects on, 2–3, 7; market influences on, 14–16
work-life balance, 214–216, 234
workplace: accountability in, 73; bilingualism in, 166–168; drug-free, 95; English-only, 158–163; fatalities in, 149; hostility in. *See* hostility, in workplace; language in, 70–73, 91–92, 157–168; safety in, 96, 149
workplace conflicts: description of, 92, 96–98, 100; discipline for, 223; history of, 217–218; overview of, 216–217; recognition of, 218–219

youth: family influences on, 46–47; sheltering of, 47
Yzaguirre, Raul, 73